Praise for *Don't Compete ... Tilt the Field!*

"Through his gift for storytelling, Louis Patler shares rich and compelling insights into the leadership qualities, attitudes and approaches that will define success in the next millennium. And like any really good story, *Don't Compete ... Tilt the Field!* stays with you long after the first reading and informs key decisions just when it's needed."

Paula Belknap Reynolds
Co-Founder and Principal of M Squared Inc.

"This book is filled with lessons for leaders who strive to maximize the value of their companies in the twenty-first century. It is a must for any leader who wants to maximize the value of human capital in tomorrow's networked economy."

Dr B. Lynn Ware
President, Integral Training Systems

"Louis Patler has set forth a brilliant work in *Don't Compete ... Tilt the Field!* This book addresses the complex issues every organization faces trying to improve itself. The unique and challenging solutions that Louis Patler formulated provides a roadmap to success in the next millennium.

"The current and future environment causes organizations to confront accelerating change. Louis Patler has produced a concise study of ways to deal with the Attitude, Perspective and Leadership requirements to succeed in this volatile environment. Louis shares his views on each subject then affirms each view with references from many of today's most noteworthy scholars and with real world examples from many of today's more successful companies.

"This book is a must for every CEO or potential CEO who wishes to make a lasting contribution, not only to his or her company, but to society in general."

Timothy L. Conlon
President and Chief Operating Officer, Viasystems Group, Inc

"Talk about attitude, perspective and leadership! Congrats to Louis Patler. This is a book written with an on-the-edge attitude, an out-of-the-box perspective, and a push-the-envelope leadership in putting forth immediately practical and useful tools, techniques and strategies which replace old paradigms with new ways of thinking and acting in today's ever unpredictable business world."

Steve Cohen

"Louis Patler's writing style demands rapt attention. At once thought-provoking, honest, accessible and rich with content. Business is personal and this is a personal business book."

Holly Stiel
Author, *Ultimate Service / The Complete Handbook to the World of the Concierge*

"I have known Louis Patler for many years and have sought his counsel on several occasions. His ability to listen to and understand the issues and lend his unique perspective on organizational behavior and dysfunction has been a tremendous help to me in understanding and leading my organization. As we work to improve, innovate, achieve, and dominate, regardless of our enterprise, Louis Patler's insightfulness, intuition, and wisdom expressed in his two books, *Don't Compete ... Tilt the Field!* and *If It Ain't Broke ... Break It!* helps open doors to new ways of thinking we may not have known were there."

Barry Gordon
Senior Vice President, Operations, Red Lobster Restaurants

" 'Thoughtware'?!! We can all use it to challenge our assumptions about business, leadership and the times. Louis will entertain you while helping you pose the right questions, at the right time to create the answers for your business."

Peter Pattenden
Managing Director, People Skills International

"Louis has done it again! *Don't Compete ... Tilt the Field!* and the new Thoughtware may very well be the first original way of looking at your business since *If it ain't broke ... Break It!* A word of warning, however – your brain had better have several megabytes of available memory before starting this book, because you will find it packed with salient information that you will want to have available to download for use in keeping your business on track in these tumultuous times."

Lowell Petrie
Director of Brand Marketing, Denny's Restaurants

"Louis didn't just tilt the field, he turned it upside down and got rid of the misconceptions, hyperbole, and 'consultant-speak' that generally permeates most business books. It's a practical, insightful exploration into the inner workings of some of the most innovative companies in America. I found myself constantly writing notes to myself on actionable ways to make our agency and our clients more innovative."

Mike Moser
Partner, Goldberg Moser O'Neill Advertising

LOUIS PATLER

CO-AUTHOR *'If it ain't broke...BREAK IT!'*

DON'T COMPETE... Tilt THE FIELD!

LOUIS PATLER

CO-AUTHOR *'If it ain't broke...BREAK IT!'*

DON'T COMPETE... TILT THE FIELD!

300 IRREVERENT LESSONS FOR TOMORROW'S BUSINESS LEADERS

CAPSTONE

First Published 1999
Capstone Publishing Limited
Oxford Centre for Innovation
Mill Street
Oxford OX2 0JX
United Kingdom
http://www.capstone.co.uk

British Library Cataloguing in Publication Data
A CIP catalogue record for this book is available from the British Library

ISBN 1-900961-74-1

Typeset in 10/14 Century Schoolbook by
Sparks Computer Solutions, Oxford
http://www.sparks.co.uk
Printed and bound by
T.J. International Ltd, Padstow, Cornwall

This book is printed on acid-free paper

DEDICATION

For my wife, Catherine ...
and my children
Kale, Elina, Caitlin, Johana and Kellin
for always helping me
keep things in perspective

To Mark McGwire and Sammy Sosa,
who practised what the title of this book preaches
and in so doing raised the spirits
of a sport ... and a nation

TABLE OF CONTENTS

ACKNOWLEDGMENTS

When I was starting out in business I got very good advice from a friend who said "ninety percent of business is half mental!" I have come to believe those numbers and have found that, if anything, 90% may be too *low*! In business, as in writing a book, so much depends upon good thinking, lots of discipline, and plenty of support.

When I was a feisty little boy, I had moments when I would forget to think, abandon any semblance of discipline, and lose sight of all the support I had from friends and family. At these times, my mother would sit me down, look me in the face, gesture with her Sicilian hand signals and say: "Louis, you think you have a photographic mind? ... Well sometimes you don't have any *film* in there!"

An author's "Acknowledgments" are very much like showing you the film that captures brief images of those who have supported me through thick and thin, those who believed in me and were so very generous with their time and wisdom. I have been very lucky. Firstly, I must thank my literary agent and friend John Willig for seeing the potential of this project. Unlike many agents, when the book was sold John was only *beginning* his relationship with me. At Capstone, I am grateful to Mark Allin and Richard Burton for their editing savvy, and to Tom Fryer and Erika Sigvallius for their design, typesetting and editorial diligence; and my assistant, Ann Luckiesh, was invaluable from start to finish.

Many clients and colleagues gave of themselves generously; principal among them are: Lynn Ware (President, Integral Training Systems); Raejean Fellows (CEO, Fellows Placement, Inc.); Peter Pattenden (Managing Director, People Skills International); Tim Conlon (COO, Berg Electronics (now Framatome, Paris)); Tom Brown (Founder, Management General); Laurie Scott (Senior Associate, Korn/Ferry International); Craig

DeWald (Director of Training, American Express); Paula Reynolds (Co-Founder, M2); Larry Rosenberger (CEO, Fair/Isaac); Mike Moser (Partner, Goldberg Moser O'Neill); Danny Altman (President, 100 Monkeys); Steve Weiss (President, Straightforward Communications); and Joe Fassler (CEO, National Restaurant Association).

Bernie Nagle, Director, Global Business Process Improvement, for Berg Electronics, has been a special friend and client through the entirety of this project. He was always there with a good thought, a constructive criticism, and a pat on the back. Bernie, along with Perry Pascarella, helped me to understand what !eadership, with conspicuous and high regard for others (hence the "!") means today. For many long talks and much guidance on "strategy as philanthropy," a tip of the hat to Claude Rosenberg, Chairman of RCM Capital Management. I am also indebted to Steve Cohen, President of The Learning Design Group, and collaborator in creation of my training program on "Break-It!" Thinking™. Not only have we been business partners, but Steve read every word of the manuscript drafts and gave me invaluable advice.

Lastly, to my family – Catherine, Kale, Elina, Caitlin, Johana, and Kellin – I need a whole roll of film just for you! Thanks, from the top and the bottom of my heart!

Louis Patler

Preface

BE "SOMEBODY!"

My sixth grade teacher, Mrs. Klages, was wise and wonderful. She had a great sense of humor and the entire class respected her tremendously, so much so that my good friend Billy – in a fit of pre-adolescent exuberance – proposed marriage to her! The Queen of one-liners, she told him she was flattered, but she suspected that her husband would not agree to step aside just yet for Billy.

Near the end of the school year, she asked each of us what our dreams were for the future, what we wanted to be when we grew up. Impetuous even then, I stood up in front of the class and proudly announced that "no matter what else, I am going to be 'somebody' when I grow up!" Without hesitating she looked me in the eye, smiled, and said "Well Louis, if you *really* want to be somebody … you'll have to be more specific!"

I have never forgotten her words, and they ring in my ears frequently as I work with executives and organizations, all of whom want to be "somebody." This book is about some of the "specifics," the lessons I have found to be the most useful in this quest.

The tone I have tried to set in the pages that follow is somewhere between that of the *Harvard Business Review* and an email to a good friend or mentor. You will read parables, metaphors, anecdotes, case studies, and "hard research" – sometimes juxtaposed on the same page – all shamelessly utilized in order to make a point. My hope is that if it is interesting and accessible reading that has both content and humor, you will remember what you read, and more importantly be more likely to put it to good use. As Shakespeare said in *The Taming of the Shrew*, "No profit grows where there is no pleasure taken." For me, the "pleasure" is in the "specifics," in the lessons one can learn and live by in the modern workplace.

The wild, roller-coaster world of business today is in a state of perpetual flux and exponential change. Technological advances have altered the nature and substance of commerce forever; and globalization of the marketplace, once only a dim light on the horizon, now fully brightens the night sky.

As the title of the book implies, given today's business environment, there is no such thing as "a level playing field." The rules of the game of commerce no longer hold, or at least they are bent and pushed and challenged at every turn. If you want to "tilt the field," simply tilt your head! Furthermore, so much time is wasted myopically watching "the competition," that many opportunities are missed – some forever. The good news is that there is emerging a new attitude and perspective that will serve tomorrow's business leaders well. To boldly paraphrase Mrs. Klages, if *you* want to be somebody ... enjoy this book!

Prolog

HORSE SENSE

My assistant, Ann Luckiesh, has a sharp eye for business wisdom. A few days ago she sent me an email from home with the heading: "If your horse dies, dismount!" Seems like a rather obvious and simple statement. Unfortunately, in business we have a tendency to delay, skirt or complicate matters, and employ a few too many strategies. As the rest of her email illustrates, too often when the horse dies, we:

1. Buy a stronger whip.
2. Change riders.
3. Say things like 'This is the way we always have ridden this horse.'
4. Appoint a committee to study the horse.
5. Arrange to visit other sites to see how they ride dead horses.
6. Rewrite the standards for dead horse performance.
7. Appoint a triage team to revive the dead horse.
8. Create a training session to increase riding ability.
9. Compare the state of dead horses in today's environment.
10. Change the requirements, declaring that "This horse is not dead."
11. Hire outside consultants to ride the dead horse.
12. Harness several dead horses together to increase speed and pulling power.
13. Declare that 'No horse is too dead to beat.'
14. Provide additional incentive funding (more sticks, more carrots) to increase the horse's performance.
15. Do a case study to see if competitors can ride it cheaper.
16. Purchase a software product to make dead horses run faster.
17. Declare the horse is 'better, faster and cheaper' dead.

18. Form a quality circle to find uses for dead horses.
19. Revisit the performance requirements for horses.
20. Say this horse was procured with cost as an independent variable.
21. Promote the dead horse to a supervisory position.
22. Shorten the track.
23. Establish Benchmarks for industry dead-horse leaders.
24. Gather other dead animals and announce a new diversity program.
25. Put together a spiffy PowerPoint presentation to get planners to double the dead-horse R&D budget.
26. Get the horse a Website!"

I laughed when I read this, because the analogies to business are so readily apparent, and so true. too often we in business are so focused on the saddle or jockey on the competing horse that we forget all about our horse's health, the changing conditions of the track, and what it takes to win the race. Therein lies the moral of the story.

Part One

ATTITUDE!

Chapter One

ATTITUDE!

Placing Lightbulbs in the Snow

A PARABLE

A long, long time ago – two, perhaps three years – Richard Branson, Ted Turner and Bill Gates all perish in a airplane crash and arrive in Heaven to find God on his throne.

God turns to Branson and asks, "Richard, just what do you believe?" Branson says: "Well, I believe in the power of *quality*. Quality of services, quality of products; total quality."

God says, "OK, Richard, very good: come, sit at my left hand!"

Then God turns to Turner and in a deep voice says, "Ted, what do you believe?" Turner, not one to waste time, answers: "I believe in *speed*, in being quick. I believe that any man or woman from any background, any nation, any walk of life can become a success if they act swiftly and follow their dreams!" God nods to Turner and says, "Excellent: Ted, please be seated at my right hand!"

God then turns to Gates and, pausing a moment to make eye contact, asks, "And Bill, what do *you* believe?"

"I believe," says Gates "that *you* are in *my* chair!"

THREE MEN AND GOD!

Three men and God ... what a way to start a book! I couldn't resist that story because within it is revealed some of the lasting truths and realities of today's zany world of business. Two decades ago business success was driven by the quest for total *quality*. A decade later, quality had become a "given" – it was the price of entry into the marketplace – and more recently quality has given way to *speed*. But today, as a new century unfolds, quality and speed are the givens and, as exemplified by Bill Gates's conversation with God, the new force that will shape the world of commerce is ... *attitude*!

It is no longer enough to have quality products and services. It is no longer the case that speed to market is the key to lasting, repeated success. The emerging major factor that is now shaping commerce is an irreverent attitude about the nature and substance of how to gain an advantage in an exponentially changing world. New times call for new thinking, and having an attitude that works in your context is the newest "given."

Ironically, this is nothing new at all. Nearly 40 years ago, Thomas Kuhn wrote a simple and elegant book, *The Structure of Scientific Revolutions* (1962), in which he invoked the old Greek term "paradigm," a word that has been used and abused ever since. What Kuhn told us was that at the base of all science there is a foundation, a set of core principles and assumptions that are not questioned and which subliminally guide all that we do. Yet paradigms do shift: they take hold, they generate unexplainable anomalies, the anomalies generate new answers and the new answers generate a new paradigm. If you doubt this says Kuhn, ask Copernicus about Galileo, Galileo about Newton, and ask Newton about Einstein.

It is the same in commerce: new eras generate new paradigms. Furthermore, co-evolving with each new paradigm are a new mindset, skillset, and toolset that shape the very core of business strategy and action on both a macro and a micro level.

GWENETH, YOSHI, AND HECTOR

In my opening parable I cited Branson, Turner, and Gates, but it could just as easily have been Thatcher, Clinton, and Gorbachev, or Monroe,

Hepburn, and Olivier, or I could as easily have mentioned Gweneth Smith, Yoshi Kobayashi, and Hector Rodriguez ... three global movers and shakers who were born somewhere in the world last year, and who are destined to impact the future of the next century.

The truth is that all of them – Bill Gates, Hector Rodgriguez, and the others – are a great deal alike, for all of them know, as you do, that we now live in a world that is small and yet limitless; that the rate of change is increasing and yet unmanageable; and that the key to success is a new *attitude* that is durable and yet infinitely flexible!

THE NEW THOUGHTWARE

In the pages that follow, I will tell you about the key elements of this new attitude. I will do this not by citing theory or ideology, but by telling the stories of real companies and real people who have created for us a new "Thoughtware," a Mindset, Skillset, and Toolset suitable for the wacky world of commerce and business, at the start of a fresh millennium.

I will take you on a voyage to the ends of the Earth – we have already been to Heaven after all – to document what the human mind can create and bring to fruition. I will show you how the new leaders are thinking, implementing, and applying the attitude demanded by our times. I will detail for you the new paradigm and the Mindset/Skillset/Toolset that I call Thoughtware.

Several years ago, the movie *Field of Dreams* told the fanciful story of an Iowa farmer who loves baseball. Hearing a voice (no, not God's voice, it was actually the baseball legend "Shoeless" Joe Jackson) he is told, "If you build it, they will come!" As the movie unfolds, he realizes that he is to build a baseball field in the middle of his cornfield, stadium lights and all, and that when built, two legendary teams will come to play. Drawing upon themes of eternal life, following your dreams, and coming to peace with your family roots, the movie was a blockbuster hit.

However, were the movie to be made today, as a new century is unfolding, *Field of Dreams II* would have a revised core theme, "If you *think* it you can build it, and if you build it they will come!"

To thrive in the global economy of the twenty-first century you have think on your feet, stay on your toes, and see in unconventional ways where the future is leading. How do you do this? How do you know where things are heading and what you should do? Well, I usually start by making a list!

THE TOP 10 LITTLE KNOWN AMAZING FACTS

As one who has analyzed trends for many years I have been keenly aware of the big "shifts" as well as the small "dots" that are connecting to form a clear picture of the future. For many years I have kept a folder, in which there is a list that I call my "Top 10 Little Known Amazing Facts." In it I place data, statistics, research studies, and quotable quotes that document emerging trends. The criterion for inclusion in this select list is that each fact must have several broad applications that stimulate much more expansive thinking about the near future, and must represent *exponential* (rather than incremental) change.

Here is an indicative list from last year:

The top 10 amazing facts

1. On average, worldwide, an innovation in digital technology is copyrighted every three seconds.
2. In the United States in 1960 there were 5000+ people over the age of 100. In 1996 there were 1,000,000. By 2010 that number will rise to over 5,000,000. In the western world, a child born in the year 2000 can expect to live well into the twenty-second century.
3. Much as movie theaters gained popularity with the advent of TV, libraries throughout the world are gaining popularity in tandem with the acceptance of the Internet. "High-Tech" therefore, continues to generate a commensurate need for "High-Touch."
4. The number one status symbol in America in 1996, according to an SRI poll, is ... a long marriage.
5. World export of services and intellectual property in many countries is now equal to the export value of electronics and automobiles combined.

6. More than 50% of many companies' revenues in a variety of industries (e.g. technology, food service, and banking) comes from products and services that did not exist two years ago.
7. 1996 was the first year that PC sales outpaced the sale of TVs; and in several industrialized nations there was more email than "snail mail."
8. By 2002 there will be a five-fold increase in the number of telecommuters worldwide.
9. There are more computer literate first graders worldwide than there are computer literate CEOs.
10. Computer power today is 8000 times less expensive than in 1966. Similar progress in the automobile industry would mean buying a new BMW for $2 that could travel at 600 mph on a thimble of gas!

Thought provoking isn't it? Well, here are the ten more facts to consider:

Global top 10 amazing facts

1. The most popular name in Latin America is ... Juan. The fourth most popular name in The United States is ... Juan.
2. In some parts of the world, on-line subscriptions are growing at the rate of 20% per month.
3. According to United Nations estimates, nearly 80% of the world's population has never flown, and half has never used a telephone!
4. In Seattle, Washington, in 1992 there were 84 startups. In 1996 there were over 1100, over 400 of which were started by ex-Microsoft employees, of whom fewer than 3% had been "downsized."
5. In Singapore, during a lifetime, the average college graduate can expect to change careers four times and change jobs every four years.
6. In China, the first McDonald's restaurant opened to long, long lines ... not because of the demand for fast food, but because of the demand to sit down and eat an American meal.
7. In the USA, the costs of feeding a family of four will have fallen from 46% of a week's pay in 1901 to an estimated 12% in 2001.
8. In spite of the explosion in technology, an average employee of a multinational corporation in 1997 can expect to work 20% more hours (48.3) and sleep 20% fewer hours (6.5 hours) than in 1986.

9. In 1984 the average product development cycle was three years. In 1990 it was 18 months. In 1997 it was six months ... and dropping!
10. On average, multinational corporations listed on the NY and Tokyo Stock Exchanges lose half their customers within five years, half their employees every four years, and half their investors in less than one year.

Both lists – the 20 facts – represent the directionality of exponential change, and the commensurate amount of opportunity each portends. They are, therefore, *indicators* of change.

Yet, what if we want more than a forecast: what if we want to encourage change, to partner with change, to consciously alter a life, a system, an organization, a city, or a nation? What kind of Thoughtware might we bring to bear?

"COUNTERINTUITIVE LEVERAGE POINTS"

Donella H. Meadows is a systems analyst who understands very well the nature of complex organizations in a time of great complexity and change. By examining the "leverage points" in a complex system – the places where, in often "counter-intuitive" ways, an organization can see a small shift in one thing produce a major change in everything – you gain a better understanding of how to dramatically change that system. (Meadows, 1997). After all, as she says, "Complex systems are, well, complex."

Of special importance here however, is the need to open your mind to "find the *wrong* direction" in order to be on the right track! Flying in the face of conventional wisdom, she offers us nine "places to intervene" in a system in order to effect maximum change. Thus, what follows begins with the *least* effective change agent.

9. numbers (such as subsidies, taxes, and standards)
8. material stocks and flows
7. regulating negative feedback loops
6. driving positive feedback loops
5. information flows
4. the rules of the system (such as incentives, punishments, and constraints)

3. the power of self-organization
2. the goals of the system
1. the mindset or paradigm out of which nos. 2–9 arise!

Like so many things today, what I will call the new Thoughtware begins by turning important things upside down, by proceeding counter-intuitively. A change in "mere" numbers, therefore, represents much less substantive and lasting change than a change in the mindset. So, if you *really* want to change your life – or that of an organization – you must change your heart and mind and soul! You must become fully engaged in an irreversible "attitude adjustment."

This book then, with its focus on the attitude, perspective and leadership skills that will shape future success in an exponentially changing world, is best understood as a radical and revolutionary inversion of what previously affected our ways of seeing and behaving in the real world. Change the numbers, the products, and the services ... and little has changed. However, change the mind, the spirit, and the attitude of a person and you will change the person and the system around her.

THE LAST STRONGHOLD OF AMATEURISM

Whew! Statistics. Systems theory. Paradigms. Mindsets. It makes *my* brain freeze ... and I am *writing* it! However, once I stand back long and far enough, what I see is a rich and fertile array of new opportunities that are there for the taking ... if I have the right attitude! How do you work on your attitude? Where are the role models?

Last year my wife was asked to lead a series of discussions for parents of school age children in our community. While doing preparatory reading, she came upon a delightful one-page article whose title was immediately both wise and humorous: "Parenting, The Last Stronghold of Amateurism"! As I thought about the title, I began to substitute a variety of words where "parenting" had been. To my surprise, each time I did this, I could readily see another valid article. Consider, for example:

> *"Management, The Last Stronghold of Amateurism" ... or*
> *"Economics, The Last Stronghold of Amateurism" ... or*

"Love, The Last Stronghold of Amateurism"!

The topics were endless ... and all quite true! One tenet of the new Thoughtware maintains that when change is as rampant and incessant as it is today, we would all benefit from trusting our own "amateurism" and naiveté. Many a breakthrough has come from exactly this process.

In the last few years, the nature and substance of successfully competing in the marketplace has been significantly – and permanently – changed. Those individuals and companies that have mastered the fine art of seeing the future before it unfolds have held a distinct advantage.

In my last book, *If it ain't broke ... BREAK IT!* (Kriegel & Patler, 1992), we proposed that the most successful companies and workers in the emerging economic order are those who understand early on that many of the old rules of running a business no longer apply. Their recent experience tells them that the traditional wisdom of "staying with the tried and true" has most assuredly been tried, but is no longer true. After all, would you want to fly on an airline whose motto is, "If it ain't broke ... don't fix it"?

It is a very different world today – there is no such thing as "a level playing field." Now, we cannot gain a wide advantage without continuously innovating, being adamantly flexible, and constantly questioning the fundamental assumptions of the game ... via a radical new attitude! In fact, the emerging business "Thoughtware" that will guide us into the twenty-first century must be as radical as the times. Today, "business as usual" means "business as *un*usual"! Witness the tale of the invention of the technique that exponentially increased the storage capacity of the silicon computer chip.

A LIGHTBULB IN THE SNOW!

The day after Christmas of 1990, a 27-year-old Bell Labs computer scientist, Taiwan-born Ran-Hong Yan, was carrying his two-year-old daughter Rose outside to build her first snowman. He had been employed at Bell Labs for four months, and was a rookie to semi-conductor research. He called to tell his boss he'd be a little late.

After hanging up, he looked out of the window and watched how the snowflakes blanketed the tops of cars without sticking to their sides.

Something clicked. He was struck by the realization that he had discovered a solution to a haunting problem, namely that the same principle for the distribution of snow would hold for the distribution of information. That single observation (connecting information flow and snow falling), and the innovative energy that brought it to fruition – a "lightbulb" in the snow – changed forever the nature of an entire industry. Thus, for example, he was able to use boron gas in "vertical doping engineering" of microchips, and a technique for transfering much more information was born.

MONKEY SEE, MONKEY DO!

Albert Einstein once observed that most problems cannot be solved using the same kind of thinking that created the problem in the first place. I never fully understood his remark until a friend emailed me the following clinical research findings:

A group of behavioral psychologists recently conducted an experiment with a group of monkeys in a lab setting with one-way mirrors. A dozen monkeys were placed in a room, in the center of which was a pole with a bunch of bananas on top. Above the bananas, mounted in the ceiling, was a shower head. When one of the older monkeys climbed the pole the scientists sprayed her with ice cold water. The monkey retreated. An hour or so later another monkey made a quick dash for the top and was also hosed down.

At this point unbeknownst to the monkeys, the scientists changed three things: they removed one monkey from the room; they brought in a new one; and they disconnected the shower head. Soon, the new monkey in the room tried to climb to the top but was stopped by others. Eventually all the monkeys were replaced and each time the new monkey was stopped when they started climbing. Finally, though no monkey remained who had been present for the spraying, no one ventured up the pole. Thus they never realized that conditions had changed and the bananas were there for the picking.

The moral of the story? Experience is the best – and at times the worst – teacher. So, if we are to solve new problems we must develop and adopt a new attitude – a new Thoughtware – that is suited to the times.

The good news is that today, after nearly two decades of transition and experimentation, there has slowly been evolving a new mindset (paradigms, attitudes, values, and beliefs), new skillset (attributes and abilities), and new toolset (techniques and methods), the key elements of which are at the heart of the remainder of this book. Further, creating a successful climate for incessant innovation in a twenty-first century organization will require fundamental shifts in our mindset, skillset, and toolset – *simultaneously*. Viable solutions will require new ways of seeing, new modes of action, a new vocabulary, a new set of images, new perspectives, and new sensibilities – and with the emergent attitude there comes commensurate perspective and leadership.

Chapter Two

THE FUTURE

There Are No Prizes for Predicting Rain ...

"Anyone can hold the helm when the sea is calm."
– Publius Syrus, ancient Greek

ORCHIDS AND KILTS

On a recent trip to Singapore to deliver the keynote address to the annual Congress of Les Clefs d'Or – the international association of concierges of four-star hotels – two events occurred that offer useful metaphors for a perspective on the future.

I can't think of a profession that has a better understanding of "service" today than that of the concierge. Les Clefs d'Or is the elite, the cream of the crop, so they had attended to every detail. Yet the first event affected the thousand or more participants who had gathered in Singapore from more than 30 countries.

Upon arrival we received beautiful and detailed packets of information and every facet of our room accommodations had been attended to. The opening gathering was an excursion to the sprawling grounds of Sentosa Island, and excitement was in the air as we met one another and boarded the buses.

As we rolled onto Sentosa we were greeted by our hosts and told that the entire island was reserved for our exclusive use and we could eat, drink and be merry at our leisure! Leave it to the concierges to know how to throw a party.

After about 45 minutes of serious mingling, in the distance I heard muted, high-pitched sounds that sounded vaguely familiar. As the sounds grew louder I could decipher a melody and then, incongruous as it was, I realized I was hearing the stirring sound of ... bagpipes!

There I was, ten thousand miles from Scotland, on a tropical Asian island, surrounded by orchids and palms – and drum and bagpipe marching songs filled the air. Then, suddenly, as if on some weird Machiavellian cue, at precisely the moment I caught a glimpse of my first kilt and bagpipe, the sky opened with the loud roar of thunder and a tropical downpour began.

Our host Jerry Soh, who was President of the Singapore Planning Committee, had literally thought of everything, but there was no way to stop Mother Nature. All the preparation and planning in the world couldn't keep it from raining on our parade!

The future is a lot like that. Plan as we may, the future has plans of its own. There is more.

CARTIER AFTER DARK

A second event – an image really – occurred the next night at the gala opening dinner at the palatial grounds of the Alkaff Mansion on one of the highest points overlooking Singapore. As we sat down and were enjoying our dinner – served outside under a huge rain-proof tent – once again music rose in the distance. Ethereal and electronic, this music created a mood of excitement and expectation. As we looked to the south, smoke began to rise from the stage and from the corners of the covered dining area, further enhancing the level of excitement and expectation. I half expected Indiana Jones, Luciano Pavarotti and Madonna to step out of the mist. However, I was wrong; I had *under*estimated the stars of the occasion!

Slowly and gracefully, out of the smoke and haze emerged a half-dozen stunning, out-of-this-world figures in full black body suits and feathered masks, tastefully adorned with millions of dollars' worth of jewels made by the evening's corporate sponsor, Cartier of Paris. The tall, sleek, cat-like models proceeded to walk slowly amongst us, moving at their own pace, visiting each table and allowing us to look ... but not touch.

As I sat there captivated by the event's stunning male and female models, I had a revelation about the future: It was not "the future" *per se* that I was dealing with, it was my *anticipation* of it, attitude about it, and reaction to it. The new Thoughtware is committed to *inventing* the future – rather than fearing it, or merely reacting to it – so I understood that I must *initiate* change and look ahead without looking back.

The future is full of paradoxes and ironies: Dark and mysterious yet sparkling and bejeweled. It is eerie, yet ravishing at the same time. It is unpredictable, but brings gifts from afar. While it may be scary, it is none-the-less quite seductive.

The orchids, kilts and Cartier "cats" served as a friendly, but vivid reminder and at that moment I felt I was seeing the world with fresh eyes.

EINSTEIN'S BRAIN, KELLIN'S SOLUTION

Upon returning to my hotel room at the Oriental Singapore that night a fax was waiting for me. Knowing that I am a great fan of Albert Einstein, a friend had sent me an article on a recent scientific analysis of tissue from Einstein's brain, one of several such studies conducted over the years since his death. Every so often it seems, tissue samples of the dear Doctor's brain are subjected to investigation by the latest breakthrough technology in the hope of determining if he had some special or unusual make-up. The results are consistently the same as the headline in the fax proclaimed: "Scientists Stumped by Einstein's Brain."

The story went on to describe just how "normal" his brain appears to be. They quote Einstein, who never took himself too seriously, as saying, "My brain ought to be studied for scientific reasons so that if anyone has a question, it can be answered." At first glance I thought that was the humorous point of the article as well as the reason my friend had faxed it to me. He knows I collect quick one-liners.

Fortunately I read on and noticed some comments by Einstein's granddaughter, Albany Evelyn Einstein. "Anything they find [by examining her grandpa's brain] will be interesting," she said. "I think it's important to look for something if it's there; and if nothing's there, to prove he was a normal guy. He was not some new, super-developmental stage of the human race," she said. "I think he retained, to a large degree, the freedom and the ability *to think like a child*!" (My emphasis.)

I was reminded by that article of something that happened when my youngest son, Kellin, was in fourth grade science class and learning about optical illusions. He taught me a great lesson that I have never forgotten, one that Albert himself perhaps would have enjoyed.

One day Kellin was looking at the Sunday comics section. In our local paper, the San Francisco Chronicle, there is a weekly feature about science written for kids his age. All of a sudden he looked up at me and said, "Dad, bet you can't get the right answer to this quiz question." Never one to dodge a challenge like that, I smiled and he handed me the paper and pointed to a drawing on the paper.

Now, you look at this for awhile, as I did. The question asked was: "*Which of these circles is the biggest?*"

Knowing a trick question when I see one, I scoured the drawing for every nuance of meaning, and reverted back to a Rolodex full of physics principles I had known.

Do you have your answer ready?

How many of you say the circle in the upper left? Why? Perhaps you see the pattern it forms and how it alters the perceived shape? Or did you select the circle at the upper right. Or maybe, you selected the lower left circle, realizing that it is an optical illusion, and appears slightly elliptical. These are but a few of the responses I have heard. I have shown this to thousands of people during the course of my speeches and consulting and am amazed by the vast array of interesting answers I receive.

Well, I turned to my son and said "Kellin, I have to say it is the upper left circle. The others are an old trick, right?"

"No," he said, "wrong again, Dad!"

"OK, smart guy," I said, "what do *you* think is the biggest circle?"

"It's easy, Dad. The biggest circle is the circle with the other circles in it!"

Can you see it? What he noticed – quite accurately – was the "boundary" circle that surrounded the other circles. Wasn't that a plausible answer? I learn a lot about having "fresh eyes" from him and from my other children as well.

Herein lies the lesson I learned from Kellin's solution: Sometimes the most obvious and logical answer is the most difficult to see. It's finding the "biggest circles" in life that we must master if we are to invent the future.

That's a basic part of the Thoughtware of today's innovators; don't just look for the predictable solution, look beyond it for what I call "the second solution." In my training programs on "Break-It" Thinking™ I often have an exercise wherein a problem is described and participants are asked to come up with a solution. The trainer then asks that the exercise be repeated, adding that the only "rule" is that you cannot solve the problem in the same way that you had previously. Inevitably, the second solution is the better solution, one that is simpler and more readily implemented.

ASKING THE OBVIOUS QUESTIONS

How do we do this, how do we keep a fresh perspective, how do we stay on the trail of life's second best solutions? As we have seen, in my consulting, managing, and research I have found that developing a new Thoughtware is a crucial step. To develop the new Thoughtware requires that we constantly shed old habits, forge new ground, then, hardest of all, break the mold! That's the foundation of all Thoughtware.

If you adopt the business Thoughtware of "shedding old habits," a useful starting point in your skillset is to ask yourself tough, *obvious* questions. The most fundamental of these questions – and by far most important – are the following threesome. Think about your own business or work and answer these for yourself:

- What business(es) am I *really* in?
- What are my core competencies and strengths?
- Are the answers to Questions 1 and 2 in alignment? How?

Many companies around the world have been asking these questions in earnest for several years. Dell Computer, Disney, and 3M are recent examples. Dell realized that they are in the computer, service, *and* the mail-order business. At Disney they know they are in the entertainment business and the "animation" business. At 3M they are into coatings, adhesives, and *un*adhesives business – thanks to their invention of Post-its. Throughout this book, we will look at the answers to these three questions by dozends of successful companies.

THE "HONOR BAR" ... IN THE BATHROOM!

Chip Conley holds a Stanford MBA and before his thirtieth birthday had bought his third hotel in San Francisco. His company, Joie de Vivre Hotels, was founded with the understanding that in the inhospitable hospitality industry, service is now a given, so there must be more. Chip understood that the basic elements of service, the smallest details, often make the guest's stay the most memorable.

His business plan called for acquiring run-down hotels in the nicer districts of San Francisco. With careful remodels, and themes in each hotel, he decided to pursue niche market after niche market. For example, one of his hotels caters to the female business traveler, another to musicians.

One day, while making the rounds of his properties, Chip had an insight ... and he implemented it. Busy professional women, he observed, have an array of products and services they need that are different from men. To accommodate that, Chip took the basic idea of an "honor bar" and moved it to the bathroom! So all his hotels have an "honor bar" in every bathroom filled with lotions, perfumes, hygiene supplies, hair brushes, nail files and panty hose. Much like the traditional honor bar, guests take what they need, check it off on a list, and are billed when they depart.

LATE BREAKFASTS AT THE RITZ-CARLTON

Sometimes the answers to the trio of macro questions produce insightful and unexpected results on the micro level. Let me give you an example of another hotel chain that understands the business it is "really" in, its core competencies, and how to align them.

The Ritz-Carlton has won just about every major award in the service and hospitality business in recent years, including America's prestigious Malcolm Baldridge Award. Senior management knows that the Ritz-Carlton is not just a five-star hotel chain, it is also in the information management, foodservice, and diplomacy business. That's not a big leap. However, what they recently came to realize is that they are in the "creative espionage" business too.

Everyday offers a new riddle, a new problem to solve. A case in point, the "mystery" of the day at one Ritz-Carlton: Guests were complaining that their breakfasts were getting to their rooms too late.

As the complaints mounted, the front desk alerted the concierge who then alerted the general manager of the problem, and the GM launched an investigation. First, he checked to see if the order sheets were picked up from the doors during the night. That was done properly. Then, he observed the preparations by the kitchen staff. Everything was prepared on time. Next, he followed the room servers to the elevators and stood with them as they waited and waited and waited for the elevators to arrive. "Aha!" he said to himself, "this is the problem!"

Impatient, he dashed off to call Otis Elevator Company to "come fix the damn elevators." By noon, Otis sent out an engineer who checked out the entire system – and found nothing wrong. Puzzled, the next day the GM accompanied another room service staffer and waited, and waited, and waited until the elevator finally arrived and the doors opened.

Out came a number of house-keepers, their arms full of linens. "What's going on here?" he demanded.

"We have no linens on the third, fifth and sixth floors," they told him. Aha! The *second* "clue" broke the case wide open: to find extra linens, the staff was tying up the elevators! Instantly he knew what to do: When he replaced his linen supplier, the breakfasts arrived on time!

Through his creative espionage, and dogged determination, he solved the problem. Even that wasn't all. He also learned an important lesson and broke an old habit: The first solution – in this case "it's Otis's fault" – is not necessarily the correct solution. Now, like a good carpenter, he measures twice, cuts once.

A HOTEL ON A CLIFF

Shedding old habits is not easy, yet such myopic and habitual thinking can get you into a lot of trouble. Let me illustrate this by telling a parable, again, from the hotel industry.

A prime piece of property on a beautiful ocean cliff came up for sale. In their wisdom, the board of directors of a prominent hotel chain decided to buy it and build a four-star hotel there. They planned every detail, projected budgets and timelines, and finally opened their doors right on schedule. Even with all the advance preparation, within the first month of the opening a major, unanticipated problem emerged: nine toddlers had fallen off the cliff and broken their arms or legs!

What should they do? Everyone had a different idea for the solution drawn from their own perspective.

The master chef, wanting to do his share to solve the problem, decided that the best remedy was to add more calcium to the children's menu! The stronger the bones, the lower the risk.

The sales manager, wanting to help (and ever the entrepreneur), thought the best thing to do would be to build a coin-operated slide from clifftop to ocean front, thereby turning a "cost center" into a "profit center."

Security wanted coiled barbed wire fencing around the parameter, and the legal folks suggested posting a sign: "Attention Toddlers, Jump at Your Own Risk," an interesting strategy considering the kids don't read yet.

The Board overrode these and several other suggestions and in their infinite wisdom went forward with their own solution: they built a pediatric clinic at the bottom of the cliff.

Is this a true story? Essentially, yes ... but I will admit that I elaborated on the suggestions to protect the guilty parties. The truth is I am writing about *your* company, *your* office, *your* department – and mine.

We've all built a clinic or two at the bottom of a business cliff. I certainly have. Driven by logic and encouraged by myopia, I've made more than my share of mistakes. The trick is to step outside your own habits so that the clear solution – as well as the folly of alternatives – can be seen. That's what innovators know how to do. A good first step, as we teach in our training programs, is to learn to ask the right questions at the right time, by looking beyond the cliff to the horizon line.

"CORE COMPETENCE," JAPANESE STYLE

A few years ago SONY sought the answer to the second basic question: "What is our core competence?" "Core competence" is a technical business term popularized in an article in the *Harvard Business Review,* "The Core Competence of the Corporation," (Prahalad and Hamel, 1990, pp.80–91).

To understand the phrase "core competence," think of a tree viewed in cross-section. Most people assume that their core competencies are obvious for all to see, like leaves on a tree. Wrong! A core competence is akin to the taproot of a tree. It is the source of strength, the avenue of all growth. Though of enormous importance, it is usually not readily visible. What Prahalad and Hamel teach us is that the trunk of the tree holds its core products, the limbs its core business units, and the leaves its end products or services which the consumer purchases.

For SONY, their core competence lies not in electronics or technology as you might have guessed. Their taproot from which all that they do grows is "miniaturization." SONY knows how to make little tiny things better than anyone in the world!

Similarly, Honda determined that its core competence was not the car or the motorcycle *per se*, but rather their knowledge of internal combustion engine development. That was the intellectual capital on which all their end products are based. Once that became clear, they re-engineered and understood that their core product was developing and manufacturing the engine and drive train; the "limbs" or business units became the automotive, lawn mower, and motorcycle divisions; and the "leaves" on the automotive "limbs" were the Civic, the Accord, the Del Sol, and so on.

Taco Bell hires and trains so many young people worldwide that they have a core competency as "the first global job corps." Toyota too, owns and operates a diversified portfolio of businesses and products, as does Honda and SONY. A few years ago they realized that they were also in the human development business. With more than 100,000 employees, the growing and nurturing of their people was a core competence that, if done well, would offer a clear competitive advantage. So at Toyota, they take their employees – and their employee's *suggestions* – seriously.

For example, according to a 1992 study by the National Association of Suggestion Systems, in one year Toyota employees submitted 860,000 suggestions for improvement. This is a high figure, even in Japan, where 66% of the employees regularly generate ideas (compared to only 8% of Americans). One reason may be that, on average, Japanese managers adopt four out of five suggestions, while American managers use only one in four. What better way to recognize and encourage employee involvement – the human development business – than to solicit and *use* their suggestions? If you use them, more will come ... and they will stay.

SICK-LEAVE "BANKS"

Similarly, employee retention strategies are becoming very creative and very frequent. Public school employees in Arizona, for example, are able to "donate" sick leave to co-workers, much like they might donate their blood or an organ in an emergency. Sick leave "banks," based on the principle of the blood bank, anchors workers' commitments to one another and makes them feel good about feeling healthy.

At Bell Canada, employees can take a leave of absence for up to one year with a guarantee of getting their job back, even if they leave to work somewhere else, or in another industry, or for a competitor! Furthermore, while they are gone, Bell pays their health and pension plan! Should they choose to return they may do so, no questions asked.

A WEDDING TO REMEMBER

Asking the right questions at the right time is a vital part of the new Thoughtware. Yet once you have the answers, then the real work begins. Often times, the role of leadership these days begins with the ability to communicate those answers.

For example, for those who have done or will do business in China, Fred Schnieter's *Getting Along with the Chinese for Fun and Profit* (1992) is a very useful book. Since 1966, Schnieter has been US Wheat Associates' Vice President for Marketing Development for China. With all that experience under his belt you would think he would know the right questions and have garnered a few of the right answers as well.

Yet even though he has lived in China for 35 years he recently described a surprising incident that happened at his daughter's wedding.

Heidi was married at St. Margaret's Church in Hong Kong. This was quite a fancy affair and just before things got underway, as guests were gathered in front of the church, one of Hong Kong's street people wandered gregariously into the crowd. Barefoot and grubby, he frustrated the (wedding) photographer ... and my wife made it clear that resolving such a situation was what the father of the bride was supposed to do.

Not wanting to create a scene, I pressed a few banknotes in his palm and said in Chinese, "Run along and get a few beers." Off he toddled.

We didn't see him again until midway through the ceremony as he came strolling casually down the entire length of the aisle, an open can in each hand, looking for the guy who'd sent him out to get the beer. Everyone agreed it was the highlight of the wedding.

That story reinforces one basic principle in the new Thoughtware: Whether doing business in the People's Republic of China, in San Francisco's

Chinatown, or on Montgomery, Sesame or Wall Street: Always say exactly what you mean.

WHINING ... AND WORKAHOLISM

Easier said than done. There are always cultural differences, nuances, personal experiences and gradations of listening skills that make human communication very problematic. Furthermore, if "men are from Mars and women are from Venus," you begin to get the picture. It's a wonder we ever get through to one another isn't it?

Yet, if we are to invent the future, our *attitude* about the future must be bold and confident. It must not wallow in self-doubt or compulsive busy-work, as the following story reveals:

A Japanese executive from a high-tech company was assigned for a three-year stint in its US offices. Accompanying him were his wife and 12-year-old son, Yoshi.

They timed their move to coincide with the American school year so that Yoshi could enter at the beginning and make the adjustment more smoothly. His sixth grade teacher was aware of his arrival and had prepared for it. She knew that Yoshi's English was good, so she concentrated on making him feel welcomed in a new country.

On the first day of class she introduced him to his classmates. "Class, I'd like you to meet Yoshi. He has moved here from Japan and will be in America for the next three years."

Then she said to the class, "Boys and girls, let's share with Yoshi a few of the highlights of American history. Class, tell Yoshi who said 'A government of the people, by the people, and for the people shall not perish from the earth'?"

No one answered. Finally Yoshi raised his hand and stood stiffly beside his seat, saying with pride "Abraham Lincoln, 1863!"

"Very good Yoshi," said the teacher, smiling curiously. "Thank you."

"Now class, let's bring this a little more up to date for Yoshi. Boys and girls, who said 'Ask *not* what your country can do for you, but what you can do for your country'?"

Total silence, blank faces, and another long pause. Then up went Yoshi's hand and he rose saying: "John F. Kennedy, 1961!"

The teacher looked at Yoshi. The class, amazed, looked at the teacher then scowled at Yoshi.

At this point the teacher turned and walked towards the blackboard when she heard one of the students blurt out:

"Damn those Japanese!"

"Who said that?," she demanded as she whirled around.

Yoshi leapt to his feet and answered proudly:

"Lee Iacocca, 1989!"

I like to tell this story because it illustrates two very human tendencies.

For some of us, when the going gets tough, as it did for Yoshi's classmates, we tend to whine, complain, and blame. Others, in the same situation, respond (as Yoshi obviously did) by working very hard, and doing their homework late into the night in order to be ready for the next long day. It's symptomatic of a bad case of constantly pushing yourself to work faster, harder, and longer ... just to stay even.

The new Thoughtware tells you that neither whining nor workaholism will keep you in the lead, happy to go to work the next day. Neither of these are sustainable business strategies.

Rather, to invent the future, we must find a balance point so that we don't burn out (like Yoshi may later in life) or grow bitter and resentful (as his fellow students might).

THE GREAT SHAMPOO HEIST

There's another old habit worth breaking which greatly enhances the ability to break new ground: the failure to incorporate the experiences and ideas of those closest to the problem, product, or customer. Quite often the person closest to the problem, to the customer, or to the product is the *last* resource we utilize.

In my "Break-It!" Thinking™ training program (co-designed with Steve Cohen, president of The Learning Design Group in Minneapolis, MN), to overcome this barrier, we utilize what I call "novice consultants," those line and staff workers with "fresh eyes" who can find the obvious amidst the obscure. Consider the story of The Great Shampoo Heist.

The purchasing agent for a country club noticed that the locker rooms were losing a lot of shampoo bottles from the shower area.

Several bottles had to be replaced every day and the expense over time was substantial. Finally, management decided to do something about it.

They held a long meeting. They tried putting in a security camera. They even made signs to induce guilt among the membership saying "Don't take the shampoo bottles. It's *your* club!" Nothing worked.

Finally, a new employee at the club said, "Let's get some input from the locker room attendant."

So, they invited him to their meeting, told him their concerns and asked if he had any suggestions.

"That's easy," he said with no delay at all. "Just take the caps off. Nobody wants a bottle that looks 'used.'"

Bingo! Problem solved!

DINNERS, DINERS AND "DUNKMAN"

I'll admit it. I am an unabashed, unequivocal dilettante. I travel frequently and work in more than a dozen industries. I read widely and voraciously. Also, I eat out often.

For these reasons – especially the latter – I have been very pleased that for the past two years many of my clients have come from the swelling ranks of the foodservice industry: restaurant chains, grocers, suppliers and franchisers. As a consequence, I have been tracking the trends in that industry with great regularity.

One client recently asked me to identify the major trends that I see in foodservice for the future. Since the foodservice industry is so large, and because it touches so many of our lives daily (it is estimated that 9–11% of all Americans work in the industry), I think that readers will find it interesting.

Compare these developing trends with your own industry.

1. Diversity: of patrons, menus, and venues. New patterns are emerging of "cross-eaters" who are looking for palatable experiences, in new and unexpected places: at airport espresso kiosks, at corporate cafeterias that prepare take home dinners, at healthy food concessionaires at the ball park.
2. Demands for consistent quality: From management, franchisees, front and back of the house staff ... and most of all from customers, consistent, quality service is now routinely expected.
3. Downgrading sacred cows: Every aspect of the foodservice business will undergo radical rethinking and process re-engineering. When work is done properly there are no sacred cows.
4. Young diners: Small children play a larger role in brand selection, product loyalty, and influencing parents foodservice decisions. Training of waitstaff to understand and cater to children's styles and needs will be crucial.
5. Coupons, discounts and deals: As the economy goes, so go the coupons, discounts and deals. As the economy improves, couponing becomes less vital. According to the National Restaurant Association's 1993 survey, at most fullservice restaurants, word-of-mouth recommendations from family and friends are the principal source – accounting for as much as 86% – of new business.
6. Sean, Juan, John, and "Dunkman": People want to eat where they feel safe, can relax from the stresses of daily living, and everybody knows their name. "Hi Mike, Hi Diane how's the house search going. Hi Darlene, how was your trip to Kenya?" Patrons want to be greeted at the door by name – or better yet by a nickname, like "Dunkman." That shows that you are valued and that your host remembered you love basketball and that although you're only 5'9", you can dunk the ball in the over-30 league at the local gymnasium.

   Hanging out is catching. So, as the popularity of alcohol continues to decline, Starbucks may be the pub of the 1990s, a "Cheers" without beers!
7. Daffy Duck, *no*! Delila's chicken, *yes*! Chicken will stay hot, as will coffees, premium baked goods, snacks and vegetarian dishes. What I call "flour power" – pasta and tortilla-based meals – will continue to diversify and expand. It's all in the price points (the spread between costs and retail pricing) my friends.
8. Leopards: New dots formed by new demographics will coalesce to form

mottled, splotchy patterns – like the skin of leopards. Those who connect the following dots will win the prizes: 58% of women work (all time high); highest birthrate since the 1954–65 boom; over 75 is the fastest growing group. The young, the old, and the female markets are growth areas in foodservice. Eating habits that they share – e.g. certain kinds of snack foods – will continue to be big winners.

9. The best, the rest. Double standards will dominate marketing strategies in smart companies. According to a recent American Express study, the best (return) customers out-eat the rest (new) as much as 15:1. The best foodservice providers are those who have one strategy to keep the best, and another to bring in the rest.

FROM THE AMERICAN EXPRESS FRYING PAN INTO THE IBM FIRE

There is something quite admirable about Louis Gerstner, Corporate Turnaround Artist. He rose through the ranks of American Express to one of the most senior positions. During this period, American Express – like Sears, GM, Kodak, and IBM – was undergoing substantive change and was clearly reeling. Gerstner, having made some progress, jumped out of the American Express frying pan to become the CEO of Nabisco, facing a new challenge in a new industry. Applying his keen marketing savvy and organizational development strengths he led Nabisco into several new ventures and some very profitable times.

Then a funny thing happened on the way to the office. Against the advice of many, he resigned from Nabisco and took the job as CEO of IBM in the wake of the worst five-year performance in the history of Big Blue. He faced record losses, a wave of layoffs, staff lethargy, low morale and lackluster products. In fact, IBM's middle management glut was so out of control that it was called "lion food," from the story of the lion that hid near an IBM office and ate a manager a day for a year before anybody noticed they were missing! Other than that, IBM was in great shape!

To outsiders, to his peers and colleagues, he was taking over a huge corporation that had almost completely lost respect for itself, and the respect of the business world as well. Having been selected a record seven out of 12 times as number one among *Fortune* magazine's "Most Admired

Companies" in America, by February 1994 and in less than two years IBM had slipped from number 1 to number 354 out of 404 cited. A staggering loss by any measure.

Gerstner knew he was facing the challenge of a lifetime. In moving to yet another industry – leaving cookies and credit cards in his wake – Gerstner leaped from the frying pan into the fire with poise and confidence, determined to invent the future of Big Blue. To him, dropping the ball at IBM was not his worry.

Syndicated columnist Jon Carroll offers a useful metaphor from juggling to describe what Gerstner faced: "Dropping," says Carroll, "is not the enemy; *fear* of dropping is the enemy ... good jugglers always know there's a next time. We know that, of course," he adds, "that's why it's nice to hear it again." To Gerstner, juggling IBM's resources was the issue.

To Gerstner, as to all innovators, the future is not the enemy. *Fear* of the future is the enemy. Gerstner, it appears, followed the new Thoughtware which says implementable change will shape your future. Therefore, "Be practical, spread your wings!"

For Louis Gerstner, being CEO of IBM requires that he spread his wings. Though the results are not in yet, it is clear that he decided to run IBM – and his own life– according to the new Thoughtware. To Gerstner, his challenge at IBM was to work in accordance with what I call The Noah Principle. The Noah Principle is based on a quote from Gerstner: "In the future there will be no more prizes given to those who predict rain," he says. "Prizes will go only to those who build arks!"

By building an ark aimed at the future, he understood the truth in the famous pair of strategies of Lawrence "Yogi" Berra, baseball hall of famer: "The future just ain't what it used to be ... (so) ... When you come to a fork in the road, take it!"

Chapter Three

SERVICE

Service Is as Service Does

"At the end of the day, we just make video games."
– Ruth Kennedy, VP, Electronic Arts
Advice on service given to new employees

COMPLEX ... YET SIMPLE!

For more than a decade, locally and globally, the ability to be or remain successful has become increasingly difficult. Chapter 1, ATTITUDE!, foreshadowed what every industry now understands: the importance of a few basic ingredients – quality, speed and attitude – in the formula for success. Chapter 2 offered a glimpse of the future. In this chapter I look more closely at one of the most important "strategic givens," customer service. The customer now feels *entitled* to top-notch service – dare I say it is taken for granted in all aspects of doing business today? As we shall see, to be repeatedly successful today is much more complex – yet simple – than ever before. Therein lies one of the great ironies of the new Thoughtware.

How do you attain a mastery of the new mindset and the new demands of service excellence? At the outset, it is crucial to ask fundamental questions:

- How can you turn service into a comparative advantage?
- How can service become a profit center (rather than a cost) of doing business?
- How do you gain greater customer loyalty?

In the remainder of this chapter we will look at what the new Thoughtware provides as answers to these and related questions.

MAXIMUM, TOP-O'-THE-LINE, PENULTIMATE SERVICE!

I am always on the lookout for models of excellence that are to be found at the extreme end of the spectrum. Often it is difficult to find such a model; but in this case, if I want to focus on unparalleled customer service, two words come to my mind: Holly Stiel!

For 16 years Holly was the chief concierge at San Francisco's Grand Hyatt Hotel on Union Square, and was the first female concierge in the United States to have been admitted into Les Clefs d'Or (Golden Keys), the elite international association of four-star hotel concierges based in Paris. However "darling, demanding, or demeaning," as she says, the customers' needs may be, they are commonly *dazzled* by Holly. She's a living legend in customer service. As you read on you'll see why. Observe the master at work!

"One guest came up to me," says Holly, "and asked me in the same sentence to order flowers for her friend's wedding shower, give her directions to a restaurant to get some pot stickers, and tell her where to get a luggage strap fixed!

"No problem!" says Holly to the guest, smiling. Pulling out her thick Rolodex, she orders the flowers, finds and Xeroxes a list of nearby Chinese restaurants, and arranges with the bell captain to get the damaged luggage repaired.

"Then this distinguished gentleman asked me 'Can you mail a bathtub to Bahrain for me?'" she recalls. No Problem: Van rental, Pack 'n' Ship company, Fed Ex. Mission accomplished ... in a matter of minutes!

"Or there was the Swiss gynecologist who was doing a workshop at a convention," Holly recalls. "Under obvious stress, and in broken English, the dignified gentleman asked me go to the airport to pick up six pigs' uteri for a seminar he was leading!" No problem ... for Holly. She contacted Air Cargo, borrowed a van, found three ice chests, and off she went!

SERVICE THOUGHTWARE

Diligent and resourceful, Holly exemplifies many of the key components of the new service Thoughtware:

- Service is as service *does*! Serving, like leading (See Chapter 12, !EADERSHIP), is what I call a "Golden Rule" profession. You must treat others as you wish to be treated – even if they do not reciprocate! Therefore, in my experience, the best servers are a bit insecure, slightly co-dependent, and exceptionally recuperative! Consequently, you *hire* someone with these inherent personality traits, and you *train* into them the skills they will need to utilize their serving abilities.
- Think – even *dance* – on your feet! There are no pat answers, only well maintained tools. Every service opportunity is a case unto itself – to the customer! Hence, the best service is provided one customer at a time by those who practice what Gary Heil (1996) proposes in his delightful book *One Size Fits One – not* one size fits *all*!
- The customer is usually right – even at those times when *you* are certain they are wrong! Top service providers understand this very well. They develop a keen ability to be *oxymoronic* for each customer by providing personal service while staying detached from the customer's personality.
- Service never sleeps! Service excellence is a round-the-clock profession. It is a "calling," to use an "old fashioned" concept. It is also replete with irony, not the least of which is that service is both temporary *and* chronic. By this I mean that most demands for service are episodic and arise from a given customer's needs and expectations. Yet service is also chronic because right now, somewhere, someone is in need of good service. At LL Bean, a clothing company in Maine, for example, planning for and executing the temporary and the chronic needs of

customers is part of their corporate culture and work ethic. In fact, they guarantee customer satisfaction. Says Leon Gorman (1998, p.15), "customer service is just a day-in, day-out, on-going, never-ending, unremitting, persevering, compassionate type of activity." Wheww!

Let's look at several examples of the service Thoughtware put into practice. Again, a Holly story comes to mind.

HEAVYWEIGHT TITLE FIGHT BLUES

"These two guys wanted to see a heavyweight boxing title defense on closed-circuit TV," she recalls. "I made a number of inquiries and got nowhere. I was slightly exasperated when my husband called and I mentioned to him the 'heavyweight blues' I was having. Perennial tease that he is, my husband didn't help much when he said, 'Yes, I understand Holly, and it should be a great fight too. I'll be watching it!' "

"Then – pardon the pun – the solution hit me! I did the only honorable thing: I invited the two hotel guests to be *my husband's* guests! The guests accepted, and they arrived with a case of cold stout, pretzels, and a pop corn popper, which they left as a house warming present!" Bill and his two new buddies enjoyed the fight tremendously.

CUSTOMER RETENTION IS NO PICNIC ... OR IS IT?

The relationship between good service and customer loyalty is well documented. However, for all the statistical validation, I still encounter corporate CEOs and board members who do not fully understand the impact of service excellence on the bottom line. In this final tale of Holly's exploits perhaps there is enough wisdom to convince them.

The story begins a few minutes before Holly was to go off her shift for a long-awaited weekend. I'll let Holly speak:

"John Thomasson (pseudonym) was very distraught-looking as he approached my concierge desk. I recognized him as a regular guest, a businessman who often arrived mid-week. He waited until no one was around, shyly walked up to me, and confided that he had been separated from his wife for several months and they were attempting a weekend reconciliation and meeting in San Francisco."

"He said, 'Holly, I need your help, I'm totally in your hands. I have no idea what to do or where to go and I'm a nervous wreck.' " Holly felt no pressure at all. "Just reconciling a marriage you understand – I really loved the *challenge* of this."

"So, I planned every detail for him: cars, food, limousines, dining reservations, flowers, champagne, even her favorite chocolate-dipped strawberries. The Works!"

Even "The Works" isn't enough for Holly. She wanted to give them *more* than the works. So she gave them. ... a picnic!"

"I knew they were both outdoors people and that they would love a hike on Mt. Tamalpais. So I went home, got my picnic basket and supplies, my handy pocket map of trails, and came in on Saturday to leave it for them as my little surprise."

Whatever it was, the strawberries/the flowers/the picnic, it must have worked. On her desk on Monday morning was a huge box of chocolates and a thank-you note. Six months later Holly got a card from the man. "Today marks our 14th Anniversary. Holly, thanks for saving our marriage."

With experiences such as this, Holly could write a book. Fortunately for all of us she has! It's called *Ultimate Service* (1993). Her sage advice offers further components of the new Thoughtware:

- *Attend to the little things, every detail has meaning.* There is a saying among poets, attributed to William Carlos Williams (himself a pediatrician for 30 years) that "The crisis in the poem is everywhere in the poem!" Service, like writing poems, is as much in the smallest elements as the biggest ones.
- *Service is not for the meek and timid.* Service – like leadership – often requires a thick skin and a warm heart. It helps to be assertive and a good listener. It helps to be resourceful and have the patience of Job. It is vital to be highly empathetic and quick to laugh. These are very difficult combinations of traits to find in the same person.
- *The best deserve the best.* To say it boldly: There are customers ... and there are *customers*. Often companies are not mindful of the "80–20 Principle." Twenty percent of your customers create 80% or more of

your business. Consequently, the new Thoughtware says *the best deserve the best*. As Jill Griffin says in her book *Customer Loyalty: How to Earn It, How to Keep It*, "Customers are not created equal ... most successful companies match the best service to the best customers." (1988, p. 18.)

NEW WAYS, OLD REASONS

Many industries have come to similar realizations, for service excellence is endemic to business growth and development today. In the marketplace, service excellence is absolutely critical to success. Consequently, many companies are hiring and training and rewarding employees in new ways, for an old (and very good) reason: profitability.

Given that most statistical forecasts in the Western world estimate that children born in the year 2000 can expect to change *careers* four times in their life and change *jobs* every four years, you can imagine the strain it places on organizations that value continuity, building relationships over the long haul, and customer loyalty. It's no wonder that customer turnover is a major problem in almost every industry. Customer turnover – like employee turnover – is a very costly problem, for it is far more efficient (and profitable) to treat an existing customer in special ways than to seek out and cultivate new ones. (See Chapters 9 – TALENT – and 10 – RETENTION – for more on this.)

Knowing this, I am always on the lookout for those companies that have high customer retention. They must be doing something right, something innovative, something out of the ordinary that breaks the pattern and alters the statistical probabilities.

COMIC RELIEF

Gathering vital information about customers is easier than you might think. Of course, email and the Internet makes this even easier, especially if you wish to survey them. Here is a sample purportedly from a major aircraft manufacturer, emailed to me recently by a friend:

AIRCRAFT-SPACE SYSTEMS-MISSILES

IMPORTANT! IMPORTANT! PLEASE FILL OUT AND MAIL THIS CARD WITHIN 10 DAYS OF PURCHASE.

Thank you for purchasing our military aircraft. In order to protect your new investment, please take a few moments to fill out the warranty registration card below. Answering the survey questions is not required, but the information will help us to develop new products that best meet your needs and desires.

1. ☐Mr ☐Mrs ☐Ms ☐Miss ☐Lt. ☐Gen. ☐Comrad ☐Agent ☐Other
   First Name: .... Initial: .... Last Name: ....
   Password, Code Name, Etc.: ....
   Latitude: .... Longitude: .... Altitude: ....
2. Which model aircraft did you purchase?
   ☐F-14 Tomcat
   ☐F-15 Eagle
   ☐F-16 Falcon
   ☐F-19A Stealth
   ☐F-007 Inflatable
3. Date of purchase: Month: .... Day: .... Year: ....
4. Serial Number: ....
5. Please check where this product was purchased:
   ☐Received as Gift/Aid Package
   ☐Catalog Showroom
   ☐Sleazy Arms Broker
   ☐Mail Order
   ☐Discount Store
   ☐Government Surplus
   ☐Classified
6. Please check how you became aware of the aircraft you have just purchased:
   ☐Heard loud noise, looked up
   ☐Store Display
   ☐Espionage

☐Was Attacked by One
☐Political lobbying by Manufacturer
☐Recommended by friend/relative/ally

7. Please check the three factors which most influenced your decision to purchase this aircraft:
☐Style/Appearance
☐Kickback/Bribe
☐Recommended by salesperson
☐Speed/Maneuverability
☐Comfort/Convenience
☐Our Reputation
☐Advanced Weapons Systems
☐Price/Value
☐Back-Room Politics
☐Negative experience opposing one in combat

8. Please check the location(s) where this product will be used:
☐North America
☐Central/South America
☐Aircraft Carrier
☐Europe
☐Middle East
☐Africa
☐Asia/Far East
☐Misc. Third-World Country
☐World Cup Soccer Match

9. Please check the products that you currently own, or intend to purchase in the near future:

Product	Own	Intend to purchase
Color TV	☐	☐
VCR	☐	☐
ICBM	☐	☐
Killer Satellite	☐	☐
CD Player	☐	☐
Air-to-Air Missiles	☐	☐
Microwave Oven	☐	☐

Space Shuttle	☐	☐
Home Computer	☐	☐
Nuclear Weapon	☐	☐

10. How would you describe yourself or your organization?
Check all that apply:
☐Communist/Socialist
☐Terrorist
☐Crazed
☐Zealot
☐Neutral
☐Democratic
☐Dictatorship
☐Corrupt
☐Primitive/Tribal

11. How did you pay for your aircraft?
☐Cash
☐Suitcases of Cocaine
☐Oil Revenues
☐Deficit Spending
☐Personal Check
☐Credit Card
☐Ransom Money
☐Traveler's Checks

12. Occupation	You	Your Spouse
Homemaker	☐	☐
Sales/Marketing	☐	☐
Revolutionary	☐	☐
Clerical	☐	☐
Mercenary	☐	☐
Tyrant	☐	☐
Middle Management	☐	☐
Eccentric Billionaire	☐	☐
Defense Minister/General	☐	☐
Retired	☐	☐
Student	☐	☐

13. To help us understand our Customers' lifestyles, please indicate the interests and activities in which you and your spouse enjoy participating on a regular basis:

Activity/Interest	You	Your Spouse
Golf	☐	☐
Boating/Sailing	☐	☐
Sabotage	☐	☐
Running/Jogging	☐	☐
Propaganda/Disinformation	☐	☐
Destabilizing/Overthrow	☐	☐
Default on Loans	☐	☐
Gardening	☐	☐
Crafts	☐	☐
Black Market/Smuggling	☐	☐
Collectibles/Collections	☐	☐
Watching Sports on TV	☐	☐
Wines	☐	☐
Interrogation/Torture	☐	☐
Household Pets	☐	☐
Crushing Rebellions	☐	☐
Espionage/Reconnaissance	☐	☐
Fashion Clothing	☐	☐
Border Disputes	☐	☐
Mutually Assured Destruction	☐	☐

Thanks for taking the time to fill out this questionnaire. Your answers will be used in market studies that will help us serve you better in the future – as well as allowing you to receive mailings and special offers from other companies, governments, extremist groups, and mysterious consortia.

Comments or suggestions about our fighter planes? Please visit our Website at:

www.boomboomboom.com

A little comic relief when you least expect it never hurts! Yet there is a method to the madness here: the new Thoughtware says that before you can get a customer to answer, you have to get their attention! Humor is certainly one such way, but there are many others.

For example, try going to where the customer is most comfortable, to their "natural habitat," as Tom Kasten (1997, p.294), Vice President at Levi Strauss calls it. When he was responsible for developing Levis products for teens, he would drive down weekly to the famous Fillmore Auditorium in San Francisco and talk to kids waiting in line to buy tickets, observing what they were doing to customize their jeans.

"This is where it all begins, so this is what I do to learn, by watching consumers in their natural habitat."

THE "ABCD" AWARDS: ABOVE AND BEYOND THE CALL OF DUTY

Let's look at an extreme example of customer retention strategies in the mid-scale restaurant business, where it is not uncommon to see a ratio of returning versus new customers of 16:1! In that business, you don't have to have an MBA to understand that customer retention is *the* name of the game!

I recently spent four days at The Enchantment Resort in Sedona, Arizona, where I was the facilitator, thought-provocateur and "catalyst" for a Food Service *Summit Leadership Conference*.

Presidents, CEOs and other senior-level managing directors from more than 20 *competing* restaurant chains gathered together to discuss mutual problems within the industry and to focus upon some shared possible solutions. It was an extraordinary challenge given that most of them are rivals and fierce adversaries on a day to day basis, yet they left having been able to "tilt the field!"

Many fresh ideas and new insights arose from the Summit Conference, but one in particular stood out for me. When I asked attendees to share a story of exemplary customer service and how they rewarded such service, Richard Laibson, Chief Operating Officer of McGuffey's Restaurants, based in Asheville, North Carolina, told us of his creation of "The ABCD" Awards.

"The ABCDs," said Laibson, "stand for 'Above and Beyond the Call of Duty.' Any employee who performs in a manner that is ABCD will be immediately recognized by their manager and some reward and/or recognition presented."

As an example of an ABCD Award he told this story: "A waitress arrived at a table to find two distraught parents trying to calm down a screaming four-year-old child.

"'I don't want *anything* here – I don't want to eat here – I want a Big Mac – I want to go to McDonald's!' the child shouted, obviously finding McG's no substitute for McD's.

"Somewhat embarrassed, the parents hastily placed their order and told the waitress to come back in a few minutes when they'd decided what to order for their child. As the entire restaurant filled with his sounds, all eyes turned to the demanding child. Nonplussed, the waitress was determined to help, and had an idea.

"Returning shortly to the table, she gingerly served the appetizers to the parents. 'I'm afraid we're not ready quite yet to order for our little boy. He's still pretty upset,' said the mom.

"'I understand,' said the waitress, 'I have three kids of my own. But, maybe this will help.' With that, she reached down into her serving cart and pulled out a bag, and on the bag were big Golden Arches, and in the bag was – you guessed it! ... A Big Mac!"

The waitress had gone next door – to her *competitor*! – and with her own money bought the child the meal of his dreams. Was she spoiling the child further? Maybe. Was she creative in her solution? Probably. Was she providing incredible, memorable service to the parents? Absolutely! Will that family return to McGuffey's? Guaranteed!

Now *that* is service "Above and Beyond the Call of Duty!" It's also very good business. But the story doesn't end there. Kudos have to go also to the astute manager of the restaurant who witnessed the whole saga and used the new mindset to *reward* his waitress for an act that in many other establishments might well have led to her dismissal! By giving her an ABCD Award, a win-win-win was created: the family was delighted, the waitress was rewarded (with a plaque and gift certificate), and McGuffey's will retain a loyal customer.

BUZZWORD-ITUS

Providing customers with the service they expect is no easy matter. Quite the contrary. Add to this the tendency to jump on the latest fad or buzzword, and the situation only becomes more problematic. For nearly a half century, W. Edwards Deming, himself a creator of a modern buzzword "TQM: total quality management," has warned us of this as he described the focus and commitment it takes to provide top quality at the lowest cost.

"Excellent customer service" is a buzzword too. Everyone wants to meet or exceed the customer's wishes. Everyone wants to build a sustainable and growing relationship with their customers. As multi-billionaire Sam Walton, founder of Wal-Mart, once said, "The only boss we have is the customer," and his customers can "fire" him simply by taking their business elsewhere.

There is a substantial amount of research that indicates that TQM is a very effective management tool, especially in the manufacturing context. Yet everywhere I go I run across CEOs and corporate VPs who espouse TQM and who delegate the implementation of it to those under them, but are not personally committed to TQM practices. It's the old "Do as I say, not as I do," approach. Consequently, when the going gets tough, it's out with the old buzzword and in with the new one.

In the early 1990s, another buzzword was "reinvention." Reinvent yourself, your community, your business – everyone was talking it up. Yet even the man responsible for coining the term, Michael Hammer, readily says that reinvention is unsuccessful in more than seven out of ten cases. Why? Not because it isn't a perfectly viable tool in the toolbox for organizational change and development, but rather because it was a tool never fully put to appropriate use.

As you will find many times in this book, fully understanding the business you are in is a central element in creating a viable business strategy. No matter what business you *think* you are in, there are always other business and industries from which to learn. This lesson was recently understood by one of America's preeminent law firms, Pilsbury Madison & Sutro.

META-LEGAL SERVICES

Patricia Rock, former Administrator for the firm's San Francisco office, became interested in reorganizing all aspects of administration, and she started at the reception desks on each floor. Noticing that a fair amount of the receptionists' time was devoted to hospitality services – making lunch and hotel reservations, doling out seats to theater and sporting events, contracting with caterers for intense in-house client meetings, booking air reservations – she concluded that her staff were involved in a new form of meta-legal services, one that could usefully learn from the techniques of good hotel and travel management.

Consequently, she brought in a hospitality consultant, and within two weeks she was able to turn "stagnant reception" activities into "vital, hospitable" services based on the hotel model. "Pilsbury, Madison & Sutro was entering the hospitality business," she said.

She gave the staff a new name, a new identity, and a new array of training programs to build their skills, referring to them as "client service assistants." In ten working days the CSAs learned the ins and outs of the transportation, hotel, and restaurant/catering business. They condensed and centralized many functions that were repetitive, and they worked on phone manners, negotiation skills, and more. They even created a "Lost & Found" for absent-minded attorneys and their stressed clients.

Perhaps most importantly, Ms. Rock worked on her staff's attitude and self-concept by encouraging a "pro-active approach" to anticipating, identifying, and solving problems. For example, when attorneys from other offices were slated to visit the SF office, the CSAs would contact the visiting lawyer in advance, just to check that proper arrangements were in place ("will you need a lap-top?") and to determine if there was anything else they might need. The CSAs even made *suggestions* to their superiors: "Are you interested in taking in a ball game? Would you like to try a new restaurant? Have you seen Phantom of the Opera here?"

Nothing was too small to pay attention to. CSAs were encouraged to take nothing for granted in dealing with the attorneys:

"If someone needs directions," the consultant told them, "there is one fundamental question that you must always ask: 'Do you have a pencil?' I can't tell you how many times I have given detailed instructions only to have someone say to me 'Run that by me again, I didn't have anything to write it down with.'"

The CSAs began to initiate things too. Many lawyers were, shall we say, "lax" about logging in and out. So they created a "Lost Lawyers Log" to keep track of the "repeat offenders."

They created an "Information Resource Book" of common questions and common – and a few uncommon– answers. Lastly, perhaps most importantly for their own pride of accomplishment and self-esteem, for the first time they made themselves business cards! A small, simple, even obvious act, but one loaded with meaning.

As so often happens, in the course of providing excellent service to the client, the servers themselves are transformed. In this case, the CSAs' perception of their contribution to the firm and their ability to solve problems escalated dramatically. "One woman had worked here for nearly twenty years," said Rock, "and she told me that it had never occurred to her that she really was the first person the clients saw when they came to the office. She set the tone!"

THE ESOTA ENVELOPE PLEASE ...

Given that excellent customer service too often merely receives lip-service, what happens when the buzzword becomes the operative word, when the "talk" becomes the "walk"?

What happens? Shifts happen! So let me once again visit the extremes for examples that may be instructive to the norm. So unexpected was this case study that I have decided to steal unashamedly from McGuffey's ABCD Awards and create one of my own: the first ever ESOTA (Every So Often Thoughtware Award)! It is not always the company serving the client. In a "win–win" relationship, at times the *customer* serves too, as you will see.

Jeff Naleway turned thirty a few weeks after seeing a life-long dream of his come true. For years he had worked his way through the ranks of the restaurant business, from bus boy, to dishwasher, to waiter, to manager. He went on to study to become a chef, and graduated from a prominent culinary academy with a single clear dream: to open his own restaurant.

Then, one Friday night, as he was walking down a main street in Alameda, California, he noticed a nondescript, family-run, Italian restaurant with only one or two diners. On impulse, he walked in, introduced himself, and asked the owners if they would be willing to sell the restaurant to him! Thinking it was providential, the elderly Italian couple talked it over for a few days, and to Jeff's surprise accepted his offer. Jeff found two other investors, completed a major remodel and opened for business within three months – with high hopes but nary a penny to spare.

On opening night there were a scant dozen or so patrons, mostly Jeff's friends and relatives. A consummate mingler, he strolled from table to table and introduced himself to each guest.

Then something wonderful happened. After completing their main course, a distinguished looking couple in their early sixties asked Jeff to tell them about the desserts. "I'm sorry to say," said Jeff, "this is our opening night, and to be honest we do not have a dessert menu tonight. We need to purchase a new refrigerator and small freezer to handle the dessert prep. And for now, cash flow just won't allow it."

"How much does that equipment cost these days, we can't wait forever for our desserts young man!" the gentleman teased. Jeff mentioned an approximate figure of five hundred dollars. Hearing this, the couple looked at each other and laughed. "What's so funny?" asked Jeff. "Well," said the gentleman, reaching into his coat pocket. "That is not a lot of money and if you can make desserts as wonderful as your fettuccini, you deserve a break!" With that, the man pulled out his checkbook. "Here's $750. That should get us some dessert soon!"

Jeff was flabbergasted. "I don't know what to say, this is amazing."

"You don't have to say anything," said the lady.

"Well," said Jeff, "I'll set up a payment plan starting the first of the month."

"That's not necessary," she said, "just give us our first dessert on the house!"

There you have it. This first ever ESOTA! goes to that anonymous couple. They added an entirely new meaning to the term *customer* service.

SPRINKLE PIXIE DUST ON CUSTOMERS

In an increasingly complex global economy, everyone is looking for ways to gain some kind of competitive advantage. Recently, companies have been paying extra attention – at last – to who their customers are and what makes them tick. Demographic research, focus groups, polling, careful budget analysis, point of sale data ... this and much more is tracked, categorized and analyzed, all in the hope of a fraction of a percent increase in profit or a percent or two reduction in costs.

At the Disney Company, long known for its quest for quality service excellence, employee training is a major factor in delivering a memorable experience to guests. At Disney Theme Parks, employees are trained as "actors and actresses upon a stage" and are encouraged to "sprinkle pixie dust" on one and all. Employees are taught to "create the magic, share the magic, and maintain the magic" of Disney, according to Jo Spurrior (1998, p.11), president of Alliance Inc., former guest relations representative and facilitator of guest relations programs for Disney University.

In order to create, share and maintain the magic it is absolutely necessary to be in constant touch with your customers. Easier said than done. How *do* you know what your customers really want? Furthermore, what if there is a product and services gap, i.e. what if what *they* want conflicts with what *you* think they *ought* to want, then what do you do?

A YEN FOR "NOH-REOS"

For me, I use the new Thoughtware to guide my own research. At times, I have even been known to substitute cookie crumbs for pixie dust! For example, I divide the world of consumers into five categories, based in large part upon the varying ways people eat Oreo cookies! I learned this technique by observing my children assaulting a packet.

- My oldest son Kale is *practical*, he reaches into the bag and puts an entire cookie in his mouth. No frills. No patience. Grab it, and eat it.
- My oldest daughter Elina is more *demure* and prefers to dunk her Oreos, one half at a time, in milk. Removing it at precisely the right time, she nibbles at the tip of the softened cookie, often rolling her eyes in ecstasy!

- My middle daughter Caitlin is a *splitter*. She separates the two chocolate halves and dunks them. One half usually has most of the frosting, and she dunks that one last, proof positive of the lasting power of the Calvinistic notions of deferred gratification.
- The youngest daughter Johana is a *plopper*. One whole cookie goes into a larger glass of milk until it is an unrecognizable mass that she eats with a spoon. Never one to rest on protocol or manners, she really *enjoys* her food.
- My youngest son Kellin is a *scraper* who loves to separate the two chocolate halves and scrape off the cream filling *with his front teeth*. It's not a pretty sight but he's only ten and I assume he'll grow out of it before he nears retirement age.

Because my world-view is seriously affected by dividing all people into these five categories of Oreo consumption, you can imagine my surprise when I read an article in Canada's *McLeans* magazine called "The Cookie Crumbles." In it reporters unearthed an example of the new Thoughtware on customer service at Yamazaki Nabisco, which makes Oreos for the Japanese market.

Shortly after their introduction to Japan, the sales of Oreos were dramatically lower than projected, and the company undertook some sophisticated consumer research. They observed, asked questions, sent out samples and, finally, struck paydirt. As it turned out, Japanese consumers have developed a distaste for high sugar products such that they actually took out Oreos' famous creamy middle, preferring the cookies au naturale! Yes, east is east and west is west. Japanese consumers actually nixed the cream, thereby forcing me to revise my whole world-view. Accordingly, I have now added a sixth category – those who have a yen for (pardon the pun) "Noh-reos" – creamless Oreo cookies!

Today, Oreo cookies – without the famous cream filling – have become a huge hit in Japan. The plain "Noh-reo" cookies, sold under the name "Petit Oreo Non Cream" sell for $1.75 a packet. The price is higher and the quantity smaller than that sold in the US, yet the customer and the company both got what they wanted: desserts and dollars, respectively. So, by *literally* paying attention to consumer tastes, Yamazaki Nabisco validated one of my key principles of the new Thoughtware, "The customer is always right, *especially* when wrong!"

Now, you are asking, "why do you mention this in a business book?"

The answer is simple: Good service is good for business! Providing quality service is a highly cost effective skill that yields exponential results, and making a customer or client feel good will be felt on the bottom line as well.

Chapter Four

"GOOD LUCKY!"

When the Going Gets Tough, the Tough Get ... Lucky!

"O, learn to read what silent love hath writ."
– Shakespeare, Sonnet 22

THE "GOOD-FORTUNE" COOKIE

Ever since I was a child I have looked forward to occasional visits to Chinese restaurants. Even now, as an adult who far too often orders Chinese take-out, the excitement builds as the meal progresses to its culmination: the reading of the Fortune Cookie!

I admit that I have consumed large quantities of won tons, spring rolls, chow mein, and pot stickers with great alacrity, but when I place that small, bent, brittle cookie in my hand, time stands still. With a mixture of anticipation and trepidation I slowly place it between my fingers and then, like the quick, painful act of removing a Band-Aid, I *snap* it and gaze at my future as it struggles to emerge from one half of the cookie.

I hasten to add that it is not just the proposed future that interests me but, as a writer and poet, the inevitable erroneous translations from Chinese to English are often a treat unto themselves: "You will emerse [sic] victorious in all you do." ... "You will meet someone soon who will change your wife." You get the idea!

So, last year, I was preparing a keynote speech for a global symposium of Sun Microsystems' "SunService" technicians. While sitting in a Chinese restaurant near Sun's northern California headquarters in the Silicon Valley I was jotting down my most profound thoughts ... on a paper napkin. My role in the symposium was to prod and motivate SunService people to look at the emerging world differently, to think "outside the box," be more innovative and unconventional, and thus provide better service.

As I finished my meal I had roughed out the key points of my talk and had a dozen more ideas rattling in my head. Then I grabbed the cookie, and time stood still! Breaking it open in one quick movement, I shattered the cookie and the message spun downwards in the air like a poorly designed paper airplane. As I picked it up off the floor and read it, I realized that I had in my hand the title for my speech – and a new concept that I had never considered before. The fortune read:

"In love and business you always find good lucky."

Good lucky? Good lucky ... in love? Good lucky ... in business? What a concept, and what a piece of Thoughtware had been given to me. I had not previously considered the role that luck plays in my life and in the lives of successful clients and colleagues. More importantly I had not known it was possible to "find" good luck. I had always assumed that on a few special occasions, luck found me.

LEVERAGING YOUR LUCK

In my corporate consulting practice I have the opportunity to travel widely and to work with a variety of industries and professions. Of course, being a professional dilettante has its advantages and disadvantages. For me, one of the great advantages is finding commonalties amidst such a diversity of industries and cultures in the global marketplace. With this on my mind, one set of universals I have observed is that all successful companies are at times lucky, and all continuously successful companies have found ways to *leverage their luck.* Said more succinctly: successful companies don't leave their luck to chance, they go out and find it. How can you do that, how can you leverage your luck?

TOM PETERS'S PRINCIPLES

If nothing else, Tom Peters has opinions. His columns and speeches touch on everything from health to humor to harassment in the workplace. Consequently, as you might expect, he is an easy target for both accolades and animosity.

In an airline magazine column I read on a flight to Alberta, Canada, Peters took on his adversaries.

"Several readers have criticized some recent columns that suggested business success was largely a matter of luck," he says. "They miss my point: if you believe success is mostly due to luck, there are strategies you can pursue to lure luck out of hiding."

To prove this, in less than a page and a half Peters lists strategies you can use to up luck's ante. Among my favorites are the following, as well as my explanation of the implications of each for today's business mindset.

No. 28. Share all information.

To me, information is like philanthropy. You don't reap its benefits unless its potential is put to good use. Hoarding information, especially within a firm, can at best lead to missed opportunities, and at worst lead to mistrust and deceit. The advances in technology in the last decade alone make the sharing of, and access to, information infinitely easier.

No. 15. Pursue failure ... success's only launching pad.

The new Thoughtware tells me that mistakes are a good investment. Similarly, failure, properly understood, is success in the making. Tom Watson Jr., founder of IBM once observed, "If you want to succeed, double your failure rate." I agree. Too bad that Big Blue has such a short memory, having in recent years succeeded too often in doubling the rate of its failure to learn from its failures.

No. 30. "Repot" yourself every ten years.

Good things come to those who don't get too set in their ways. Peters suggests that we voluntarily change jobs or careers every so often, just to stay alive and fresh and flexible. A decade is plenty of time, almost an eternity these days, and people burn out, get stale, need new challenges. "Repotting" helps you jump-start yourself and rejuvenate your passion for what you do.

No. 34. Spread confusion in your wake. Keep people off balance ... don't let the ruts get deeper than they already are.

Most of us are creatures of habit, yet in today's helter skelter world, the new Thoughtware says you're better off getting into the habit of breaking your habits. That's how you get on top, and stay there. It also helps keep the competition confused: they never know what to expect, or when or where, because a moving target is much harder to hit.

No. 5. Read odd stuff. Look anywhere for ideas.

Lucky people in lucky companies are insatiably curious. They read an eclectic mishmash of materials, attend widely diverse events, frequent out-of-the-way places, and generally keep their eyes on the stars and their feet on the ground.

To Peters, as you can see, luck doesn't just "happen." It is not simply a fatalistic, passive experience. Rather, luck can be *leveraged*. In keeping with the new Thoughtware, being proactive with the forces around you enhances luck's odds.

Inspired by Peters, I offer seven additional fortune-cookie length axioms to help you "find" your own "good lucky"

1. Anything worth doing is worth overdoing. Learn from your excesses

What you do is worth a look, and what you *overdo* is worth a second look. Chances are, your passions rest in those things you tend to overdo. Excess – rather than moderation – is a good barometer of the areas in which you focus intense energy and passion, two well-established predictors of success.

To attract luck and to then leverage it takes work, hard work. Hard work that is work you like doing, work that you find valuable and worthwhile, is work that is pleasurable. So pay attention to your passions and excesses and learn from them.

2. Do something backwards every day

In our left-brained, deductive world most of us learn early on that logical and analytical skills are linked with career advancement. If something works, keep doing it. "If it ain't broke, don't fix it." That's the conventional wisdom.

Yet recent research on productivity and innovation reveals that quite the contrary is true. The breakthroughs, the inventions, and the new ground are broken by those who go against the conventional wisdom, who do something backwards from the prevailing paradigm.

Most of us miss many opportunities for luck to come our way by routinely repeating that which we have done before, never varying the formula, sticking with the same old habits and methods. To leverage your luck, it is necessary to break the old ways, to do something in an unconventional way. So, try this: take a different route to work; eat dessert first; open this book at random, and start reading.

3. Spoon-feed your hunches

Most good ideas arise from the passionate pursuit of irreverent intuitions. In a recent *Fortune* magazine survey of CEOs, it was found that the most successful of them said they mixed "doing their homework" with following their intuitive "gut" reactions. They are quite skilled at following their seasoned instincts, or, as a friend calls it, "following their gizzard."

Take your hunches and intuitions seriously, however irreverent or off-the-wall they may seem, and you will stack the odds of finding luck in your favor. After all, it has been demonstrated that if chimpanzees throwing darts at the New York Stock Exchange listings on New Year's Eve can consistently out-perform 80% of the market analysts, what do you have to lose?

We all have hunches, flashes of insight, lightbulbs that turn on in our heads. The problem is, when we are momentarily on fire with a new idea or hunch, we too often turn on the faucet and firehose ourselves! In my last book, *If it ain't broke...BREAK IT!*, I describe the myriad forms of firehosing in great detail. Suffice to say here, those who leverage their luck are those who can stave off the conventional impulse to firehose a new idea. In fact, the lucky ones are those who encourage and "spoon-feed" their hunches and use the new Thoughtware principles to bring them to fruition.

4. Chaos is order in the making

To many, "chaos" is seen as the evil first cousin to "change": scary, unpredictable, and to be resisted at all costs. However, the new Thoughtware says chaos has its own patterns. In the midst of chaos things are drawn towards other things in strange ways and for unknown reasons. In science's recent development of chaos theory, popularized by the movie Jurassic Park, "strange attractors" operate that are both temporary and chronic. They attract, almost magnetically, what they need in order to flourish. They are temporary in that they are always around, and chronic because new ones are always emerging. People, places, products and particles can therefore be strange attractors.

In the last few years, scientists, mathematicians, and management theorists have been intrigued by the chaos phenomenon. No wonder, in a world as fast-paced and zany as ours is today, chaos is a way of life, and it is here to stay. The new Thoughtware seeks to make chaos our friend, our partner, our ally. Therefore, chaos is understood not as random *dis*order, but rather as order about to unfold – *order in the making.* In Chaos Theory, order unfolds once something is introduced into the chaos that can provide an ordering principle. The same principle applies to "luck." It is attracted *to* you, rather than simply something that happens to you. Understood like this, luck is more pro-active than reactive, more interactive than passive.

5. Pay attention. Then, pay attention to what you pay attention to

Art, like life and commerce, is not merely a matter of paying attention, giving 110%, staying focused. We all notice things, but only a few among us take note of *what* we notice. Fewer still do something about it. You can observe a lot just by looking! Art – and business success in the new century – is always more than the sum of the parts. THough the grammar is lacking, the following is true: the artist has to pay attention, *sui generis*, to that which he or she pays attention to.

For example, I have a long time friend, Martha Benzing, herself an emerging force in American painting. For many years Martha's work has been keenly attuned to color and pigment, and her canvasses and collages reflected that interest. One day a few years ago she did a very Warholian thing. While staring at the brilliant colors in a bowl of M&M candies, she decided that those pigments in and of themselves had aesthetic value. Thus she began a series of acclaimed works, the colors in which utilize melted M&Ms! She had "noticed what she had noticed" – and applied it!

6. Always ask "Why?" Why not?

Children, bless them, are both our legacy and the bane of our existence. I know because I have five banes. Yet these youngsters can be our novice consultants who can help us to see things differently, which is frequently the crucial part of changing our luck for the better. The new Thoughtware says that adults should do more of what children do: ask basic, naive questions, especially the most essential question, "*Why*?"

For example:

- "Why does this stick and *un*stick?" That is how "Post-its" were created.
- "Why is that cat "visiting" my automotive cleaning solvent?" That is how "Kitty Litter" was invented.
- "Why do all these burrs and leaves stick to my sock?" That is the fundamental question, the answer to which led to the invention of Velcro!

To leverage luck, ask simple, fundamentally "dumb" questions: Why *have* our clients come to us in the past five years? Why *are* we profitable right now? Ford Motor Company asked some naive questions not long ago when someone pointed out to them that 89% of their operating profits were coming from the *financing* of automobiles, thereby raising the additional question, "Why are we making cars?" As it turns out, *making* the cars is but a "loss leader" on which to hang a "profit leader," the financing of the cars!

7. Open your childish eyes

One of my neighbors has a sticker on the back of the car which reminds me of most companies: "The hurrier I go, the behinder I get!" ... to which I would add: "The longer I live, the older I get!" In both cases – hurrying up, and growing old – one major pitfall that the new Thoughtware seeks to correct is the tendency to lose the ability to see things as if you were seeing them through the eyes of a child.

Quite aware of this, California developer Maxwell Drever, founder of Drever Partners, has added a new element to his quality control process.

He personally inspects every apartment and building complex at the completion of construction ... *and* he brings his eight-year-old son with him! His son is asked to tell him what he "sees," what needs fixing, and what makes no sense to his youthful mind. Only after his son has spoken will Drever sign off on a project, and then only after any of his son's ideas or concerns are resolved! For his consulting expertise, young Master Drever is paid the handsome sum of one US dollar!

So, Mr. Peters, I thank you for the provocation! One final comment though. The new Thoughtware tells us that it's true in business, romance and ... life: being lucky is rarely a matter of luck.

COMIC RELIEF: LUCK, RAISING CHILDREN ... AND ANIMALS WITH RABIES!

Recently, when discussing the "luck" involved in finding my literary agent, John Willig, he mentioned that Tom Peters had given a speech in which he quoted Ann Beattle from her book *Picturing Will* (1989). John keeps this on his bulletin board above his desk, and it guides him in keeping a keen perspective on life, business and family. Now I keep it handy too!

Do everything right, all the time, and the child will prosper. It's as simple as that, except for fate, luck, heredity, chance and the astrological sign under which the child was born, his order of birth, his first encounter with evil, the girl who jilts him in spite of his excellent qualities, the war that is being fought when he is a young man, the drugs he may try once or too many times, the friends he makes, how he scores on tests, how well he endures kidding about his shortcomings, how ambitious he becomes, how far he falls behind, circumstantial evidence, ironic perspective, danger when it is least expected, difficulty in triumphing over circumstance, people with hidden agendas, and animals with rabies.

THE LUCK OF THE LAW

Having had luck on my mind, and striving to apply my own Thoughtware, I found myself asking everyone I met to tell me stories about a recent instance of good fortune in their life. It became *my* good fortune to run into attorney Tom Zimmer at a neighborhood swim-meet.

Tom is a partner at Haight, Gardner, Poor & Havens. He and I attend the same church, live in the same community, and our kids go to the same schools. We have been friends for over a decade. So I see him regularly, but we never seem to have enough time just to talk. This time, though, I was determined. So I asked him about luck, particularly about the role luck has played in his legal practice.

"Have you noticed where your clients come from? Is there any rhyme or reason – or luck – to it?" Describing a conversation he had had with another attorney, Tom suggested that most of his firm's business comes from people he has met or worked with before, and with whom he has had direct contact *within the last 48 hours!*

"And it suggests to me," he said, "how important it is to be actively involved in various activities and to reconnect with people on a recurring basis."

In my company's (The B.I.T. Group) corporate consulting work the buzzword for this is "relationship-building," and it is vital to any industry. Return business is good business, cost-effective business, and profitable business.

"Most people have a short-term memory," he said, "so you can't just sit back and wait."

"How does luck work when you are doing research for a specific case or client?" I asked.

"Well, here's one example," he said: "It's not uncommon for me to use advance sheets (on forthcoming changes in legislation) to keep up with current material. Often-times my 'In Box' piles up with these sheets and I have noticed that frequently when I sit down and plow through them I'll pick up some gem or new piece of legislation that gives me a new approach to an issue I am currently working on."

"In fact," he continued, "sometimes, when I run out of ideas, I sit down with the assortment of advance sheets that have piled up and inevitably find something that I wouldn't have found using a more rational approach."

BEYOND "NYET"

By now I was more curious than ever. As a layman, I always think of lawyering as one of the most rational of professions. So, I pressed Tom for examples from his experience that demonstrated to him the role luck plays in practicing law. He thought for a few seconds and related this story.

Tom was doing a major aviation-related transaction involving a former Soviet Republic. At a certain point it became clear that additional information on the Republic's aviation laws and regulations was necessary, but he was having a hard time finding an appropriate governmental official to contact. He tried the Federal Aviation Administration and other agencies. No leads. He generated a long list of Soviet specialists. No help. Finally he looked up the phone number of the Soviet Consulate, dialed and asked to speak to the first available officer. No one was able to speak to him immediately, but "They pulled the name of a gentleman at the Consulate totally out of a hat," he said. "He was at lunch and called upon his return."

The consul asked Tom to describe his needs to him. "And guess what?" Tom said, "as luck would have it, the consul had been at lunch with two Soviet businessmen who were working on and supportive of the same transaction!"

With the consul's referral, Tom gained access to precisely the right people who had detailed information on the venture, enabling him to successfully complete the transaction.

Was Tom's experience coincidence? ... or serendipity? ... or providence? Nyet!

Does luck just happen? No.

Being lucky is rarely a matter of luck. Good luck comes to those who go out after it. You don't win the lottery if you don't buy the ticket. You don't ride the waves unless you get out far enough in the water.

"It may be that our lives consist of a series of concentric circles," Tom told me, waxing metaphysical, "which occasionally intersect, and it is at these points of intersection that we find good fortune. Perhaps good luck is nothing more than a process of narrowing down our options and taking advantage of the opportunities that inevitably result."

Part Two

PERSPECTIVE

Chapter Five

IDEAS

Let the Clouds Touch the Bottom Line!

"When memory is full
Put on the perfect Lid –
This Morning's finest syllable
Presumptuous Evening said."
– Emily Dickinson, Poem 1266

NO DINOSAURS IN THE KITCHEN!

There is hardly a speaker or business writer these days who doesn't shout about innovation as a crucial element in future, and on-going success of a company. It's almost a "given." Yet, few concepts are as readily espoused – and as problematic to implement – as "innovation."

It's tough to walk the innovation talk. Telling someone to be more innovative is roughly akin to telling someone to "be wealthy"! The goal is admirable, but the pathway lacks specificity! However, fear not, there are lessons taught by the new Thoughtware that make the path clearer and the power of innovation more understandable. Once again, *attitude* and *perspective* help.

Barry Diller, Chairman of entertainment and retail behemoth HSN Inc., is a man with both attitude and perspective. He understands the power of innovation too – and the risks individuals and companies run if they are not innovative and choose to rest on their laurels. "Don't ever ignore the little guys," he says, because "it's a battle between the insects and the dinosaurs." In such a battle, he asks, "Who should you bet on? Well, here's a hint. Those aren't dinosaurs running around your kitchen." (Diller, 1998, p.C1).

In a fast-forward world, the prizes will go to those who are flexible, anticipatory, and creative – essential components of an innovative process in an innovative organization. Inevitably, the seeds of future innovations are found in a single idea, ideas which come from simple sources at unexpected times via regular people like you and me.

So important are ideas to today's volatile marketplace that some very shrewd venture capitalists are willing to pay perfectly good money to get perfectly good ideas. Remember when you needed an actual business plan to elicit funds out of venture capitalists? These days, a simple resume will do the trick. Some venture firms are setting up aspiring entrepreneurs in posh offices and giving them carte blanche to figure out what business they would like to start. The firms dub their recruits "entrepreneurs-in-residence." "We'll give you $250,000 to come up with an idea," offered venture capitalist Joseph McCullen. (Useem, 1997, p.29). A series of good ideas is worth much more than that!

If the venture capitalists can identify and reward good ideas, so can any company, especially when you consider that the "entrepreneurs-in-residence" were typically in residence *elsewhere* ... but unnoticed, unappreciated, and unrewarded!

In many parts of this book we look closely at the role of flexibility and anticipation in today's marketplace, but in this chapter I will focus upon the starting point in the innovation process, the "idea." Where do they come from? What are the myths and misconceptions that the new Thoughtware reveals? What is the role of good ideas?

BILL GATES'S GATE

In recent years, considerable attention has been paid to innovation, with many proposing that it is *the* independent variable, the true key to lasting success. I make no such claim. I will say one thing with total assurance:

Innovate ... or die! Without innovation, sustainable, recurrent success is unlikely. There, I've said it. Now, let me – and others – explain why.

"In the personal computer industry," says Microsoft Chairman Bill Gates (1998, p.C1), "innovation is the path to success." That's why, he says, as new features and capabilities change continuously, as chips, peripherals, software and hardware grow cheaper and faster and stronger, "It's truly exciting to work in an industry that is so motivated to always do better."

Like him or not, Gates has always understood that the path – or the gate – to success, now depends increasingly upon *chronic* innovation and the generating of good, *implementable* ideas. (The role of "implementability" *per se* will be discussed much more in Chapter 6, INNOVATION.)

"Every product on the market today will be obsolete within a few years. The only question for my company," says Gates, "is whether we'll be the ones to replace our products, or whether some other company will do a better job ... if we don't keep up with technology and the market, we'll quickly become irrelevant."

To stave off irrelevancy, an environment conducive to innovation is a must. At Xerox, for example, having learned the hard lessons of the 1990s they turned things around using unconventional methods. Mark Chow helped put together a think tank comprised of 12–18 year-olds as one way to keep things alive! He observed that "we weren't focused on creating a result ... we were focused on creating an environment. What we wanted to do here was capture, in the purest state we could, what these young people thought, how they behaved, how they reacted." (Weil, 1997, p.104).

"WRAP" MUSIC AND OTHER ECONOMETRIC MEASURES

Ideas do not appear out of a vacuum, they usually are rooted in experience, laced with flexibility, and seasoned with large quantities of chutzpah! Even in the so-called "dismal science" – economic forecasting – ideas run along a lengthy range of plausibility. The difference between an innovative idea and a more static one can be found in the most seemingly "scientific" business forecasts. The objective of annual economic forecasting (predicting next year's economic trends) is admirable, but the tools are inaccurate at best, and obsolete at worst!

Though a "creative economist" would be considered oxymoronic by some, a close examination of the *accuracy* of their forecasts using the most sophisticated of methods is at the very least, enlightening. Like clockwork, from mid-December on, business magazines and newspapers, Internet crystal ball-gazers, and corporate Annual Reports repeat this archaic bit of ritualized guessing.

For example, many economic pundits and prognosticators annually try to forecast what the next year will bring via sophisticated projective measures. By analyzing such measures as the balance of trade, dependency ratios, and a nation's debt-to-asset rate, they are rarely able to match the forecasts of random guesses made by laymen. You think I am joking? Hardly.

Here are my Top Five choices for most zany methods in the "dismal science" of economic forecasting:

The "wrap" music theory

The handwriting on the walls of commerce takes many forms, and none struck me as being quite so wild – and predictive – as the following: one of the strongest indicators of economic activity, it is proposed, is the relationship between the sale of gift wrap and growth in the retail market.

This theory is quite simple and logical: through mid-December, retailers will order amounts of wrapping paper in line with their sales projections, and from mid-December through Christmas they will reorder in line with actual sales. Lo and behold, if you track fourth-quarter sales over the past ten years, this indicator has been extremely accurate. It's no wonder that a given year's upturn in the sale of gift wrap is music to the ears of most retailers in the Western world.

The World Cup Indicator

This is a fascinating one. This econometric model argues that as the outcome of the World Cup soccer match goes, so goes the economy. Here is how this works: the World Cup Indicator – or WCI as insiders call it – says that if you track stock market performance over the last twenty-five years, a nation's World Cup performance predicts economic growth. High ranking in soccer means a successful year ahead!

The "accuracy rate" here is above 80%. Don't dismiss this. It's worked in almost every year since the World Cup began. Except in the United States where we *never* do well in soccer.

The pub, chimp and dart theory

In this econometric model, a panel of prestigious economists from the business and academic world gathers at year end and selects the Top Five stock picks for the forthcoming year. Using advanced computer projections, careful analysis of profit and loss statements and balance sheets, the best and the brightest forecast where things are going.

Recently, however, a number of newspapers have made some interesting additions to their panels adding, for example, someone from the local sports bar who throws five darts at a copy of the New York Stock Exchange's listings. Wherever the darts land, that's their pick. The lady dart thrower at the local pub who aims at the stock market listings posted on the wall while holding a Guinness Stout in her other hand is at least as on target as the economists!

As you may have guessed, the dart players rarely finish lower than third place out of ten. A few publications, well aware of this capacity, have gone one step farther and have substituted chimpanzees for some of the economists. All things considered, this may not be a bad idea.

The January barometer theory

In this systematic theory, first made famous by Yale Hirsch in the memorable work *Stock Traders Almanac* (1994), "as January goes, so goes the year." Therefore, if January's close is higher than the previous year's close in December (using the S&P 500 Composite Index as a yardstick) the market follows suit for the rest of the year.

Wacky you say? Well, as January has gone, so have 33 of the last 38 years! That's an accuracy of 87%!

The Volume Reversal Index

Few among us like uncertainty and no one likes uncertainty less than stock market gurus and corporate economists. Each seeks out unique measures, methodologies, and theories. This is serious business. Market technicians, like Mark Lebovit, publisher of the highly respected *Volume Reversal Survey*, admit that no method is perfect science. "You're not looking at a balance sheet," says Lebovit (1994).

In Mark's case he weds the careful tracking of volume of sales with astrological and lunar data as a predictive measure! As one of Lewis Rukheiser's stock market "elves" on the USA's syndicated show "Wall Street Week in Review," Lebovitz' ideas and forecasts represent millions of dollars in investment decisions. Most investors rely on his track record with little understanding of his methodologies. "You're trying to quantify human emotion," he says, "and ultimately, that's a subjective call."

Half a brain

So, if creativity sets the stage for innovation, and innovation presumes implementation of an idea, then what must we do to gather the right people in the right organization at the right time? The answers – the keys to success – like most lasting solutions, are fairly simple. *If you train them ... they can think!*

The Kepner–Tregoe consultancy in Princeton, New Jersey, recently surveyed more than 1400 employees from over 1000 firms and, according to their president, T. Quinn Spitzer (1997, p.CL23), found that, "Workers and managers believe their organizations are operating on less than half their collective brain power, work in the dark, and are not thoroughly trained to think."

Among their list of the most creative companies are Sony, Honda, British Airways, Corning, Chrysler, Johnson & Johnson, Hewlett-Packard and Harley-Davidson. Moving critical and creative thinking into the innovation cycle is no accident, it takes a firm commitment, the allocation of plenty of resources, and on-going training. For example, when Bob Lutz was president of Chrysler, he was so intensely interested in building up the thinking skills of his employees, that in one 18-month period they trained the top 25,000 employees.

My own training program on "Break-It! Thinking" was similarly presented to more than 7000 branch managers and employees of the Bank of America in a 12-month period, where groups of as small as 12 and as large as 900 a day received training on creative problem-solving and innovative service skills.

QUESTION EVERYTHING!

Creativity sets the stage for innovation, and innovation presumes implementation of an idea, but where do we begin? What should we know in order to generate good ideas? The simple answer is ... question everything!

I know no more direct way to venture into the realm of the Land of Innovation than to cite an obvious transition that has occurred in the last decade or so. An innovative company – and this may seem ironic – is one that has very few answers, but asks very good questions. More specifically, there are three deliverables that accrue from good questions under certain conditions:

- To *catch up* you need to ask the right questions.
- To *get ahead* you need to find the right answers to the right questions.
- To *stay ahead* you need the right answers to the right questions at the right time.

Innovation-friendly companies are adept at staying ahead, and they provide systems, incentives, and resources to perpetuate new ideas. The three organizational tools – the right questions, the right answers, at the right time – they employ as a matter of course. They question everything at every juncture. The tougher and more unsettling and irreverent the questions, the better. Foe example, ask:

- What ten things will lead a customer to "fire" us?
- Where did *that* policy come from?
- Who can do my job *better* than I can?

THE VERY *IDEA* OF INNOVATION

Asking tough questions is crucial to the idea-generation process. Susan Greco (1998), understands the role of ideas and idea-generation in the innovation process, and she offers a number of insightful and stimulating examples.

Mike Stephenson, the president of Great Lakes Hybrids Inc., an agricultural seed supplier based in Ovid, Michigan, had an epiphany, she says, as "the by-product of what can happen when entrepreneurs and alcohol mix."

While he was dining in a noisy Manhattan steak house with his accountant, a German investor, a New York City investment banker specializing in agriculture, and assorted lawyers, Stephenson found himself reading the wine label aloud. He openly admits that he can't even remember what kind of wine he was holding when the idea came to him that would remake his business. After all, it was not the *wine* that intoxicated Stephenson, it was the wine's *label and packaging*.

On the label "there was a personalized message," he recalls. "The vineyard owner talked about harvest conditions, this list of the things the crop had gone through to bring these grapes along. There were family details, and he'd signed the label."

Ultimately, the message on that wine bottle was a catalyst to his own thinking, eventuating in a new line extension, christened "Signature Seed." This single idea Signature Seed helped boost the company's sales from $7 million to $18 million in four short years. Five years later, it is still the company's premium brand.

Yet, as much as Mike Stephenson's story may sound like the proverbial "lightbulb" experience, what happened *after* that dinner is much *more* illuminating. Stephenson, like many entrepreneurs, considers himself "a world-class snoop" – he fishes out ideas. That's *his* job. Then, more importantly, he is able to let go of the idea and send it on for refining by others. That's *their* job, to bring the idea to fruition. Stephenson does his part, they do theirs. The lesson here, for leaders and managers, is that there is no shortage of ideas, but, like luck (see Chapter 4, GOOD LUCKY!) you have to go after ideas, scavenge for them, *and* implement them.

If you are looking for a "steady brood of well-behaved ideas," Greco writes, it takes time and energy. Indeed, it also takes unconventional toolsets and skillsets to find viable, workable ideas in likely and *un*likely places. You can no longer rely on tradition or convention these days. *Incessant* idea generation, says the new Thoughtware, often from varying and unexpected sources (such as a wine label), is crucial to winning in today's global marketplace.

As industries blend and combine (for example, telecommunications and computers) and product cycle times are drastically reduced (in some cases down to hours and *minutes*), even the best ideas – with patents to back them up – run into competition practically upon arrival. Hot products too, no matter how unlikely their success (such as "Pet Rocks" or Beanie Babies), are the most obvious of these endangered species, yet they represent a much larger array.

"The market changes so rapidly," says Jim Amos, CEO and president of franchiser Mail Boxes Etc., "that at any moment you have to give up what you *are* for what you could *be*." (My emphasis).

These days, what you "could be" in the future (see Chapters 2, FUTURE, 7, STRATEGY, 8, PERSPECTIVE) is often limited by what you "are" today. In great part this is the case because who you are today is conditioned by an obsolete (but unnoticed) attitude, a mindset, skillset and toolset, all of which rest upon a series of false assumptions about ideas, creativity and innovation. Let's turn now to look at five such "myths" (quotations from Greco, 1998).

Myth 1: ideas will come when you need them, be patient

I often hear people propose that there's a mystical component to generating ideas, thus allowing them to assume that the process of idea-generation is out of their hands. To them, a good idea comes via divine intervention, lightning bolts, or a long bath!

Yet ideas grow, much as a garden does, via watering, good soil preparation, the right climate … and a half-way decent gardener! Inevitably, the most consistently innovative companies (such as Hewlett-Packard and Rubbermaid) have leaders who have made explicit trade-offs, with the aim of weaving idea generation into their daily discipline. It's not so much that they have to oversee the process at every juncture. However, they do have to respect it, they do have to encourage it, they do have to champion it.

Cameron Kuhn, CEO of EnviroChecks, represents an instance of this knowledge. When he knew he needed good information quickly so the operations people could perform faster, he developed a "dash report," a weekly rundown of six key marketing and finance ratios that told him how EnviroChecks was doing. Analyzing such succinct data was the easy part, the tough part for Kuhn though was psychological. Being an entrepreneur at heart, he did not know much about giving up operational control. The dash report forced him to delegate, because though the data was succinct and well organized, the work was complex and taxing. Kuhn did the only rational thing he could: he cut his own involvement by half! Whatever administrative tasks he couldn't complete "in about 20 hours a week," he passed on.

Gary Schroeder, CEO of Oakshire Mushroom Farm Inc., suggests that ideas take time to grow and develop. Schroeder spends more than half his time doing what he loves: nurturing new ideas while getting his hands dirty in the greenhouse, and calling impromptu brainstorming sessions. In fact, to do better what he does best, he left the premises! He voluntarily vacated his office and moved into another building.

"I was too involved (in day to day operations)," he admits. So, he moved out!

When you are growing shitake mushrooms, pardon the pun, you have to make some radical changes to make shitake happen!

Myth 2: all ideas are good ideas

In recent years CEOs have been battered – by competitors or, even worse, by business pundits – into making employees and customers part of the idea-generating process. Many – but not I – even propose that "there is no such thing as a bad idea." As anyone who has been at this process for a while knows, more often than not, the early ideas are typically resoundingly bad! Nonetheless, from many a bad initial idea has arisen a good subsequent one.

The first blush of ideas *should* be no more than half-baked. "Ideas are the raw material for solutions, not the solution," says Arthur Van Gundy, a professor of communication at the University of Oklahoma. If one studies the history of good ideas, he urges, one finds that the *best* of them tend to come from the *worst* of them, "with high frequency." Silly putty, for instance, started as a wartime substitute for rubber. The list goes on.

Let's look again at the great shitake maker, Gary Schroeder of Oakshire Mushrooms.

"We kicked around a lot of ideas (to grow the business), franchising (or), expanding geographically to be more local to the supermarket and restaurant customers," Schroeder explains, but their other competitors "were already there."

So Schroeder and his team arrived at an unconventional solution*: they'd sell their expertise to rival growers* rather than grow their own business units. I'll explain. Oakshire Mushroom's claim to fame is a sawdust log used for growing shitakes that reduces the harvest time from four years to four months. Shroeder and his team reasoned that they could sell their *knowledge* to their competitors for a far better profit than they could sell their mushrooms to new customers in new markets. With three managers he created a simple plan for selling information *to competitors*. The choice has paid off. Revenue increased 45%, to $5 million the first year, and Schroeder expects to double sales within a year.

Now consider Scott Reeves, president of Jinwoong Inc. USA, a $57 million division of a Korean camping-equipment powerhouse that's turned out more than 2000 tent models. Even so, Reeves's recent meeting with an Arizona inventor quickly led to the development of the "Connection tent," a two-room tent connected by a tunnel. The original inventor had a good idea, but a terrible sample product. The idea could have been seen as crude and simplistic, but Reeves knew the concept behind the sample was viable. Consequently, Reeves and his team built a better test product, refined it, and finally saw sales of the connector tent account for more than $5 million in sales in its first year.

Not resting on their laurels, one of Jinwoong's latest creations is an ungainly two-legged sleeping bag. The idea originated from a New Zealand inventor who came to Jinwoong with a rough prototype. Again, Reeves's expertise and vision combined with the imperfect ideas of someone else proved a potent combination for him, not to mention a much more comfortable night's sleep for campers around the world.

Myth 3: customers know what they want, they have lots of good ideas

"I love my customers," says EnviroChecks Kuhn, "but to meet with them would really muddy the water.

"I just want to bring them better new products. I have a great sales team. They have the customer relationships – why would I want to step into the middle of that?" His team comes up with the ideas, then shows the customer the impact of those ideas for them.

More extreme perhaps, is the approach to customer's ideas taken by the Sunnyside Cafe, in my home town of Mill Valley, California. A favorite breakfast spot for local residents, all of the waiters and waitresses wear T-shirts on the back of which is emblazoned their motto, "The Sunnyside Cafe: where the customers are rarely right!"

Even CEOs who see the virtues of quality time with customers believe in the new Thoughtware that says that ideas are only as useful as the process of which they are a part. Customers can contribute to the process by identifying unmet needs, but to distill a workable idea from what customers propose requires much more than nodding attentively and affirmatively. Suggestions must be filtered through an ever more detailed screen of knowledge about what ideas suit the company and the customer, each juxtaposed upon the other.

"We listen to our customers," says Brad Cary, president of CIBT Inc., a $12 million provider of visa, passport and other international travel services in McLean, Virginia, "but not in a traditional sense. You have to read between the lines," something that takes both skill and discipline. As simple as it sounds, a handy tool that CIBT's Cary uses is to write down every business idea he has – a habit he developed in business school. "The exercise is as valuable as the idea itself," says Cary. After all, as the new Thoughtware says, any idea worth keeping ... is worth keeping track of!

Myth 4: ideas are a dime a dozen

Many ideas are frequently best shaped through an ongoing company-wide dialogue in unlikely places at unexpected times. For example, CEO Jim Amos knew what happens *between* meetings and get-togethers at

Mail-Boxes Etc., can be every bit as crucial as what happens during them. "Ideas come *out* of those meeting, if not at them," Amos says. "Every company has a collective mind."

Knowing this, within his first 90 days of taking over as CEO, he solicited ideas that would take the company forward and still fit its culture. The result, he says, was "an explosion of ideas."

Last year an employee stopped Amos in the hall and placed a bunch of papers into his hands. Amos listened intently as this member of the accounting department detailed an idea he had for how Mail Boxes Etc. could offer more technical services to the home-office market. His idea "merited looking at" recalls Amos.

Fortunately, rather than pay lip service to this, Amos had a *mechanism* – a procedure – for such an evaluation, a place to put ideas when they arrived and a criteria for determining a good idea from amongst the many not-so-good ones. He created what he calls his "new business development group."

Every such blast leaves a mess in its wake. Amos, fully aware that following up on the best ideas would be the only way to make them viable ideas, gave the six-member group its mandate: "to evaluate, track, and refine the ideas" that flood in, and enter them into a centralized database. Presently, for example, the team tracks an average of six ideas or suggestion per *day* that arrive via the company's Web site, phone calls, letters and E-mail. Furthermore, Amos holds monthly two-and-a-half hour "renewal" meetings for all employees, to provide updates on ideas in development.

To play a more active and consistent role in generating ideas, employees need to be educated. The invitation to participate is most effective if employees know that their ideas can have an effect. So, Amos's instinct to have monthly renewal meetings is a sound one, because it reinforces the principle that employees ideas are valued, and listened to. In so doing, he is opening the rest of the process up to them.

Will Rapp, CEO of Gardener's Supply Inc., a $26 million mail-order business based in Burlington Vermont, understands this too. He recently granted a half-dozen employees their dream assignments. For six months, with the help of mentors, the employees spent eight hours per week developing new product ideas. The results were more than encouraging. Four staff members proved to be so skilled at developing good products that it's become part of their permanent jobs.

Adhering to a lesson of the new Thoughtware, and given the program's success, Rapp took the only logical next step: he junked it! Then he put something else in its place, because he knew that what he had was too potent to limit to a few people.

"We broadened the initiative to increase the awareness that we need new products and that anyone can come across them," he explains. Today, all 120 employees know the critical target numbers (such as the average gross margin dollar per square inch of the catalog space), so those who want to come up with a great new product idea know what their goal should be.

So, as the new Thoughtware states: if ideas are a dime a dozen, it'll take a fist full of dimes to find the right one.

Myth 5: thinking it is easier than doing it

Very often, coming up with an idea seems more difficult than implementing it. Myopia, bad habits, the blindfolds of too much experience – all of these can contribute to making the mind grow stale and the brain freeze over. Furthermore, assigning the task of idea creation to a chosen few only exacerbates matters, because ideas are everybody's business! But we all need tools.

Once you have adjusted your own role to make room for idea gathering, once you have motivated and educated your employees or colleagues to work with the raw material of ideas – there's one more tool you'll need to join the ranks of the top ideas generators: a Suck Index! Yes, you read that correctly. Since some ideas "suck," (as any teenager will readily tell their parents) you may well need to index them accordingly. Read on.

A Suck Index is what Tom Lix calls it, using language that sounds borrowed from those revered business strategists, Beavis and Butt-Head. Lix, CEO of NewMarket Network, a Web-site developer and marketer in Boston, Massachusetts, has his eight employees rank ideas on a scale of 1 to 10 in five areas, including up-front resources required, technical complexity, and legal liability. What the Suck Index offers is an early-warning system to catch newborn ideas that aren't likely to thrive.

What makes a Suck Index system necessary is the simple fact that if both the company and its employees make idea generation a priority, the pipeline can quickly jam up. "We come up with hundreds of ideas and bring a few to market," says CIBT's Brad Cary.

Cary is by no means alone. A similar approach is found at Mail Boxes Etc. where they grade each of 20 weighted criteria as scoring either a 1 or a 2 to arrive at a total score. At Jinwoong, the sporting-goods marketer, they use an "eight-link chain" model for managing decisions about potential new products, where each link details the company's strengths, such as distribution and in-store merchandising. Ideas are then rated and categorized.

Furthermore, ideas are not always connected to products. Many times the best ideas focus in on the process itself. At Jinwoong, for example, Scott Reeves points to a simple project management tool he called a "product-development system," a calendar that enables managers to keep better track of key deadlines as they create multiple new products. To Reeves, this was an idea that did *not* suck!

There are many other myths I could cite. Suffice it to say that the innovation process is fueled by the combination of an influx of ideas and the steady management and implementation thereof.

"The key to creativity," says Sony's advertisement in *National Geographic* (May 1998), "is yanking convention inside out." If this is true – and I suspect it is – few of us yank hard enough or long enough or often enough. Innovation is enhanced when innovation is well understood. Ideas are one part of the innovation process, and their important and disparate contribution can be well defined and understood. The potent combination of idea and implementation then, supported by an organization committed to innovation, will yield the grand prize: *repeatable* success.

Chapter Six

INNOVATION

Learn How to Back Into a Clearing

"He's certainly not playing any game we're familiar with."
–Jack Nicklaus on Tiger Woods, 1997

DAY OLD BREAD

Innovation is a word – like "electricity" or "intelligence" – that may well be easier to measure than define. As noted in Chapter 5, IDEAS, innovation is on everyone's lips these days, one of the buzzwords of the decade. Yet in my experience, few organizations fully understand how to encourage it, let alone repeatedly achieve it on an organizational level. As if this weren't enough, there are further complications: few are clear about the relative role of ideas in the innovation process, and even fewer have an attitude inclusive enough to distinguish the creative from the innovative.

For example, one of the many enemies of innovation is complacency. More specifically, success (which often breeds complacency), frequently engenders false confidence at best, and lethargy at worst. Indeed, good enough is never good enough these days, so to rest on your laurels is a sure-fire recipe for becoming old news.

Nowhere is this more obvious than in the laser-fast world of technology and many of the big winners in the industry have been those with the lowest tolerance for complacency. As Elyse Mall (1997, p.23) says about the exploding growth in website development, "remember there's no such things as a completed site. Even at the best designed Web location, information is as perishable as a baker's goods. Today's aromatic loaves are tomorrow's day-old bread." Blending a bakery metaphor with the new Thoughtware, Mall concludes: "Don't let your site get stale."

The further question you may well ask is: What blocks companies from innovation, from getting products to market? The answer, for starters, is that nothing fails like succeeding! Success itself often blocks innovation. Initial success can be the death knell for a company, because success frequently reduces your passions. Also, innovation is a process. First you generate the ideas. Then you come up with the new products and take them to market. Then the marketplace tells you if you have a success on your hands. Finally, with each success there begins the quest for the *next* idea. As any great writer will tell you, their greatest book is always their *forthcoming* book!

Chronic success requires a corporate *culture* which encourages innovation. Management's role, these days, should be to free up the rest of the organization to be more innovative.

FUELING FIRE WITH FIRE

I have known for some time that in addition to staving off complacency, the innovation process is part *perspiration*, part *exasperation*, and part *motivation*. It takes discipline to enlist the first, letting go of false solutions to provoke the second, and a fire in your belly to evoke the last. Furthermore, if the "discipline" is there, the "perspiration" comes naturally. If the myopia is diminished so is the "exasperation." But where do the passion and the fire come from? And once present, how can you or your company keep the fires of innovation fueled?

I recently paid a visit to a friend at a large computer company in the Silicon Valley. When we sat down to eat lunch we were joined by a software engineer who talked our heads off for nearly an hour. This guy's ego was bigger than the French Alps, but he was funny and quite charming in his own way. Rambling on by free associating, he described his passion for boxing, the price of Balinese wood-carvings, and his recent trip to Helena, Montana, in search of cowboy memorabilia. He went on and on, and every story seemed equally important ... to him. You know the type.

As we were finishing dessert, my friend said something semi-sarcastic about going off to get some Milk of Magnesia to settle his stomach, a not-too-subtle reference to the engineer's ramblings.

Not missing a beat, the engineer said, "That reminds me of a story about ... magnesium.

"I know a lady who is a scientist experimenting with some possible applications for magnesium for use in industrial production," he said. "She has assembled an enormous amount of information about its properties, its uses ... and about its dangers. It is very flammable you know and needs to be handled with extreme caution."

"One of the most dangerous aspects of magnesium is that it can ignite instantly and once ignited it burns at extremely high temperatures." Then he looked up at us and asked: "Do you know the best way to put out a magnesium fire?"

"I think you can ..." my friend started to say, when he was interrupted in mid-sentence. "With water? *No!*" said the engineer, answering his own question "Carbon dioxide? Absolutely not."

"Shake up a bottle of Pepsi Cola?" I chided.

"Well," he said, "I didn't know either until my friend explained it to me. You put out a magnesium fire *by pouring gasoline on it*!"

I am not making this up! He said that you extinguish a magnesium fire by pouring gasoline on it because gasoline burns cooler than magnesium and, once the gasoline is added, the temperature *drops*, allowing you then to use more conventional means to extinguish it.

I suppose this is one instance of literally fighting fire with fire. I believe that life sometimes offers us "dark angels," such as this engineer, so his magnesium story lingered with me and I thought about it all the way home. I knew there was a lesson in it for business ... somewhere.

Then it came to me. Magnesium is like a creative idea: fueling it is part of the innovation process. The innovation process doesn't extinguish anything, it simply makes the fire more manageable, and thus more likely to reach the marketplace. In the marketplace, our dreams and ideas sometimes burn as hot as a magnesium fire. For innovation to work, we have to let the dream expand and play itself out before we even consider trying to extinguish it.

Unfortunately, most of us are much better at fire*hosing* than we are at fire *stoking*. For example, we have an idea or passion and we bring it to our spouse, friends or boss and they immediately give a million reasons why it will never work, why it isn't worth pursuing. By their reaction, they are firehosing the idea as well as our enthusiasm for it. It's no wonder that after being drenched a few times we get pretty good at turning the nozzle on others – on our kids, our friends, our co-workers, even our customers and clients.

However, most insidious of all is another kind of firehosing much closer to home. We frequently turn the firehose on ourself! Next time you run into someone who is "on fire" with enthusiasm and passion about an idea or dream, try fueling their fire. At the very least, add some gasoline.

Innovation 2, Creativity 1

To the average manager or executive, the terms "creativity" and "innovation" are often used interchangeably. Yet the new Thoughtware rightly makes some useful distinctions which, when part of the new mindset, readily help guide growth and development. To illustrate this, I begin with a description of an exercise to help organize and draw out my thoughts. This tool in my toolset I call the Monty Python Interview Exercise, or simply the M-PIE. (A special "tools" section, the Tiltset, is found on pp. 227–33.) Here's how it works: whenever I have an issue or topic that puzzles me and find myself at an impasse, I find the smartest, zaniest person I know and ask them to interview and push me on the topic. I keep track of the Q & A, have it transcribed, reread it, and refine it until I strike paydirt.

In this case, since I am trying to make a distinction between "creativity" and "innovation," a fairly esoteric notion, but a crucial one for this book. So I asked my friend, Rick Crandall, Ph.D. to interview me on the subject. Rick is the editor and publisher of *Executive Edge*, a very interesting management newsletter in the US, with regular columns by Tom Peters, Ken Blanchard and myself. Having written for him for several years I knew he understood quite well the current business climate and the implications of my "quest." He also asks really tough questions.

Here is the transcription of part of my M-PIE with Rick.

Q Why isn't the average business creative?

A I think it's largely because there is very little perceived need or encouragement for creativity. Until recently, there's been a sense that it's not a necessity to be creative, with much more emphasis on operations, cost-containment, and the like. Worse still, many companies finally decide to be more creative only when the competition has dramatically surpassed them ... and by then it's a catch-up game at best.

Q So what is the difference between creativity, and what you mean by innovation?

A Well, as you know, I don't use the terms synonymously. I think of creativity as the generative side. It's coming up with the ideas, the lightbulbs, and the flashes of insight. There are dozens of games one can play to elicit this in others or in yourself. Relatively speaking, coming up with ideas is the easy part, although for some people, even that is tough.

The harder part is on the innovation side of things ... taking it to the marketplace, making the core breakthrough, setting the new standard. Today, there is no "level playing field." *An innovation is an idea brought to fruition that redefines the game and tilts the playing field.* Innovation is such that it not only creates a new product (like Post-its) or concept (like a fast food restaurant), it often alters or furthers the industry itself. Therefore, real innovation involves making breakthroughs that are by definition unprecedented. An innovation, therefore, is an instance of a paradigm shift.

Q So, it's a major change, not just a variation on a theme?

A Right. It's not just polishing the stone. It's the introduction of a new stone, which others may subsequently polish, but which you found.

Q What can the average employee do if they're not in a creative – let alone innovative – environment?

A First of all, it's probably an understatement to say that creativity is not reinforced. The truth is, more often than not, creativity is punished! There is retribution. People get blamed – or firehosed – for having come up with an idea in the first place! ("We tried that a few years ago to no avail," "That'll just cost too much," and so on.) Furthermore, there are *dis*incentives creating barriers to new ideas (like old policies and procedures). So it's even worse.

Most companies are much better at blaming than they are at encouraging. So these days, an employee, when in that kind of environment, has very few options. I often see employees mentoring or coaching their bosses, rather than the other way around! Little by little, they find ways to positively reinforce the boss or get her or him to believe the idea was the boss's to begin with. The ultimate option, of course, when all else fails, is to protect yourself and your ideas, gather as many skills and resources as you can that coincide with your values, and then … leave. Many a start-up began from a put-down.

Q Tell me more about people maintaining their own enthusiasm, creativity, morale, in an organization in which they're underpaid, overwhelmed and under appreciated.

A That, of course, certainly describes the majority of organizations these days! I think that part of the answer is to stay somewhat detached, above it all, almost aloof. You know the old cliché about not allowing "who you are" to be defined by "what you do." It is still true. Especially true in today's workplace. One of the practical things that a lot of people have successfully done is to find balance in other parts of your life that replenish and nourish, and make you fulfilled and important in the world. (See also Chapter 10, RETENTION)

If you're really lucky, for a few days or weeks at a time, it may even be that what you're doing on the job makes you feel that way. Even for people who say, during the course of their given day, "Well, I'm doing what I love, I would do it even if I didn't get paid," there is a lot of drudgery.

I think that finding a balance is important – keeping a perspective, a little detachment. You need self-discipline to be detached … and a few tools.

For example, take a tool like Edward DeBono's "six hats." You say to yourself: "I'm going to look at my day-to-day activities from the long range perspective of the "yellow hat" (the strategic hat) or the "green hat" (the financial hat)." The tool doesn't matter so long as it works! Whatever works for you. Take a close look and then reflect.

Q Could an individual change the culture of an organization by planting the first grain of sand that irritates the organization to create a pearl?

A I think it would be very rare that one individual reshapes a fairly large company. However, there are ways to juxtapose everyday job necessities and practicalities with creativity and innovation. For example, prioritizing your time. Time management, from an innovative perspective, is a little different from time management in the "day runner" mode. If you see innovation as a small "I" process, rather than a big "I" process, if you take being innovative off the pedestal, you have made great strides.

Q But we all tend to react. How can you really take control if you feel you're subject to external forces?

A Some of it is your mindset, your attitude. You have, at some point, to become *committed* to innovation. You then get into the habit of keeping your eyes open for those little gemstones and bright lights, whether they are people in your organization, or they're things you read that come across your desk. That's certainly something you could do, but it requires paying attention to that task, that opportunity, or that which matters most.

Q So it sounds to me as though an innovative person, like an innovative organization is very perceptive, right?

A Yes, absolutely. I remember Andy Warhol once said that an artist is somebody who "notices what they notice." Often in business it's a similar phenomenon. The art of business today is to notice what you're noticing, *especially* when what you notice runs contrary to conventional wisdom. That's the irony of innovation, when you think against the grain, and your intuition is that such thinking is sound, and you act upon that, you have a distinct advantage over others.

Q It's a level of self-awareness, that detachment, or ability to look at yourself. What about big companies like IBM or British Airways or Sony? How can they be more creative?

A I think that a lot of those companies became complacent by assuming that what they'd been doing was – and would remain – right, ad infinitum.

I think *they fell into the trap of assuming that creativity is the delegated pursuit of novelty*. With that mindset, it's no wonder that creativity gets pushed to R & D or to a precious few "creative people." By making this assumption, they can readily *label* creative people and then discount them as "blue sky" or "touchy-feely" types. This is both counter-productive and counter to fact. Pardon me for mixing metaphors, but since innovation begins with the creative idea (see Chapter 5, IDEAS), by pigeon-holing creativity and isolating it, they shoot themselves in the foot.

Q What about this argument? Most innovations tend to fail, at least in terms of new products that come to market. How do you handle that problem?

A: The way you handle it is just like you would handle your own finances: You have a portfolio. You don't put everything into "high risk, high yield" investments. You balance it. You mix it up. You continually have a certain percentage of your holdings which are the high-risk, high-yield options. Incidentally, this doesn't require that an organization create the high-risk, high-yield opportunity in-house. Imitation expedites creativity and moves you directly to innovation. Nowadays, it is just as easy – sometimes easier – to *acquire* a new idea rather than generating it yourself! You can do that by partnering with another company, buying certain rights/licenses, or just being the "second one" to market, but with a greatly improved product.

Q So, creativity gives you the raw materials and innovation gives you the tools to make things happen. If you expect eight out of 10 to fail, that means you just have to set them up inexpensively, quickly, and easily and see which ones survive.

A Right. And also you doggedly pursue innovation without a lot of emotional baggage attached to what fails – *or* what succeeds! If you worship the successful innovative products, you're not any better off necessarily than if you never created it in the first place. Innovation is a continuous cycle. You can see the merits of something. You can see its market potential. You can be a true believer. But, then it hits the shelves and nothing happens. You're really in hot water if you don't have something else ready to roll shortly thereafter.

Q So success can be counterproductive?

A Yes. That's the irony.

Q Isn't it possible to worship creativity?

A Yes, you can worship "creativity" in the same way you can worship "productivity" or "profitability" or any of those buzzwords. That's one of the ways I try to nudge companies that perceive themselves as having a "creative culture." I make them look at how they have organized structurally for the innovation process – and thereby, typically, atrophied the process.

What organizations sometimes do is use creativity as a platform rather than a springboard. They elevate it to the point where that's their organizational self-concept. The problem is, then they can readily fall prey to the same thing that happens to painters, dancers, poets and other artists. They get so self-possessed with the life of the "artist" that they're unable to function in the real world, let alone produce any more art. The poet Charles Olson once observed that "what's private, is public. And the public is where you behave."

Similarly, you can have a great culture of creativity that has no pragmatic sense to it. Therefore, in any separation of the two terms (creativity vs. innovation) you can have a creative company, but not necessarily a very innovative one.

I see this in graduate business schools, too. Those who believe in creativity, sometimes base their belief on an understanding of creativity as an extension of projective processes (such as planning, forecasting, and modeled projections) which rests on a very interesting assumption. It's another paradox: the assumption that projective measures are best if based in the past, funneled through the present, and thereby become predictive to the future. Increasingly, I have seen that not to be the case.

Q I am not sure I understand.

A Let me try a different track here. I've always liked the history of ideas. So right now, for example, I'm very interested in the evolving history of "fuzzy logic," because we're right in the middle of the creation of that history. By analogy, I think of the standard MBA strategic planning models as being ostensibly a yes-no approach wherein the switch is thrown once all the data is in. They plan as though the past and the future worked like a toggle switch!

On the other hand, I think the marketplace operates really on best "guesstimates." Within boundaries of X, you do this. Within parameters of Y you do that. That's the fuzzy logic toolset that the new Thoughtware fosters.

Q Define "fuzzy logic" for us.

A Fuzzy logic works within ranges of probability and then goes ahead and makes a best guess that is logically derived and is likely to encompass the vast majority of outcomes, say 90–95%. In other words, if it knows 85% of the time such and such is going to happen, it will not have to wait until it happens 100% of the time to go into the yes-no. It will say: "If we move along this path the likelihood is this result." Fuzzy logic is used in computer programs in Japanese washing machines now. You just throw all the clothes into the washer, the fuzzy logic chips then "decide" what your clothes need, and the water temperature and cycle is set automatically while the proper amount of soap is released for that load. The only fuzzy part is what gets trapped in the lint filter!

Q Fuzzy logic would fit with your earlier point about having a portfolio, having a lot of little creative shots, of taking – yet minimizing – risks.

A I am going to take it a step further, beyond fuzzy logic if you will. Chaos theory has fascinated me for years. In chaos theory, there is a notion which I find very, very useful. It's the idea of "strange attractors" (see Chapter 4, GOOD LUCKY!, for more on chaos theory). I think that every organization has within its product capabilities, within its resources, and within its people, a wide array of strange attractors.

Q How would a person be a strange attractor for an organization?

A You have people in any company who are "naturals." Sometimes we refer to them and say, "Oh, she's a natural negotiator, or he's a born leader." They attract to themselves situations which allow them to practice their trade. They are adept at detecting, being sensitive to, or on the lookout for, provocative, magnetic forces within that organization. They attract the necessary resources and energy to them that is needed to make innovation happen.

The irony is, for example, that it is very rare that the best negotiator in an organization is utilized as the company's negotiator. "Officially" they will be performing some other role that may have very little to do with utilizing their negotiation skills. So the organization has to have processes to discern a person's strengths, then free them up to perform the right roles, roles that enhance the strange attractor quotient.

Q Let's say you've stimulated creativity in the organization, put in an idea-friendly, suggestion system, and made a commitment to innovation, then what?"

A First of all, a suggestion system to generate innovation doesn't necessarily stimulate or aid creativity. It may also stimulate bad habits done in a new way. That aside, if you want to add value, perhaps to the creation of a new product, it has a lot to do with the allocation of resources, the commitment of management, and the self-confidence and self-esteem of the individual employee or champion of that idea. Again, an idea – however creative it may be – that is left unimplemented has never yielded an innovation. That's why creative people are expendable today, innovators are not.

Q The first two – allocation and resources management – are basic necessities for innovation. The latter point – the self-esteem – can you talk more about the individual champion or the organizational culture's self esteem?

A For starters, we are once again talking about "attitude" here. If you have low organizational self-esteem it is no different from individual low self esteem: it is a draining, depressing milieu in which the best thinking is hard to come by. Further, some of the most innovative people in organizations are the last to think of themselves as being creative. I have seen this over and over again. From their perspective, they're just doing their job. Yet they seem to know what "matters," what will contribute to the success of the organization.

Q This sounds a lot like Steven Covey's writing too.

A It's not too far afield from what Steven Covey in his book *Seven Habits of Highly Effective People* (1989), was talking about when he showed how the "urgent" gets in the way of the "important." For the most part, organizations encourage and reward reaction to the urgent, the urgencies of day-to-day, quarter-to-quarter, client-to-client pressures and crises. If there are some tools in the toolbox, people who want to have more options than triage or crisis management, they'll need a new array of skills and tools.

For example, if a major bank or insurance company, like Lloyd's of London or Bank of America, wants to find some way of blending customer service and the selling of banking products, they may not be well-advised to begin with a sales training course for their tellers or agents. Rather, they may want to begin with something that has more to do with self-esteem or communication or people skills. When you encounter resistance in the sales process, such skills may help to get a sale if you understand the ways in which the person you are addressing is resisting you, and your reaction to it. Some people, when somebody resists them, push harder. Others let go and say, "Okay, I'm going to go with this potential customer's priorities." In other cases, they don't have the skills in active listening. So they don't have a clue as to what is happening right in front of them.

Q So, creativity and innovation are similar – but different?

A Creativity and innovation go hand-in-hand. That's a given. However, far too few creative people are innovative. Whereas the reverse is not true. Most – no, all – innovative people are creative. Innovative people have all of the traits of a creative people plus some. In psychological terms:

- They have the ability to sort, cull, and select from a wide range of creative ideas those ideas that can be taken to the marketplace.
- They have an entrepreneurial confidence about the future.
- They have a higher level of comfort in a changing environment.
- They closely tract the pulse, pace and preferences of the customer.
- They initiate independent action.

These are the five most common characteristics of innovative thinkers and innovative organizations. The good news is innovation can be taught, encouraged, and supported. That's what the smart companies are doing these days.

Try an M-PIE of your own some time soon. Remember too, what was proposed early on in this chapter, the importance of asking the right questions at the right time. By inviting someone to ask you tough, even unsettling questions, you often can make considerable progress in a relatively short period of time.

TAKE A "THINK WEEK"

Bill Gates has managed to utilize the advantages of the M-PIE via his widely syndicated column. In it, he often utilizes a Q & A format with readers asking him critical questions. Recently a college student wrote in to ask: "In my college computer class we're studying your book, *The Road Ahead* (1996). I can see your vision coming true but I want to know where you get your ideas about the future."

"I think a lot," says Gates (1997, p.D1). "Sometimes I take a whole "Think Week" away from my office routine. I have a lot of people working with me who ponder the future, too. Like many businesses, ours is built on looking down the road and preparing for what we foresee." Gates goes on to acknowledge the value of diverse reading (he likes science fiction, for example) and good listening skills, but says none of this *per se* offers a good "road map."

"When I think or write about the future, I'm trying to draw a map that connects the present to the future," says Gates, "and my key message about the future – that everybody will be connected, and that computers will see, listen, and learn – have all been said before by other people."

Perhaps most importantly, he offers an insight into the lessons of the new Thoughtware when he says "most ideas about the technological future come along when they're completely *impractical*." (My emphasis). Unlike most of us though, he says "I am in an unusual position because my company is doing a lot of work to define future software."

Therefore, as we teach in the Break-It! Thinking™ training program, Microsoft is of the mindset that actively seeks to "invent the future!"

HOW TO THRIVE!

Forecasting *who* will survive (let alone thrive) isn't easy, and knowing *how* to do so is even harder. What do the innovative companies do in order to plan for their futures? How do they operate such that innovation is a chronic condition? What attitudinal sets shape their endeavor? The following five case studies of the new Thoughtware provide some simple and telling answers:

1. Do what Rubbermaid does

Named repeatedly by *Fortune* magazine as "the most respected company in America," their Chairman and CEO, Schultz, gives us his four word formula for success: "Innovation and steady management." Sage advice when you consider that, on average, Rubbermaid introduces a new product *every day of the year*! To accomplish this feat, the entire company – from new employee to CEO – must be aligned for innovation-conducive actions. As we have seen, nothing can *fail* an organization like success. So, these days, the new Thoughtware exhorts us to create an organization that can develop and implement a process for perpetual innovation.

2. You don't need names on the uniforms, just good people in them

Recently, Penn State University went undefeated in American college football, including a resounding Rose Bowl victory over Oregon. In an era of huge egos and even bigger salaries amongst many professional athletes it has always been the policy of Penn's coach Joe Paterno not to put the names of his players on their jerseys. Football, like business, is a team effort and as such it is always more than the sum of its named parts.

An organization built upon egos and personalities, or one with large spotlights on the "rising stars" to the exclusion of the average workers in the pressurized modern world, will have a half-life that is roughly equal to that of whipping cream in the hot sun! (See more on this in Chapter10, RETENTION),

3. Don't hesitate, imitate

Imitation may be the highest form of flattery, but it is also often the highest form of profitability. Steven Schnaars's book *Managing Imitation Strategies* (1996) shows how companies coming into the market second, often end up first. Schnaar cites dozens of cases. For example:

- Ticketron pioneered telephone-based ticket sales until Ticketmaster moved in.
- RC Cola pioneered diet and decaffeinated colas, but Coca Cola and Pepsi stepped in later and captured the market.
- Diners Club lost out to American Express in the early days of credit card sales, and AmEx is now trailing VISA. The list goes on and on.

So, if you don't have the innovativeness of a Rubbermaid you can still build an organization to *acquire* an innovation by mastering another's idea, perfecting the execution, and/or improving the service. If Robin Hood were alive today, his adage might be: Steal from the rich ... you might get richer than they are!

4. Do it unconventionally

"Finding out where conventional wisdom is in error, that will give you business advantages," says the $3 billion dollar man Larry Ellison, co-founder/CEO of Oracle. "It's where you make your discoveries. When everyone is doing it one way and you do it another way, you have a huge advantage in art, business, or anything you do." My last book, *If it ain't broke...BREAK IT!: Unconventional Wisdom for a Changing Business World*, examined this in great detail. Contrariness pays off!

5. Stop getting sick

In the pages of Gary Hamel and C.K. Prahalad's insightful book, *Competing for the Future* (1994), downsizing, restructuring and re-engineering are portrayed rightly as "simply the penalty a company pays for not having anticipated the future."

As an example of a better way to go, they offer us the case of Chrysler CEO Tom Eaton. Shortly after taking over the job, Eaton brought in dozens of senior executives to compliment them on quarterly earnings, quoting several industry commentators who had praised Chrysler's turn-arounds. However, there was one slight omission in his remarks. The articles he cited were written in 1956, 1965, 1976, and 1983. Once a decade, he mused, Chrysler had become ill and then undergone a miraculous resurrection. "I've got a better idea," Eaton said. "Let's stop getting sick ... My personal ambition is to be the first chairmen never to lead a Chrysler comeback." The new Thoughtware therefore teaches: the best way to stay healthy is to stop getting sick!

THE KEYS TO THE KINGDOM

The 1990s have often been characterized as a decade of change and transition, and the smart companies are those which understand and *maximize* that change and transition process. As we enter the new century, sufficient perspective now exists to enable us to discern and articulate the nature of this change, as well as honing in on the direction of the transition. Having now looked at some of the common myths surrounding the innovation process, the question remains how do we create an innovative organization?

All *repeatedly* successful companies have found there are *three* keys to success. In examining the characteristics of successful companies at The B.I.T. Group, as well as providing tools to individuals and organizations through our training programs, we have identified three core operating principles that, in combination, form a practical, organizational pattern to create an innovative organization. All continuously successful companies have learned how to:

1. break old habits
2. break new ground, then
3. break the mold!

The success stories of the twentieth century have been companies that were faster, more innovative, and better able to think differently about their markets, products, processes, customers, and employees. This will be a recurring theme in the twenty-first century as well. Playing by the traditional rules will be at best problematic, but for the foreseeable future, the innovators will thrive!

EPILOG

For the want of an innovation, creativity was lost.
For want of creativity, the idea was lost.
For want of an idea, the product was lost.
For want of a product, the customer was lost.
For want of a customer, the business was lost.
For want of a business, the company was lost.
All for the want of a single innovation.

Chapter Seven

STRATEGY

It's Better to be Useful than "Correct"!

"THIS is what history is: COMPANY, what we all keep right now."
–poet Charles Olson

STRATEGY AS PHILANTHROPY

To my mind, good strategy is like good philanthropy, it becomes "good" only when put to good *use*. Left isolated in the realm of the macro, the hypothetical, the abstract, or the theoretical, most strategies have little impact on business success. As the managing director of a huge financial institution once told me, "Managers with a thousand ideas are easy to find. But the rare bird is one that knows *which* three will actually work!"

Unfortunately, more often than not, strategy is put to no particular good use at all. In part this is the case because there is a great deal of confusion about what strategy is (and what it is *not*), what its proper role and function may be, and how to align the walk (implementation) with the talk (the strategy). Worse still, the development of strategy is relegated to an annual event or facilitated offsite. Strategy therefore gets set apart. You wouldn't think of devoting a day-and-a-half per year to serving customers, you wouldn't think of improving your products only at an off-site retreat center. Au contraire! Like good service and good product development, everyone in the organization must assume responsibility for it every day of the year. That is what the new Thoughtware teaches us.

Fortunately, the new Thoughtware has much to offer in this area, and the remainder of this chapter will address these and related issues.

As we shall see, sound strategy is:

- the result of good information, sound instincts, and regular detached "reflection"
- truly flexible and pro-active
- a dynamic process, not just a "plan."

SERVE 'EM ... THEN BUY 'EM!

Tim Conlon is the CEO of the fastest growing connector company in the world, Berg Electronics, recently purchased by Paris-based Framatome. At the age of 47, he is wiser than his years, and thinks better on his feet than almost anyone I know. Most importantly, his sense of strategy is developed and acute. He knows his company, his industry and the business he is in.

"We connect everything between the silicon and the customer," he recently told his senior management team. In saying that, he wanted to drive home the point that Berg is playing in a much bigger game, with much bigger opportunities, and much bigger payoffs than his team may have imagined. It is no wonder that in less than four years, Berg (which initially bought DuPont's connector business), grew from a $200 million company to one that is now at $1 billion.

I have had the pleasure of working with Tim for some time now, and am always impressed by his ability to see the big picture, to motivate and lead his company, and to retain an incredible commitment to personal, even spiritual development.

Last year, for example, I was asked to be the consultant on organizational change and innovation for a gathering of the dozen senior managers, to do some long-range planning. A devout Catholic, Tim was to introduce me and with a series of well-choreographed accolades, transfer his full "authority" as CEO to me! He stepped to the front of the room, looked at everyone, briefly mentioned the context for the meeting, then asked everyone to bow their heads while he led us in a word of prayer!

In over 20 years of consulting in more than a dozen industries and over 50 countries, no one – Catholic, Buddhist, Jewish, Muslim, Protestant, CEO or new hire – no one had ever started a meeting with a prayer. It signaled to me that Tim had deep values that were the basis of all he did, including the development of strategy.

In my preparation for the sessions, I had conducted a number of interviews, developed a set of what I call "strategic givens" (fundamental assumptions that I felt were guiding their current strategies), and had read everything I could about Berg, both internally, and from outside sources.

During the course of this preparation, I paid special attention to the Annual Report to try to determine the basic elements contributing to the incredible "rate of ramp" (growth) they had created. I saw that their growth had been largely fueled by acquisitions (such as buying the connector divisions of Lucent Technologies, Ericksson, and DuPont). I also noted that they had a strong commitment to customer service and to the quality of their products.

Of course, there is no real news here. Many a modern success story has been built on service and acquisition strategies. However, in carefully reading the Annual Report, the new ingredient, the essential ingredient of the Thoughtware mindset, was Berg's uncanny ability to *buy* customers!

Yes, you read that correctly: Berg Electronics buys its customers! Sure, Berg *acquires* companies, some of which are potential competitors. It also targeted a number of its own customers and locked in *their* customers simultaneously. For example, Lucent had subcontracted with Berg to provide a number of its connectors and cable assemblies. Part of the agreement to acquire Lucent's connector division was the provision that for a specified period of time, Lucent would agree to use Berg connectors in its telecommunications equipment. Thus Lucent got out of the connector business and Berg gained a guaranteed customer volume! A true symbiotic, "win-win" arrangement.

SHOW AND TELL AT DELL

It is the win-win that now characterizes a basic new Thoughtware strategy. I was in Austin, Texas, recently for meetings with senior training and development management at Dell Computers. Dell, as you may know, was founded in the mid-Eighties by the then 18-year-old, and now legendary Michael Dell. In a decade they are now about one lap-top sale away from adding yet another billion dollars to the company.

Dell grew a phenomenally successful business based upon three simple elements which guided their strategy:

1. maintain direct relationships with customers
2. develop high quality products that are custom-configured and sold at reasonable prices
3. provide industry-leading service and support.

"We have built a company," says Michael Dell, "and we have prospered, by sticking steadfastly to this principle."

I was invited to talk to them about new ways to *think* about business in the 1990s. So "why," you might ask, "would such a dynamic company want to mess with the success of their proven strategy?" The answer is obvious, they understand that the best time to "partner with change" is when you are riding high, not when you are in a slump.

In today's confusing, cat-quick world, Dell is breaking new ground daily and is committed to continuing to do so. This is easier said than done. The new Thoughtware requires that individuals and organizations learn to ask the right questions if they are to find the best solutions.

MANAGING 1, MANAGERS 0

"Chevron to Lay Off 750." "GM Cuts Another 12,000 Jobs." "PacBell Cuts Workforce by 3000."

Welcome to the world of downsizing, rightsizing, and corporate triage. Spawned in the 1980s and perfected in the 1990s, this cut-your-losses strategy is going to be with us for quite a while.

I see this mindset as being extremely simplistic and myopic. Cutting jobs to appease shareholders or to effect a change on the proverbial "bottom line" has not been sufficiently documented as a viable means of creating a sustainable, successful track record. It's a Band-Aid mindset. The data suggest that lean may be "mean," but lean may not mean "more productive and profitable."

In fact, recent research indicates that there is little or no relationship between the conventional cost-cutting measures and corporate profitability and productivity. For example, The *Endicott Report* on productivity in the 1980s found that even amidst the halcyon days of reductions, mergers and restructuring, productivity rose a scant 1.2% per year or 10–12% for the entire decade!

Now, compare this with the 1950s, when the productivity rate was 3.5% a year – or 35% for the decade – and you get a sense of the proportionate differences. However, these numbers do not tell the whole story. They never do.

The major difference between, say, the 1950s and the 1980s and 1990s is that in recent years most of the job reduction has occurred in the ranks of the middle managers.

In a rapidly changing world economy we need *more* "managerial skills" from employees at all levels. As we will see in Chapter 10, RETENTION, we need to develop flexible strategies in order to retain top talent and keep them productive. One of the great ironies of the 1990s is that despite the downsizing within many companies, especially in middle management, as the *position* of manager is eliminated, the *skills* of a good manager are even more in demand.

Or said another way using a sports metaphor, today's economic box score reads: Managing 1, Managers 0.

There is a way out of this situation and it is to adjust your attitude, and retrain your workforce. If you eliminate managerial positions you have to train your remaining people so that they can become little "m" managers in everything they do, and feel comfortable in that role.

In my company's work in corporate training and education we have found that the top managerial skills can be taught. That's the good news. The bad news for many is that the successful, practical application of these skills is directly related to the attitudes and values of corporate leadership.

The top executives have to create a climate that encourages the use of good management skills throughout the workforce. It is not enough to provide training, because skills can be *taught*, but the enthusiasm and encouragement to apply them must be *caught*!

Here are some of the most important skills, attitudes, and values these new little "m" managers must possess. They should be:

- agents of change
- extremely flexible
- practical and strategic thinkers
- assimilators of disparate and eclectic information
- quick decision makers
- highly innovative
- high in integrity
- motivating to others
- risk takers
- able to thrive in a team environment
- prepared to break bad habits in order to break records!

By learning such skills employees – and their company – gain a competitive advantage. Employees will be better equipped to exceed their own personal goals, the company's mission, and the customer's needs. Let me illustrate this.

SWEETS FOR THE SUITE

Founded in the 1950s to provide small portions of sugar to the food industry, by 1983 New York based Sugar Foods Corporation had a highly profitable business providing sweets for the suite.

Their business? Selling little packets of sugar and Sweet 'N' Low. Nearly every hotel, restaurant, and dormitory in the world offered their mini packets of saccharin, and business was booming.

Then the new kid came roaring into town. With the entry of NutraSweet many people began to switch from saccharin to aspartame. Did he look at the "competition" with fear and trepidation? Did this put the fear of God into Sugar Foods Corporation? Hell no!

Donald Tober, whose father founded the company, took it over in 1958. For him, the new competition was a new opportunity. In his mind, not only did the arrival of NutraSweet expand the whole category of artificial sweeteners, it also afforded him a chance to completely rethink – or in today's jargon, reinvent – his company.

Tober must have asked himself what sort of business his company was in. He could legitimately have said that the company was in the sweetener business. He could also have said it was in the diet business.

If it was in the sweetener business, NutraSweet would expand the sugarless industry and create new markets for Sweet 'N' Low. If it was in the diet business, weight conscious people would continue to create a demand for Tober's products once the dust cleared from the NutraSweet invasion.

Using the new Thoughtware, Tober also came up with an innovative answer to the question "What other businesses are we in?" Tober decided that his company was in *packaging*.

Not only did Sugar Foods have a product, they had what the business gurus refer to as core competencies, sophisticated know-how and intellectual capital which become natural resources to a savvy business leader.

That realization led Tober to the idea of brand leasing. From his experience, Tober knew that consumers like brand name products whether they are at home or out. A bit of Sunkist lemon juice here, some Earl Grey teabags there.

Understanding that he was not in the business of creating brand names, in 1988 he moved quickly and developed an ingenious scheme. Sugar Foods began leasing brand name condiments from manufacturers, repackaged them into individual portions, and sold and distributed them to the food service trade.

Even after this, he wasn't done yet.

He negotiated 10-year leases and offered manufacturers a percentage of his company's gross from millions of packets priced at between a cent and five cents each.

Manufacturers pay good money to get their product sampled. Under Tober's scheme, the samples themselves become an instant profit center! He identified the top brand name condiment in every category and leased the rights, thereby creating a win-win-win game: for Sweet Foods Corp., for condiment manufacturers, and for the brand name conscious public.

In 1989, Sugar Foods had revenues of $90 million. By 1992 his sales were over $150 million. In 10 years sales revenue had climbed to $250 million. How sweet it is!

BACKBOARDS AND BOARDROOMS

One of the tools in the Thoughtware toolset is the ability to use metaphors for factual benefit and strategy development. A metaphor often gives you a window into your career or your industry, helps to reveal something hidden to normal frames of reference. For example, I often ask CEOs with whom I work, "If you were to describe your company using a sports metaphor, what sport best captures the essence of your company?"

- Many will talk about football or rugby, tough gritty games that are decidedly competitive and traditionally macho. It's hulk vs. bulk.
- Others like something a little faster and will identify with a relay team, where working at top speed you are able to hand the baton to the next runner in a seamless, synchronized act.
- Some will cite platform diving where you step to the edge, select your dive and the degree of difficulty, and with all eyes watching leap into the warm, moist air totally focused on a spot in the water.

In America, my favorite metaphor for the nature of business today is basketball. Springtime is "prime time" and "show time" for basketball lovers around the country. What are the lessons that transfer from backboards to boardrooms? What lessons about the new Thoughtware's strategy formation can we learn from a game that evolved from throwing ears of corn into a peach basket hung from an old barn?

Here are five of my favorite bits of basketball wisdom:

1. See the whole court

Every player will tell you that the best separate themselves from the rest because they have the broadest field of peripheral vision. Michael Jordan, Elgin Baylor, Dr. J., Larry Bird, Magic Johnson, and Shaquille O'Neal all have the innate ability to see the big picture as it unfolds at high speed.

In business this is vital these days. You have to see beyond your company, your product, and your niche. You have to see the entire industry on a global basis from the perspective of the emergent future if you are to have a sustainable record of achievement.

2. Move without the ball

The great players perform some of their greatest moves *without* the ball. They keep running, they never stand still, they get into position, and they anticipate what's to come.

Successful companies do this too. The company's new product rises on the charts, gains greater market share and – guess what? – that company puts *more* money into R&D, busily creating the *next* product. That's how you get from "good" to "great"!

3. Use the backboard

Though the media and many fans love the power slammin' jam or the swishing three pointer from 24 feet away, the best athletes learn to use the backboard wherever possible. It gives you more options for scoring. It's a softer, finesse shot that lets you put some "English" (spin) on the ball and allows the backboard and the rim to be your friend.

I remember UCLA's legendary coach John Wooden pulling players off the practice court when they failed to use the backboard. He knew what he was doing too, he still holds a record number of national collegiate titles.

In business, there also are some fundamentals that we should keep in sight: listen to your customers, treat your fellow employees well; and don't lose sight of your core values.

4. Make your free throws

Shooting free throws is a luxury. They are a "sure thing," an ideal opportunity to score. Think about it. When shooting, you are not running. You can bounce the ball innumerable times. You can take a deep breath or two. No one can guard you. You can set your feet exactly where they are most comfortable.

Making your free throws, however, is more problematic. That's because it is largely a mental part of the game. You have to concentrate. You have to focus. You will have only yourself to blame … or congratulate.

In business, as in free throw shooting, many things are within our control but we lose our focus and our discipline. We get too complacent, we tend to "leave well enough alone." We play it safe, and that's dangerous!

5. Know thy teammates

Basketball, like business, is a team sport. No one does it all by themselves. That's one reason why the team with the highest scorer in the league rarely wins the championship. The great players are the ones that know what their team mates can – and can't – do. The great players are the ones that cater to their team mates' strengths not their weaknesses. The truly great players make everyone around them play better. (For more on this, see Chapter 12, !EADERSHIP.)

Let the best ball handler break the full court press. Set a screen for the player with the quick release jump shot. Throw a high lob pass to the power forward trailing you on a fast break. Play to *their* strong suit. Make playing to their strengths *your* strong suit!

Unfortunately, business doesn't quite "get" this. Most companies spend an inordinate amount of time identifying, classifying, and criticizing an employee's weaknesses and far too little time fine-tuning, and encouraging the employee's strengths. The most successful companies are the ones that match personal strengths with organizational needs.

So, as you watch the highlight reels from the world – in Europe, or North America, at the high school or Olympic levels – think about what you can learn about work, and about life, from those women and men who so effortlessly put a round ball through a round hoop. Think too about the insights that can come from the simplest of metaphors.

BUSINESS'S BEST OLYMPIC SPORT

Now, some non-Western readers, and perhaps some men or women may find it hard to understand my preference (and passion) for basketball as a metaphor for doing business. So I offer the following alternative.

The XXV Olympiad in Barcelona, Spain, got underway with a spectacular opening ceremony filled with angular galleons, surrealistic suns, flamenco dancers, perspiring human pyramids, and a hobbled archer with pinpoint accuracy whose flaming arrow ignited the massive Olympic torch, striking it dead center from 150 yards away! The thrill of victory, indeed.

Then came the agony of defeat. We watched tiny gymnast Kim Zmescal fall from the balance beam, climb back up and continue. We watched Inga Thompson fall off her bicycle, crawl out of a ditch, get back on her bike and nearly recover enough ground to win a medal. What drama.

What does this have to do with strategy and innovative thinking in the world of work?

Well, as intense and memorable as these Olympic moments are (and as perfectly suited as the analogies between sport and business can be), all of these athletic performances are not nearly as useful in today's business world, nor do they perhaps have as much to teach us, as another Olympic sport. Please read on.

Ted Cocheu, former Director of Training and Development at a major technology company in the Silicon Valley, is a very bright guy who has that rare ability to see the forest and the trees simultaneously. His company, Conner Peripherals, grew to a billion dollar level at record speed, fell almost as fast, and was then merged with another, Seagate Technologies, and yet neither company existed a decade and a half ago.

Being insatiably curious I was determined to try to find out from Ted what made Conner run and fall. I asked Ted: " How do you balance the risky and volatile nature of your industry with the constant demands for growth from shareholders? How do you "plan" in such an environment? How far do you look down the road? What special kinds of research do you do on the market and new products?"

He stopped my marathon list of questions, smiled, and said: "Around here we have a model we use all the time ... skeet shooting!"

"Skeet shooting?" I said, incredulously.

"Yes," he said "skeet shooting!" One shooter. One rifle. Several laser-fast clay pigeons. "You see," he continued, "the target markets and new customers are moving so fast, and they come from out of nowhere ... there is no way we can keep them in our sights long enough. So, like a good skeet shooter, we have learned that we have to shoot ahead of the target to stand any chance at all of hitting it!" Of course, you hit some and you miss some.

Think about it. Things are changing so fast, and the world is so full of clay pigeons, we all have to learn to take an educated aim, shoot according to our best hunches, learn from our misses and failures, and move on to try again. Ted Cocheu is right. Nowadays, the strategic business marksman's motto is: Aim. Fire. Ready.

OK, now it is your turn! Pick a metaphor, any metaphor. It needn't be sports, it can be almost anything. For example, answer the following questions about your company:

1. If your company were to be described as a kind of footwear (or motor vehicle, or food), what would it be?
2. Why did you pick this answer, and what insight does it offer you about your company?
3. Now answer questions 1 and 2 again, this time using yourself in place of your company. (What kind of footwear best captures your style and personality, and what does this reveal about you?)

HOW HEWLETT-PACKARD RECYCLED THEIR RECYCLING PLANS

When Hewlett-Packard was designing its terminals assembly plant in Roseville, California, the project leaders gathered around them what I call a "diagonal slice" of the company's workforce. New employees, senior managers, cafeteria personnel, architects, engineers, and assembly line production workers formed a design team with a single mission: create an assembly facility that met both cutting-edge production standards *and* reflected the human values of those who would work there.

For example, not far into the design process consensus emerged around the value of environmental awareness, and the team decided to create a mini-recycling center within the facility. When the Roseville Plant opened, parts arrived from the supplier, were removed from the boxes and placed on a conveyer belt. Simultaneously, the boxes and packaging material would head off on another conveyer belt into "recycling land." Not a bad idea, and trees throughout the Pacific Northwest no doubt breathed a small sigh of relief! They thought it! They designed it! They built it!

However, after about three months in operation, a new employee approached his supervisor with an ingenious idea: "Let's get our suppliers to send the parts in boxes packaged and printed with the H-P logo and specifications on it," he said. In other words, instead of cartons arriving that read "Acme Terminal Parts," suppliers would redesign the containers and packaging to allow the assembled terminals to be shipped in the same boxes in which they had arrived.

This simple, obvious idea saved H-P a significant amount of money. And the savings will accrue annually thereafter.

Think of all the materials you recycle (or throw away) only to replace them with a fresh supply. Think too about all the times you've made perfectly logical plans and missed the obvious – and better – solutions.

The new Thoughtware says: in the future, be prepared to recycle *all* your plans.

COMIC RELIEF

Let me illustrate why it is always necessary *to plan on changing your plans* with the following parable e-mailed to me recently by a friend:

The plan

In the beginning was the plan.

And then came the assumptions.

And the assumptions were without form.

And the plan was completely without substance.

And darkness was upon the face of the workers.

And they spoke amongst themselves saying, "This plan is a joke, and it stinketh."

And the workers went unto their supervisors saying, "The Plan is stale and moldy, and none can abide the odor thereof."

And the supervisors went unto *their* managers saying unto them, "The Plan stinketh, and it is very strong such that none can abide it."

And the managers went unto the directors saying, "The Plan is best used as mulch and fertilizer, and none can abide its strength."

And the directors spoke amongst themselves, saying to one another, "The plan contains that which aids plant growth, and is therefore very strong."

And the directors went unto the managing director saying to her, "The Plan promotes growth and is very powerful."

And she went unto the CEO saying unto him, "This new Plan will actively promote growth and efficiency of our company."

And the CEO looked upon The Plan, presented it to the Board Chair and said, "Trust me! This is good!"
And The Plan became policy.

Indeed, today, far too many companies are guided by far too myopic a Plan. In part this happens because in our rush to please our superiors we make inferior decisions. Worse still, The Plan often determines the direction and tone for the company, and when The Strategic Plan is seen by the employees as The Disaster Plan, there is serious trouble! To change The Plan, however, is no easy task … but often it can – and must – be done. You start this change with an "attitude adjustment," top to bottom, bottom to top.

A FEW RECESSION-BUSTING WORDS

As the story goes, a waitress once asked Yogi Berra if he wanted his pizza cut into four or eight slices. "Four please," said Yogi without hesitation, "I could never eat eight!" Plans often are like pizzas: we could never do eight, so let's plan on four!

A lot of people these days are looking at the continuing wave of downsizing like Yogi looked at his pizza, thinking that if you somehow make the numbers smaller it all becomes (please forgive the pun) more palatable. Cut jobs, cut inventory, cut training, and cut benefits, they reason, and you'll ride out an economic storm or add value on Wall Street or the Tokyo Stock Exchange. That's the conventional wisdom.

As I travel around the globe I am always on the lookout for new perspectives, skills, and strategies … fresh approaches to our most difficult problems. I didn't have to go very far to get a wonderful example of the new Thoughtware applied to downsizing and re-engineering. It came right to my front door with the Christmas mail.

I received a holiday message from a marketing communications group in Minneapolis, Minnesota, which shed more light on the problem than anything I had seen in many months.

Instead of the usual artsy marketing materials you see at so many agencies; the company fosters clients who value their unique, strategic thinking and "big picture" perspective.

Consequently, when their card arrived under a pile of mail it was the first one I opened. The basic design was unlike any other I'd seen. On slate gray construction paper was glued a torn white "page" that looked as though it had been ripped out of an etymological dictionary. I reprint it here so that their few recession-busting words can be fully appreciated. Here is their prescription for how to move your Plan from half (or more) empty to half (or more) full:

recession/ 1: a period of reduced economic activity 2: returning conquered territory 3: withdrawing to expose formerly covered areas 4: a procession back, as a choir after performance 5: the action, appearance or process of *recessing*

recess/ 1: an indentation in a line conceived of as straight 2: to interrupt for a period of time 3: a period that intervenes, used for rest or play 4: a suspension of usual business, a *holiday*

holiday/ 1: time exempt from usual vocational activity 2: a period of relief 3: a good time, a festive occasion 4: *holy* day

holy/ 1: set apart 2: spiritually sound, good, unimpaired, pure 3: filled with mysterious spiritual *light* or power

light/ 1: something that makes vision possible 2: that which gives life or individuality to a person 3: an inner *vision* that enlightens or informs

vision/ 1: the sense that distinguishes the true quality of things 2: a momentary sight, a glimpse 3: an experience of unusual discernment or foresight 4: the power of perceiving by other than ordinary sight.

At the base of the card it read: "In lives that often seem defined may this season give us new meaning." Short and sweet ... and true.

We all have mental recessions as well as economic ones. To move quickly from "a period of reduced mental activity," you must rely on "the power of perceiving by other than ordinary sight." Good advice in both the best and the toughest of times.

Is the ability to see other than the ordinary an ordinary skill? Increasingly, among the successful business people of the world, the answer is "Yes!" ... with a little help from the new Thoughtware.

DO YOU THINK LIKE A SUCCESSFUL CEO?

Research on more than 6000 mid-size companies that were highly successful throughout the 1980s revealed that a remarkably consistent way of thinking characterized their CEOs. The results, published in the book *The Winning Performance*, by Donald Clifford, Jr., and Richard Cavanaugh (1991), offer some useful lessons on what works and what doesn't in today's laser-fast world.

Two things struck home. First, the vast majority of these CEOs were gaining an advantage by doing all the "wrong" things in terms of conventional wisdom. By being *un*conventional in their approach, the most successful CEOs led their companies to new levels of growth and productivity.

Secondly, I noticed that their business paradigm formed a clear *pattern of thinking*. There was a consistent configuration of beliefs, as though they were all following the same pied piper of prosperity and productivity.

I have encapsulated the key elements in this pattern into the following six questions. Give them a try. How would you answer these, and how do your answers measure up?

1. It is better to be competitive on a broad scale than to narrow the market and serve the needs of a few. Yes ☐ No ☐
2. By careful cost-containment and lowest pricing you will gain a competitive advantage. Yes ☐ No ☐
3. Creating additional products and services is preferable to enlarging your successful markets. Yes ☐ No ☐
4. Emphasizing the values your company stands for is more important that emphasizing the bottom line. Yes ☐ No ☐
5. The most effective way to have employees share in the company's vision is to encourage them to become owners or shareholders. Yes ☐ No ☐
6. Successful CEOs rely as much on hunches and intuition as they do on analysis and logic. Yes ☐ No ☐

There's an old joke: "Here are today's soccer scores: 2–2, 3–1, 1–0!" Well, here is how today's best and brightest CEOs answered: No, No, Yes, Yes, Yes, and Yes.

How did you do? Where did you agree and disagree? What, if anything, surprised you? Would you have been a successful CEO and score a perfect 6–0? A growing body of substantive research supports the "correct" answer to each of these questions. To succeed, think like a successful CEO ... or at least heed the wisdom of comedian Jonathan Winters who once said: "I couldn't wait for success, so I went ahead without it!"

FIVE FUNDAMENTAL ASSUMPTIONS OF THOUGHTWARE STRATEGY

We all have to "go ahead" with life, especially considering the alternative. It helps to remain insatiably curious and to have a terrific sense of humor. It also helps to find a way to claw and fight your way "outside the box" to venture into the unknown from time to time.

The anomalies of the world fascinate me and raise fundamental questions that I ponder far into the night. For example:

- Why is it that a team of experienced senior executives with individual IQs of above 130 have a collective IQ of 71 when they are asked to solve a problem or be the least bit innovative and/or creative?
- How can there be such a thing as a self-help *group*? Or a self-directed work *team*?
- How can a market or niche be seen as a standard *deviation* from the norm?

We know that groups of individuals can – and do – learn. In fact, there is convincing evidence that the advantage almost inevitably will go to those groups who learn to make their collective whole greater than the sum of their individual parts.

We see it in sports, in the performing arts, in science, and occasionally even in the workplace. If we look at the Asian and Continental European paradigm, for example, we find a deep-seated belief that real learning takes place in groups. Knowledge accumulates *within* organizations and *between* individuals who understand how to share information, pool resources, and creatively collaborate.

It is helpful too, to understand the assumptions which underlie your strategy, to identify what the basic premises of your paradigm are.

According to the new Thoughtware, here are some of the more important assumptions in today's business world:

1. Today, the rate of change is exponential, not incremental

This is a crucial starting point. Things are changing at a fast-forward, willy-nilly pace. This makes it very difficult to use the conventional modes of thought, measurement, or planning. Often things don't build up or add up, they just explode to a new level.

2. Things will never get "back to normal," this is normal!

The so-called glory days of the bygone past have gone by fast. They won't be back. So, the new Thoughtware says: "Get over it! Get used to it! This is normal ... from now on!"

3. Plan as we may, the future has plans of its own

Because exponential change is here to stay, we have to look down the road with 20/20 vision, focusing on the next 20 minutes and the next 20 years, simultaneously. The bad news is the number of senior executives and key managers who possess 20/20 vision is very small. The good news is this is a learnable, cognitive skill that can be taught.

4. Organizations that "learn how to learn," ask the right questions, at the right time, and "find out how to find the answers," will thrive in a global economy

Astute organizational theorists, such as Warren Bennis or Peter Senge or Peter Drucker, are absolutely correct in proposing that a continuously learning organization is a healthy – and highly productive – organization. In the new Thoughtware, the organization's "verbs" supplant its "nouns," By this I mean that diverse *methods* and responsive *processes* will be more powerful than "tried and true facts" and "off the shelf systems." Asking the right questions *at the right time* will determine the most sustainable and viable answers.

5. The productive organizations that will excel in the future will be ones that value: flexibility, diversity, integrity, cooperation, and innovation

It is no longer sufficient to "add value" to products, we have to add values into the process and the product. Customers, creditors, consumers, and our conscience now require it. (Much more is found on this point in Chapter 6, INNOVATION; 10, RETENTION; and 12, !EADERSHIP.)

These "high five" premises are extremely useful, because they stimulate dialogue, raise provocative questions, and, at the very least, increase the collective IQ over the century mark! But more importantly, they provide the context by which strategy moves to a higher level, perspective.

Chapter Eight

PERSPECTIVE

Don't Compete ... Tilt the Field!

Question: "What is your assessment of the French Revolution?"
Answer: "It's too soon to tell."
– Mao Zedong, 1975

NEVER SHAKE A SPOON AT A NUN!

Some of my earliest and fondest memories of my mother center around her proclivity to offer up a seemingly endless succession what she called "life's little lessons." She had a quote or aphorism for every imaginable occasion. Some I understood, such as "Leave your favorite food for last and you'll have a clean plate." Others left me clueless: "Never shake a spoon at a nun!" Recently, one came to mind when I was developing this chapter on the necessity and role of perspective in the new Thoughtware:

"Wisdom doesn't always come with age," she would say. "Sometimes it just shows up all by itself."

If there is any wisdom I have accrued over time it is that few individuals, and even fewer organizations, take – or make – the time to pause and observe, let alone provide the opportunity to feel what Michael Hammer (1997) calls "the power of reflection."

Consequently, according to the new Thoughtware, reflection and seeking a creative perspective are perhaps the last stronghold of amateurism.

SET YOUR HAIR ON FIRE!

Sometimes, in its simplest form, you exercise perspective by being disciplined and patient. As Nancy Austin (1997) says, "You have to hang in there long after someone else has given up. Your hair has to be on fire to build great companies or write great books or raise great kids."

Although the flash of insight and the great idea or the big dream are important variables, the ability to *build* and *implement* them requires a constant state of what I call "pent up rapport" – within yourself, with others and inside an organization. (For more pent-up rapport, see Chapter 12, !EADERSHIP.) The real power of reflection is then revealed through a perspective that is "wise" enough to be made real.

How can we employ perspective to further our dreams and meet our goals? The remainder of this chapter will illustrate what the new Thoughtware offers that can, indeed, set you hair on fire!

JACKDAW MANAGEMENT TOOLS

"Continuous Improvement is no longer a procedure carved in stone that we follow like a cookbook," says Bernie Nagle, former vice president, Grocery Products, at a major food manufacturer. Nagle directed the manufacturing of products as diverse as salsas, soups, and evaporated milk, and was responsible for a division with a budget in excess of $375 million a year. Three of his seven plants had budgets of over $70 million dollars.

Like so many manufacturing operations, his company had been utilizing Total Quality Management (TQM) and Continuous Improvement processes for many years. However, unlike other managers, Nagle has always refused a single-focus, buzzword-of-the-month approach. He is a jackdaw operations expert – gathering up that which sparkles and using it to feather his company's nest!

He walked in the door, hit the ground running, and quickly decided that to make a substantive difference in his part of the company he would have to build an integrated team of corporate and plant management. He wanted to increase quality while reducing cost, develop both long-term and short-term strategies of change, and create a flexible, innovative organization. In short, Bernie Nagle is a manager addressing the strategic "givens" of today and the challenges of the new century.

"I told my team that we had to be a learning organization," he told me. Consequently, Nagle saw himself as part manager, part mentor, part provocateur, and part visionary. The whole of his perspective was greater than the sum of his parts.

In our work together over the last few years I have come to understand his approach to business by way of a metaphor. For him, running a business is like running down a massive hallway where doors are constantly opening to your left and to your right. The winners are those who see the doors first and know which ones to walk into and which ones to pass by. An avid competitive runner, Bernie Nagle runs a very good race through today's crowded business corridors.

How do you tell the good from the bad doors, the breakthroughs from the buzzwords? To Nagle, one key is to keep the big picture in mind, while actively staying open to new developments. "We aggressively search out new methods, determine whether or not they will add value and move us toward our vision." he said. "Then we implement, evaluate, and integrate the new method into our evolving skill-set." For him, no business principle or axiom is "a monolithic religion" existing in a vacuum. The marketplace is alive and tells those who listen closely where to head next. That's where perspective comes in and gives you a competitive advantage, and with perspective comes a sense of *sequence* and *priority*.

At a recent plant managers' meeting in Philadelphia on which he and I collaborated, Nagle introduced a conceptual model to help his team understand where they have been, where they are now, and where they are headed. By aligning vision, strategy, and perspective, he was able to give them a picture upon which to build and develop the business processes needed to reach their objectives. These tools are not only interrelated but they bring yet more value when used simultaneously. They are also applicable to industries that have no relation to the canning of minestrone soup and the hand packing of jalapeno peppers. Here is his toolbox for the future. The vertical axis lists "Evolving Core Capabilities," and the horizontal axis is "Time."

ONE JACKDAW'S TOOLBOX

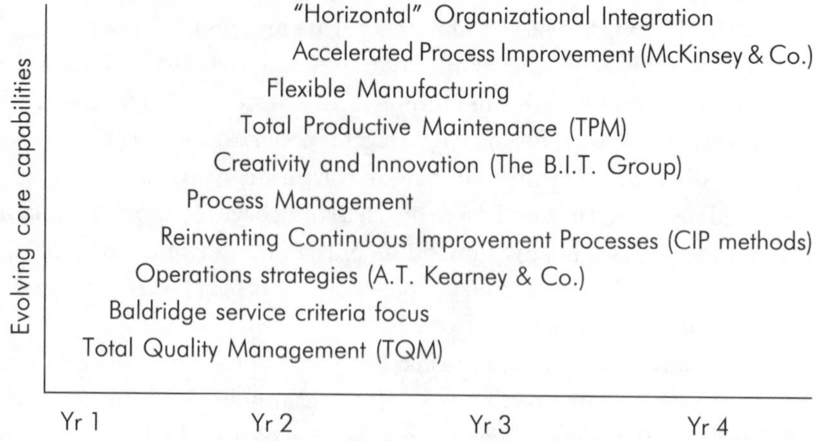

"I don't want people to be too parochial about any (of these)," he said. "We must be flexible, responsive and able to change." So, for example, my research and consulting company, The B.I.T. Group, worked with his team on the "Creativity and Innovation" tools level, which Nagle has integrated with each of the preceding tools so as to add value to the *successive* tools.

"The point is to always have a conceptual toolbox, and over time keep adding new tools to the toolbox." In so doing, he set – and reached – his three-year goal by attaining "Top 4" status in the packaged food industry.

"We're pretty bullish on our prospects for the future. When we fail to keep learning," muses Nagle, "that's when the competition will declare us legally dead."

A MAN OF FEW WORDS

To learn continuously, it helps to be curious. And being continuously curious is crucial to keeping your perspective. There is so much information out there today, however, that mere curiosity is not enough. This is where perspective and the ability to synthesize and simplify vast amounts of data come in very handy.

For example, if I were a principal in the independent investment counsel firm of Schultz Collins Lawson Young & Chambers, Inc., I would be well-advised to be a man of few words in an industry prone to incoherency, obscurity, and confusion-by-the-numbers. With a corporate name that long you could use up half your client's available time on the rudiments of simple introductions before getting down to business.

Fortunately, my friend Dale Schultz uses few words, and his San Francisco-based company's newsletter *Investment Quarterly,* provides many valuable numbers. I was therefore very pleased to receive the first edition of *IQ* and was anxious to see if Dale's imprint was to be found on it. I was not disappointed.

In clear succinct language *IQ* helped me to understand some fairly complicated financial and investment issues and supplied the evidence to back it up. Let me offer two illustrations.

I have been puzzled for some time in understanding why, over a decade or more, two companies could have the same *average* annualized return and yet one would still have a greater ending wealth than the other.

"The answer is found," according to *IQ*, "in the mathematics of compound interest." For example, a dollar investment that loses 10% in year one (making it worth 90 cents) must earn a rate *greater* than 10% in year two ($1.12) just to get even. Similarly, a 20% loss will necessitate nearly a 25% gain to get back to square one, and so on.

From this *IQ* states *General Rule No.1*: "If two assets have equal average historical returns, the asset with greater variability of returns will produce less ending wealth." Now I get it! This is why slow and steady often wins over wild and woolly!

The second illustration is even more fundamental and insightful for today's investor to understand. Before I disclose it, let me show you the way Dale's competitors (who remain anonymous) make the identical point in another newsletter. Please pay close attention as you read this and see if you can understand it. Then try to reduce what is said here to one simple sentence.

The market's rise after a period of re-accumulation is a bullish sign. Nevertheless, fulcrum characteristics are not yet clearly present and a resistance area exists 40 points higher in the Dow, so it is clearly premature to say the next leg of the bull market is up. If, in the coming weeks, a test of the low holds and the market breaks out of its flag, a further rise would be indicated. Should the lows be violated, a continuation of the intermediate term downtrend is called for. In view of the current situation, it is a distinct possibility that traders will sit in the wings awaiting a clearer delineation of the trend and the market will move in a narrow trading range.

I read this three times to be sure I had read what I thought I had read. Indeed I *had*, and was left with the distinct feeling that with advice like this from their competitors, I ought to take wing and fly over to Schultz Collins Lawson Young & Chambers, Inc., post haste!

In contrast to the verbosity of the competition, *IQ*'s perspective was infinitely more clear and certainly more succinct: "In light of our analysis, we will make our first market prediction." *Market Prediction No. 1* says: "In the near-term, the US stock market will either go up, down, or remain flat." Now these are honest people with a sense of humor – and a perspective – about today's market.

The moral of this story? With the enormous amount of raw information now instantaneouslyavailable, the advantage is going to go to those who can say the most first, and most clearly.

In the era of the new Thoughtware, under the malaise of massive amounts of information, simplicity wins!

A CURIOUS LITTLE BOOK

Simplicity often comes from having perspective, and both are crucial when doing business outside your own culture. For those who do business in China, for example, Fred Schnieter's *Getting Along with the Chinese for Fun and Profit* (1992), is a real eye opener. With over 30 years' worth of business experience in China, Schneiter has written a chatty, useful book full of practical wisdom that is nearly devoid of "business-babble."

Though conversational in tone, it is nonetheless packed with little details that will often make the difference between a successful – or disastrous – encounter. Perhaps most importantly, his 35 years of experience gave him a perspective ... and a sense of humor.

For example, he describes how for three to five thousand years the Chinese have been deeply involved in Feng Shui, an elusive pseudo-science involving warding off evil, bringing good fortune your way, beckoning ghosts and offering talismans. If you doubt the scope of its power and influence, Schneiter illustrates the force of beliefs on architecture, citing the design of the new Hyatt Hotel in Singapore.

On the advice of a geomancer, the fountain at the front of the hotel was relocated because it was believed that if the waterspout was maintained at a certain height, it would insure prosperity. The entrance doors were also rebuilt and placed slightly askew from the cashier's desk because a basic rule of Feng Shui says that a door directly in front of a cash register "would cause the firm's money to 'go out.' "

In doing business with the Chinese, here are ten pearls of wisdom from his book. Let's make this interesting! I'll list them, you circle your answers as a True/False Quiz:

---

1. When approaching a door,mildly protest your host's offer to let you go first two or three times. Then proceed. T F
2. Escort a departing visitor to the elevator or, if they are special guests, all the way the front door. T F
3. When you get shoes or other goods repaired, examine them closely before you pay to show your approval of the workmanship. T F
4. Anything offered to you with two hands should be taken with two hands. It demonstrates mutual respect. T F
5. When drawing up a contract, the line for your signature should appear respectfully below the Chinese names. (However, Schnieter notes, "you're probably better off with goodwill, friendship, and a handshake") T F
6. If you enter a hall and the group applauds you, slowly clap back. "It's part face, part egalitarianism." T F
7. Any business trip where your spouse comes along is considered a holiday to the Chinese. T F
8. You are not defined by your personality or character, but by family relationships. English has 30 family words; Chinese has 120, including 16 ways to describe a cousin, 10 for brothers-in-law, and six kinds of nieces. T F
9. "Eating is the first happiness." Meals are a big part of life and of business dealings. So knowing chopsticks etiquette is important. Remember that chopsticks were not made for tapping out the solo to *Wipeout* or Beethoven's Fifth! If you drop a chopstick it's bad luck ... so, drop the other to cancel the hex. T F

Lastly, my favorite, because of the fresh perspective it brings:

10. The word "criticism" in Chinese is referred to as "medicine for the ears." No-one gets it right all the time, but everyone can *try* to do so. Consequently, do not criticize and blame, speak only of how something could be done *differently*. T F

Do you want to see how you did? Well, that should be easy to tally, since *all* of the above are "True"! Do you have a slightly different perspective on China now?

America's executives and managers would do well to learn these pearls and dole out such medicinal remedies.

THE POWER OF FRESH EYES

"In the hills above Stanford University, at a research center famous for its digital breakthroughs, a seven-member team is brainstorming about the future of work," writes Elizabeth Weil (1997, p.93). She describes how using sophisticated communications equipment and high-speed internet hookups, the team is creating a series of multimedia presentations for an audience of scientists and engineers.

At the same time, in a consumer-research laboratory owned by a fast-growing computer manufacturer, a beta-tester is pushing the limits of a cool new product. "Scenes like these unfold every day in Silicon Valley," Weil says. "With one big exception. The oldest researchers on *these* projects – at Xerox, Autodesk, and Compaq – are 18. The youngest is seven ... the under-21 set is where the new visionaries are: they have the fresh eyes."

Weil quotes John Seely Brown, the chief scientist at Xerox PARC, who believes that success in an era of technological discontinuity requires not simply modification or enhancement but, rather, "a fundamental shift in cognitive styles." He calls this new style *bricolage* – the capacity to build new things from whatever's available – and this is precisely what kids do. Says Brown; "You're going to ask *me* what the workplace will be like in the year 2010? I can say with almost total certainty that I won't be in the workforce in 2010. However, today's students will. They're going to create the environment."

At Xerox they understand this, and so seven high-school students "have just finished their six-week stay here," says Brown. "These kids have been working on computers since day one. That makes them different people. To them, computers are not new or cutting edge. They're like refrigerators or cars. They bring a perspective on technology that we adults simply can't have."

One of the skills of a child is the ability to render fact and metaphor indistinguishable! Metaphors are treated as facts, facts as metaphors. In the BREAK IT! Thinking™ training program, we practice this, and extend it, to practical issues within organizations. By using the power of metaphors, many a barrier has been broken down via a simple process. As the Japanese teach their children: when you come to a brick wall, find the first loose brick.

"WELCOME TO THE 9-DS"

"I want to ask you a question," said Joseph Wahed, Chief Economist of Wells Fargo Bank. "What is the difference between a bank regulator and a terrorist?"

Hearing no reply he said: "You can always negotiate with a terrorist!"

Mr. Wahed was addressing the Sixth Annual "Real Estate and the Economy" Conference in San Francisco, where I was the guest of my friend, Realtor Diane Martin. As Wahed continued he offered us some thought-provoking economic forecasts and remarks – a mix of good news and not-so-good news.

From his perspective there are five "D" words that encapsulate the essence of change in our times. These are the D's that are signaling fundamental, structural change (as distinguished from cyclical or incremental change). Coincidentally, that same morning my youngest daughter had heard me refer to the "nineties," but what she heard me say was the "Nine D's!" She asked me, "Dad, how many D's *are* there for you?"

So, I had "D's" on my mind and found this mnemonic device worked so well that the more I thought about Wahed's forecasts, the more D's came to mind. So, to Wahed's list I have added four D's of my own.

So, if you'll pardon the pun, "Welcome to the 9-Ds!"

1. *Debt*: Personal debt has altered the nature of our socio-political-economic fabric. Compared to many other industrialized nations, the typical American's debt-to-savings ratio is far too high.
2. *Deficits*: On the governmental side, our debt is even worse and has been characterized as ransoming future generations. Our officials will have to focus on breaking the cycle of taxing and spending, an archaic but incessant paradigm in Washington.
3. *Decline in defense spending*: The shift from the Cold War is restructuring the job base and skillset. Regions that had flourished in great part due to defense contracts, such as Southern California, are very hard hit, while small businesses are consistently generating new jobs in large numbers.
4. *Disposable income*: The amount of disposable income is subsiding, both in real and in psychological terms. In real terms, we are working more hours for proportionately lower wages than at any time in the last four decades.
5. *Demographic diversity*: The face of America is changing, Wahed argued, and these changes are not cosmetic. The indicators are everywhere: racial and ethnic enrollment levels in colleges and universities; percentage of women in the workplace; average life span. Salsa now outsells ketchup in most American groceries! According to recent data, there are three times as many lawyers as there are fire fighters!

To Wahed's list, I will add the last four D's.

6. *Downsizing*: Though by now downsizing is old news, it ain't over yet. We are witnessing the continuing diminution of the dinosaurs. Recent casualty lists read like a *Who's Who* in business: IBM, GM, United Airlines, Lockheed, Boeing, and Sears. Most economists, including Paul Erdman and Joseph Wahed, agree that this will continue well into the next decade.
7. *Deregulation*: The era of deregulation has been upon us long enough now for it to have affected major systemic change. The airlines are still groping. The banks appear to be coming out of a tailspin. What we are seeing today is a cycle that moves from regulation to deregulation to reregulation. No area will be untouched ... nor unscarred.
8. *Dazzling databases*: The quantity and quality of information and data available today is staggering. We can instantaneously get information about people, products, places, and procedures. The technological revolution of the 1980s and the on-going software explosion of the 1990s

is dazzling indeed, but will seem minuscule compared to the changes brought by the new century.

9. *Dalmatians*! The world is changing from hard-edged, blacks and whites that form tidy bar graphs and pie charts into a more mottled, flexible and idiosyncratic world of splotches and spots. We are now a world whose values, ethics, and priorities are gathering in *ad hoc* areas such that the face of citizenry and of commerce now more closely resembles the skin of a Dalmatian than that of the proverbial blank slate. Strange bedfellows, says the new Thoughtware, are forming limited partnerships!

As Wahed quipped: "Have you heard the new definition of child abuse? Leave your children property!" Welcome to the 1990s!

COACHING FOR LIFE

One common set of metaphors used to gain a better understanding of your business and career is that of sports. Using sport as a metaphor for greater perspective and insight allows old assumptions to be broken down. In America, where football is a major sport, many men often invoke it and its strategies when describing themselves and/or their companies.

As a card-carrying football fan I was reading recently when struck by two contrasting pictures on opposite pages, one at the end of an article and the other in an advertisement, in *Sports Illustrated*.

In the ad, a muddy, discouraged football player is sitting on the bench with a towel over his head, his taped and padded hands under his chin, his eyes looking at the ground, traces of blood, sweat and, yes, tears on his uniform. The controlled violence and uncontrolled emotions of having lost some big game were clearly visible. The ad, for an insurance company I think, made a pitch for one of those football clichés about "when the going gets tough the tough get going." Designed to be motivational, the ad only reminded me of all the disappointments I'd faced on the athletic field and how ill-equipped I was to handle them.

On the opposite page, at the end of an article, was a photo of a man in his seventies balancing on one foot on the end of the bench along the sidelines of a football field. The article was about Roland "Ort" Ortmayer, head football coach for more than 40 years at tiny La Verne College in Southern California. *Sports Illustrated* calls Ort "the most unusual coach in the United States," and the college's president refers to him affectionately as "a kind of Socrates." When I saw Ort's photo, I felt good inside.

Why these accolades? What is so special about this man poised lightly on one leg? Why would America's largest sports magazine devote so many pages to him? Consider the following examples of Ort's approach to the game:

On winning: "Sometimes I have the feeling that justice will not prevail if we win" So, each season Ort schedules a few games he thinks his team can win, a few they'll probably lose, and maybe three toss-ups. After nearly a thousand games he has lost about a dozen more games than he has won.

On authority: "If players would rather run something out of the 'I' formation than out of 'splitbacks,' that's okay with me. I teach that it's alright to use your brains. All I insist on is that they come up with something I can understand so I can stay with the program."

On planning: "I call a few plays during the game. It's just that the players don't choose to use them. That's okay. I feel like I should try to make some sort of contribution."

On recruiting: He doesn't believe in it. Whoever walks onto the field at the beginning of the season is on his team. Recruiting, Ort believes, will only "bias" him and alter his expectations in the off-season.

On scouting the opposition: Ort tried that for a while, but gave it up as a hopeless cause when he missed the entire first half of one cross-town "rival's" game because he was eating popcorn and chatting with old friends in the stands.

On leadership: Ort is notorious for picking up wet towels in the locker room, chalking the field at dusk, repairing the sod after a game. He'll literally do anything that needs doing. With his wife, he even *washes and irons* all the uniforms the night before each game! Says Ort "It gives me a chance to think about each and every player, each week."

It's no wonder that one of Ort's former players says, "all Ort will do is change your life."

Ort would like that kind of praise because, as you can surmise, Ort sees himself as coaching *life*, not football. His players learn that there is life before, during, and after a football game. They understand that building character, learning to cooperate, being gracious in victory and learning from defeat is how you "win" in life. Consequently, Ort's players live out many of the basic tenets of the new Thoughtware.

Sure, competitive sports are a wonderful metaphor for life, learning, and work. Unfortunately, from my point of view, too often the metaphor is used too narrowly in the business and educational worlds I frequent. Competition ruins lives. That's the proverbial bad news.

The good news is that more and more people in business, the best managers and leaders (See Chapter 12 for more on !EADERSHIP), are really a lot like Ort. They know the importance of keeping priorities straight, communications open, and plans flexible. That's why they are usually the best "coaches" and their entire team joins them in a one-legged dance on the bench.

They also understand the unconventional wisdom of Shakespeare when he said, "No profit grows where there is no pleasure taken." In the game of life, isn't that how you really win?

A "PACKET" COACH TO WINNING THE BALDRIDGE AWARD

I never know where I am going to find the new Thoughtware, so you can imagine my elation as I finally catch hold of something when and where I least expect it.

For example, recently while preparing for a series of meetings with a prospective client I wandered in to grab a cup of coffee at Coco's 24-hour cafe in Austin, Texas. When the coffee arrived, I reached for the cream and sugar and noticed something printed on the back of the sugar packet. In large capital letters it said "PERSPECTIVE: Perspective, like experience, is a wonderful thing. It enables you to recognize a mistake when you make it again." As we have seen, *humor* and *metaphor* can aid perspective, but at Coco's I realized that *serendipity* is an ally of perspective as well.

Since a great deal of my company's consultation and training work involves helping organizations learn from mistakes so they will *not* repeat them, I paid special attention to the cryptic message at Coco's. Juxtaposing the message and the wishes of the client I was about to meet – a client dead set on winning the Malcolm Baldridge Award "within three years" – I sketched out some notes on how to use perspective in yet another form.

Six value-added tips for my client quickly filled my napkin, key elements to be kept in mind if the client was striving to gain recognition as a leader in "total quality" products and "total quality" services. With these six tools in the Toolset, there would be a greatly increased chance of winning a "Baldy." By using a creative methodology, a new perspective could yield a competitive advantage.

1. Read the application form backwards

Start by using content analysis and look at the brief descriptions they provide of past winners. This is a great way to identify key criteria and the panel's priorities and vocabulary. Then sprinkle those values and terms into every aspect of your company … and onto every page of the application. Furthermore, while you're examining the application materials note, for example, that "Customer Satisfaction" is given 300 out of 1000 possible points; while "Strategic Quality Planning" gets a maximum of 60 points. That should tell you something.

2. Assemble a diagonal slice of your company's resources

"Top down/vertical slices" and "side-to-side/horizontal slices" won't suffice. Find everyone's core competencies, summon (and employ) all your resources, and get *everybody* into the picture.

3. Avoid the temptation of placing too much reliance on quantitative measures of qualitative processes

Find a balance that works for you *and* your customers. For example, measuring telephone "response time" by the number of "rings" means little if the caller is met with a fully automated menu.

4. Remember that collaboration and innovation are encouraged every step of the way

This should apply in all areas – in business process improvement teams, as well as in union and management partnerships. Collaboration and innovation are necessary to win a Baldy and, more importantly, to better serve the customer.

5. The Baldridge Award is an "abstraction"

It comes and goes like Christmas Day. It is your people – from the CEO to the newest, entry-level employee – who will insure true quality implementation and who will provide your customers with quality products and services that are "real" ... and sustainable ... and truly worthy of the best of all awards: customers' continued business.

6. Think twice before applying in the first place

Some of the most likely candidates for the award have decided that throwing their hat into the ring would be a *dis*service to their customers and an even greater distraction for their company. The quest for it may better serve your vanity than the needs of your customer. There's an old saying amongst carpenters that applies here too: "measure twice, cut once." "Think twice," I advised the client, "before you apply."

At the very least, if you do nothing else, have your key decision-makers gather for a leisurely cup of coffee at Coco's first!

TO DO ... OR NOT TO DO, THAT IS THE QUESTION

Ever wonder how companies like 3M and Motorola grew from small innovative companies into large innovative companies? In terms of perspective, these companies have flourished over time in large part because they know what they have to add and, they also practice the "discipline of removal," as Jim Collins (1997) says. Indeed, one key to 3M's success lies *not* in its ability to generate a plethora of new opportunities but rather in the fact that its people can say without penalty, "Hey, that's not such a good idea after all; let's unplug it and move onto something else." They know when to hold on ... and when to let go. In so doing, they continually free up resources for more promising fresh opportunities.

Had 3M, for example, not had such a perspective, one of its major breakthrough products – Post-its – would never have reached the shelves, for up to that point 3M's "to do" list included products that would only adhere, not a product that would stick and *un*stick!

In another instance of bold removal, Motorola jettisoned its television business at the high point of its success in the1960s. To fill the vacuum, it sought out exciting new fields, such as microprocessors and cellular communications. "Instead of milking cash cows," says Collins, "Motorola slays them."

Peter Drucker, one of the leading management theorists of the last three decades, is well aware of the power of perspective in helping us know what to do ... and what *not* to do.

Drucker suggests making both a "To Do" list, and a "Stop Doing" list! An excellent tool in the Thoughtware toolset, you could extend Drucker's logic to every aspect of your company's activities - people, products, systems, structures, and even how you spend your leisure time. You should, says Drucker, create a "don't do" list to complement your "to do" list. That will greatly help keep things in perspective. (Rubin, 1998, pp. 62–68).

TURN, TURN, TURN

In the end, whatever tools you use matters less than making the commitment to invoke the power of reflection and the wisdom of perspective. To do so, to insist on keeping things in perspective, one has to stand back far enough and long enough and often enough. Gaining a perspective often boils down to getting sufficient distance to see the forest for the trees.

Sometimes in business there is a fine line between taking a stand and being a stand-up comedian! Humor is a great tool for gaining such distance and for laughing at that which is closest to you, because if you can laugh at it, at least you are assured that you see it in the first place. Consequently, I am a great fan of comedy and love nothing more than arriving at my office in the morning to find an email (email me at bit@nbn.com) with a funny story or a terrific joke to start my day. Thank God for my friends and their varied senses of humor!

Recently, a friend sent me such a missive in the form of an e-mail's worth of one-liners from the zany minds of Mel Brooks and Carl Reiner, which help me find perspective.

- "Want to enjoy a long marriage? Marry someone who can stand you," says Carl Reiner, married 54 years to wife Estelle. Mel Brooks and actress Anne Bancroft have been married 33 years.
- "Want to gain a perspective on life? Turn, turn, turn. We don't turn enough," Brooks says. "Turning gives you perspective." Reiner adds, "If you're looking right, look left. If you're looking forward, look backward." (Zaslow, 1997).

The new Thoughtware agrees. Turn, look right, look left, look forward, look back, keep your perspective ... and read on!

Part Three

LEADERSHIP

Chapter Nine

TALENT

The Waves are in the Water

"Why did you go on that wave?" Shawn Briley asked.
"If you don't go, how are you going to know if you would have made it?"
– Chris Malloy, champion surfer, 1997

ALL THE WORLD'S A STAGE

Finding, casting, and directing top talent is a vital part of the new Thoughtware. Talent is the name of the game in a Networked Age, and smart companies understand this and are being very innovative in their never-ending search. "It's a major trend in the workplace," says consultant George Bailey (1998, p.B8) of Watson Wyatt Worldwide, in Bethesda, Massachusetts. "Companies are finding what they're really competing for isn't just market and customers. It's employees."

Firms are going to incredible lengths to identify and attract fresh talent, and they are doing so in creative ways, using every means available, and on an on-going basis. For example:

- Says Cognex's Shay Tressa, "In the Boston area, there's a lot of competition for good employees." To distinguish themselves from other firms, they have developed their own identity. For example, they have a corporate "salute" – a right hand to the bridge of the nose like "The Three Stooges" – with which they greet one another. Funny? Irreverent? Self-effacing? Yes. Good business? Yes.
- At Sprint Business's creative marketing center, new recruits are told of free ice cream, karaoke machines, rubber pig noses and juggling balls that are used to encourage brainstorming and creativity. Says Margie Tippen, at their center in Dallas, Texas, "It has absolutely helped in our recruiting, as well as the retention of our employees."

Considerable research over the last two decades, including a recent survey by Interim Services, a Ft. Lauderdale staffing and consulting company in Florida, shows that "nearly 75% of employees feel promoting fun and closer workplace relationships would make jobs more attractive." As consultant Matt Weinstein from Berkeley, California observes, "companies are saying, 'If you like fun, we're the place to come.' " Interim Services' survey also found that "fun" is the "key for wooing workers ages 18–33." So, if you want to lure top young talent, remember: the world is a stage!

COMIC RELIEF

The quest for "top" talent ... actually for *any* talent ... can be stressful and frustrating, so it helps to keep your sense of humor *and* your perspective. When the going gets tough, the tough read the funnies! If that weren't true, then Scott Adams, creator of "Dilbert" would still be working in a mundane job at Pacific Bell in San Ramon, California.

His keen and witty insights into the trials and tribulations of the workplace have made him a wealthy man. Specifically, here's Dilbert's view of the job market today:

Catbert: I'm having trouble finding qualified external applicants.
Pointy-haired boss: (Stares at him.)
Catbert: All I have are a headless man, a mime, and a frozen cro-magnon guy we found in a glacier.
Pointy-haired boss: Does the mime bring his own invisible cubicle? I love those! (Waving his hands happily in the air.)
Catbert: Only if we pay his relocation costs.

WE'VE FLAT RUN OUT OF PEOPLE!

The *Wall Street Journal* (1998), ran an article in which several business people lamented the lack of skilled labor. Over the past year, Michael Ottenweller, head of the family's metal fabrication business, has lost both sleep and several millions dollars for the same reason: a tight labor market. His firm, Ottenweller Co., had to turn down nearly $6 million dollars in orders from their major client, Caterpiller Inc., because he "simply couldn't find enough workers to do the job."

In many parts of the world, Ottenweller's story is now being repeated. In an expanding economy, where capital is readily available, there will come a point when there will be a collision between economic growth and availability of labor to fuel that growth. "We're slowing down because we've run out of people to employ," says Diane Swonk, economist at First Chicago NBD. Even after luring students, importing immigrants, and courting retirees, the dearth of skilled labor is a serious problem.

"Put boldly," says Tom Guthrie, an economist at Purdue University: "We've flat run out of reserve labor."

The short supply of labor in a booming economy has been cited many times – in Singapore, parts of Scandinavia, the Silicon Valley of the USA – to mention only a few.

Michael Ottenweller though, is talking about Indiana ... and Iowa ... and Nebraska! The heartland of America, the industrial hub, has also been hit hard. In terms of labor availability, there is a famine, a dustbowl of human resources that might have John Steinbeck writing new novels were he alive today!

This shortage of labor in the presence of orders and opportunities left unfulfilled has finally reached the attention of executives worldwide. What should have been clear on many levels and long ago ... that *people* make businesses run ... is only now garnering systematic attention. For example, when Promark Electronics decided to open a new plant in labor-rich Georgia, far from its headquarters in Columbus, Ohio, president Phillip J. Glandon said "we're not so concerned about saving 50 cents an hour, we're just concerned about finding people, period."

If you are having trouble finding good employees, you're not alone. According to a 1997 survey by George S. May International Co., finding and training new employees is one of the biggest management challenges that the owners of US and Canadian small and midsize businesses face. Furthermore, a study done earlier in the year by the same company revealed that finding top-notch people is even harder than it used to be. That survey of 838 company owners found that 56% believe it's more difficult today to find qualified employees than it was five years ago. Worst hit were manufacturers, who complained about the high cost of turnover. The obvious expenses of the casting search process? Recruitment fees, training costs and lost productivity are but a fraction of the cost of lower productivity and/or lost opportunities.

Taken cumulatively, the cost of replacing a good employee is a significant factor affecting every major company in the world, yet few companies have a perspective (let alone a process or plan) for addressing this key issue.

The good news is that a greater understanding of the value of finding a viable labor supply is now openly being discussed. The bad news is that this discussion only covers half the scope of the real problem! What the new Thoughtware reminds us is that the difficulty of *finding* a work force often pales in comparison to *keeping* that workforce productive and employed for the long haul. (See Chapter 10, RETENTION, for much more on this.) Today, the "long haul" has a horizon line of three to five years!

In some parts of the world, the annual employee turnover rate is 60%

or more. In some industries (such as fast foods and financial management), the annual rate exceeds 100%.

Further exacerbating the problem is that today's work force has few loyalties and moves willy-nilly from company to company ... and with little hesitation and few, if any, regrets! So, even if you find, train, and invest in your emplyees they may be recruited from outside and turn right around and go to work for the competition, and they'll do so in a nanosecond! Indeed, times have changed. Things will never return to "normal," says the new Thoughtware, *this* is the new normality.

Further, do not be deceived into thinking that this is only a phenomenon of a vibrant, expanding economy. Nothing could be further from the truth. In fact, all substantive studies on productivity as it relates to downsizing in a slowing economy report the same thing. If you cut your workforce, the productivity and commitment of those still employed drops.

So though the bottom-line looks better in the short-term aftermath of downsizing, the long-term impact can be devastating on future growth and revenue. Consequently, boom *or* bust, the recruiting and retention of top talent, says the new Thoughtware, is an issue that is here to stay.

Fortunately, many organizations have come to this realization years, even decades, ago and they have paved the way for the rest of us. In the remainder of this chapter we will look at some of the best practices addressing the issues of the recruiting *and* the retention of talent. Make no mistake about it, these are serious, bottom-line factors in today's marketplace. Consequently, companies have developed some very innovative search techniques.

HIRING ... MICROSOFT STYLE

The answer: "I hired a lot of smart people." The question: "What's the most important thing you did last year?" The speaker: William H. Gates III, Chairman of Microsoft Corp.

In a *Business Week* article in the early days of the company, we were given an insight into the policies, procedures – and priorities – of what would become one of the most successful companies in economic history. Mavericks from the start, they continue to push beyond the boundaries of traditional business wisdom.

To some extent this unconventional bent is a reflection of Gates's management style. Gates seems to understand that good people make for good companies, and good companies are very good to their customers. However, there's more to this than meets the eye. Gates also understands that in a competitive industry, to get good people to come to work for you requires some daring new strategies.

Consequently, Microsoft recruiters have been given the freedom to develop a talent-scouting process that seeks out idiosyncratic candidates who possess many of the basic skills of the new Thoughtware: attitude, perspective, and tenacity ... as well as a good sense of humor!

Microsoft recruiters include all employees. For example, President Steven A. Ballmer explains the legendary open-ended questions that are at the heart of their talent search interviews. "They don't have to get the right answer. But I want to see how they go through the process," says Ballmer. "If they're good, I make the game harder."

Here are some of the most commonly asked questions by Microsoft's interviewers.

1. How many gas stations are there in the US?
2. Why are manhole covers round?
3. Why do jukeboxes have both letters and numbers?
4. How many square yards of artificial turf would you need to cover all the baseball fields in the Major Leagues?
5. If you were a product, how would you position yourself?

How would you answer these "quirky questions"? Now, how did you do? What mix of logic and creativity did you use to answer? Would Microsoft hire you? Would you want to work for a company that was as interested in the rationale for manhole covers as they were in your academic degrees or software programming experience?

Perhaps Marshall McLuhan was correct in pointing out that "the medium is the message." The hiring process – unconventional questions and all – delivers a clear message to applicants: Microsoft does things differently.

James Allchin, former Chief Technical officer for a networking software company, was personally recruited by Bill Gates. "(He) convinced me of one thing. If you want to change the world – and being the silly kind of guy I am, I do – I would have a bigger impact at Microsoft."

Incidentally, Allchin not only left his old company, he voluntarily took a 35% cut in salary.

HIRING ... SUN STYLE

I have had the pleasure of working with Sun Microsystems for a number of years in a wide number of capacities. I served as a consultant to senior management at Sun University and Real Estate in the Workplace, keynote speaker to SunService, and creator of a training program which more than 1000 employees have taken on "Break-It! Thinking." I have done satellite down links, conference calls, surveys, and emails galore. Yet my fondest memory is my first memory, of a conversation I had at lunch the first day on their "campus" nearly ten years ago, when Sun was in its infancy.

I was there to meet several people and prepare a proposal and Scope of Work on an organizational development issue. My host, who I will call Tom Perkins, was a big man. He looked more like a professional wrestler than a corporate director, but he was charming and talkative and very bright. As we sat down to eat our sandwiches, I asked him how he came to Sun. This is his story.

Three years ago I was sitting at a bar in Jackson Hole, Wyoming, where I'd found work after a serious injury. Sitting next to me at the bar was a tourist and he bought me a drink. I told him I had been a diver in high school, and my hobby was cliff diving. I mentioned that I was on the mend after two near-death experiences, and he wanted more details. Well, I went on to explain that I was doing a very high cliff dive in Mexico when the wind suddenly picked up. As I was hurling towards the cliff, I felt I left my body and I 'watched' myself hit the cliff, and die! Next thing I knew, I watched again as the surgeons in the operating room were pronouncing me dead for a second time. Obviously I somehow recovered, rehabilitated a little, and got a job in Jackson Hole.

As soon as I had finished telling the guy this story, he hands me his card and he says, "I'm with this company near San Francisco. You're just the kind of guy we're looking for. If you ever need a job, give me a call!"

I laughed, bought him a drink, put the card in my wallet and thought nothing more of it for more than a year. Then, one day, the card appeared in my wallet and I recalled his invitation. So even though some time had passed I called him. I said, "you probably won't remember me, but I am Tom Perkins and ..." He interrupted me saying, "Hi Tom! How's Wyoming?" He remembered me immediately, said the offer was still good, paid my way down, and hired me on the spot!

He was my boss at first, now he's moved on, and I am in his old position! Fate works in interesting ways, doesn't it?

The moral of Tom Perkins's story? There are several really.

- The search for talent is incessant.
- The search for talent is everybody's job.
- Top talent has a new array of skills to die for!

This story may be a bit extreme, but it is also quite exemplary, and common. Talent is hard to come by, so finding it is everybody's job. Ultimately, it is people who will be the greatest asset base of any company.

THE RACE IS ON

What factors are driving the changes in the labor market and presenting challenges to those who seek to improve their company's people assets?

- *Downsizing* in the 1980s and 1990s has altered forever the notion of reciprocal "loyalty" among workers and corporations. Gone are the days when people spent their entire careers with a single employer. What has emerged is a new employer-employee contract, one that is agreed to for the short-term rather than the long-term.
- *Low unemployment rates* put potential employees in the driver's seat. Stories abound of job offers that include six figure starting salaries, one year's mortgage payments, six week vacations, paid tuition – and this to 27-year-olds with two years experience!
- We have become a *free agent nation.* Increasingly, people no longer even entertain the possibility of working for a corporation. Rather, they will freelance, or contract with companies for specific projects over specific time frames. In fact, the largest employer of the twenty-first century ... by far ... will be "Me, Inc."!
- Of course, the free agent market has been largely made possible by *the laser-fast changes in technology*. The Internet has made it possible to seek jobs all over the world, and provides infinite amounts of information to job seekers.

On that last point, here is a story to illustrate how this can work.

I coach Little League baseball and posed a question over the Internet to a youth sports "chat group" about how to teach kids to slide into a base. The first response I received was from a "chap" (his term) in London. He told me he had never played baseball, but loved cricket and was trying to get more information on baseball in order to try the sport. He then said: "To be honest, I noticed you are in California ... I just became engaged to a girl from there ... and in four months we are to marry and I will move with her to America. Got any job leads for me?" I complimented him on his tenacity, told him of the website for Sun Microsystems which I knew was hiring, and three hours later got a message from him: "I got a job at Sun doing HTML ... my fiancé is happy ... I am elated ... Thanks so much!" As my mother said: you *can* change your life in an afternoon!

- *Gen X values and attitudes* are another factor to take into account when developing a plan. (Much more will be said about understanding Gen X later in this chapter).
- Lastly, there are also to be found in every company an array of *hidden issues*. For example, the special attention paid to the rising stars or the "best and the brightest" often come with a hefty price: the loss of productivity of the duller stars and the "rest but not brightest." These will be the vast majority of the workforce, who will then leave the workload to the chosen few stars and move on to a job where they feel appreciated.

OUCH!: MANAGERS IN PAIN

There is only one word to describe what managers feel when they wrestle with issues of acquiring and retaining top talent: pain! Consider the scope and depth of the problem. There is a shortage of labor. There is an even greater shortage of talented labor. Even if you can identify the talent you need, you may not have the budget or resources to lure them. This is just the front end of the problem!

Once you hire them, you have to train them, get them up to speed, orient them to the company culture, get to know their strengths and potential, give them challenging projects, mentor them, push them, and reward them.

It's no wonder that when I asked the Vice President of human resources at a $2 billion Silicon Valley company to describe his current thinking on hiring and retention, he had only one word to offer: "Ouch!"

This is an endemic and deep-rooted problem. It calls for a clear perspective, adequate resources, a wealth of information, and more than a bit of chutzpah! So, what's a manager to do? Gaining a perspective on the issues is a crucial first step ... and moving beyond "denial" of the new "commitment" won't hurt either.

ATTRACTING TOP TALENT

Some of you may have lived long enough to be tempted to say that the issue of finding top talent is cyclical, that is it a by-product of a boom economy, that it is not an issue that merits much attention. The new Thoughtware disagrees and tells us instead that the rules have indeed changed, that retaining top talent is critical in a boom or bust economy, and that the nature of the employer-employee relationship has changed in both form and substance.

What we are seeing now, at the opening moments of the next millennium, is a new commitment emerging that defines not only the nature of work, but the fringe benefits and (what I call) the *fringe deficits* of today. Emerging factors and demographics contribute to the new commitment between employee and employer.

- More women and ethnic minorities are entering the workforce and moving higher and higher in organizations.
- A record number of families now require dual incomes.
- The level of higher education among ethnic minorities in many nations is at the highest levels in history.
- The skills of workers are infinitely greater than ever before.

The question then for a manager is not so much "is there or is there not a new commitment, a new labor contract emerging?" The real question is

"How do we attract and retain members of this new work force?" Here are some tips from the new Thoughtware:

1. Offer "meaningful" work

In the early part of the 1990s, I was the special consultant to the Minister of Labour for the Province of Alberta Canada, the Hon. Elaine McCoy. While involved in the two-year project ("Alberta 2020") which looked at the future of work over a 30 year horizon line, I met with a very wide range of Albertans ... from native Indian tribal chiefs to the local police chief. Alberta's police chief told me that he was having a difficult time advancing and promoting from within, because so many officers liked what they were now doing and found their work meaningful. The officers did not want to move up the career ladder, because they were afraid that they would lose the part of their work that they enjoyed most!

2. Maximize lifestyle-relevant choices

People no longer have careerist employment assumptions, so they make job-related decisions on a new array of factors such as family preferences (such as availability of childcare); hobbies or passions; flexibility (such as the opportunity to telecommute); or the company's role in the community.

In my community, for example, LucasFilms is one of the most coveted employers, in part because they are environmentally aware, have terrific childcare facilities, and have a creative culture.

3. Treat your company "culture" as if it were a "brand"

At Hewlett-Packard, for example, being an "employer of choice" is a key value frequently found in their *hoshin* (Japanese for "breakthrough thinking") strategies that guide their goal-setting for a given year. I recently did a survey on behalf of Sun Microsystems that sought information and opinions on various aspects of their corporate culture, and among the questions I asked was: "If you were not working at Sun, where would you most want to work, and why?" The first choice of Sun employees was Hewlett-Packard. Their most common reason was that Hewlett-Packard "consistently treats their people very well."

4. Provide a "cafeteria style" customized menu of benefits and challenges

Let employees select their unique array of benefits to create a "mass customization package," rather than assuming that "one size fits all." Also, provide an assortment of challenges and professional development opportunities to future employees. At Nissan Design International in La Jolla, CA, they hire people in "divergent pairs," not in spite of their differences but because of them.

A PROSPECTIVE EMPLOYEE'S "CHECK-LIST"

In the Network Age, intellectual capital and intellectual skills are a hot commodity. Therefore, in those intellectually intensive industries, top talent is in the greatest demand. If you are recruited by a company, or are applying to one, or have multiple offers and have to make a choice, Lynn Ware, President of Integral Training Systems, offers this check-list of points to consider (1998, p.8A):

- *What are your first impressions*, your "gut" reaction. As an analogy, when you were thinking about colleges or universities, if you visited campuses you no doubt had an intuitive sense of how it would "feel" to be there for four years. Since, on average, that is now the average length of employment at a given company, the same criteria may apply.
- *How will they orient or mentor you*? How quickly will they do so? How long will it take you to "get up to speed?" The longer that process is, the higher the likelihood of frustration and of a feeling of low productivity.
- *What is the scope and the extent of professional development opportunity*? As Peter Senge rightly observed, most companies have to become "learning organizations" if they are to thrive. If you are not likely to be given new learning opportunities on a regular basis, you are losing ground *vis à vis* your future employability. Further, are the learning opportunities aligned with promotions and/or career-building opportunities?

- *Is there a fair distribution of rewards*, and easy access to company information, policies, and vision? If you are kept in the dark, you are quite likely to produce sub-optimal work, with sub-optimal rewards.
- *Who will be your peers*? Walk around the premises, get a sense of the people and the work environment. Seek out your future peers and colleagues rather than accepting the description and/or assessments of those officials hiring you.
- *Does the work fit with your values and self-image*? Is there what Lynn Ware calls a "psychological paycheck" that will add value to working there? Will you be proud … or embarassed … to tell friends and loved ones where you will be working?
- *How engaged and committed is your direct manager or boss*? Is she enthusiastic and knowledgeable? Can you work with her? Will she listen to your ideas and suggestions? How good are her communication skills? What is her management style and does it mesh with your disposition? how long is *she* likely to stay there?

Isn't it interesting too, the many things that I *omit* from my list, which until very recently would have come up? Where are factors such as "job stability, parking, corner offices?" Lynn Ware has the bold, simple answer: "They're all gone!"

TIME FLIES … WAGES WALK!

A study by the New York City Department of Consumer Affairs indicates if you think you have been working harder and bringing home less money, you are probably right. The study offers plenty of chilling documentation in the data.

"This is the first generation of American workers," says Mark Green, the city's consumer commissioner, "who are living less well than their parents. People have to run harder to stay in place …"

Does this sound like your life? Do you have to work longer hours, perhaps moonlight on a second job, and/or have your spouse working too?

The study calculated wage-price relationships and determined the cost of living in 1972 compared with 1992. The numbers are sobering. For example:

- **1972**: Total annual household expenses (food, clothing, health care, transportation, housing, and utilities) for an average family took 65.4 weeks' work (@ $145per week).
- **1992**: The same expenses took 82.2 weeks' work (@ $345 per week).
- **1972**: It took 3.68 years' worth of income to buy a median-priced home.
- **1992**: It took 5.37 years' worth.
- **1972**: A full-sized Chevy cost the equivalent of 25.4 weeks' wages.
- **1992**: A new Chevy cost 42 weeks' wages.
- **1972**: A routine doctor's visit cost 2.48 hours' wages.
- **1992**: By then it cost 7.46 hours' wages!
- **1972**: A college education averaged 20.63 weeks' wages.
- **1992**: A 92% increase, to 39.59 weeks'.

These figures are significant enough on their own merit, but let me make an additional point. Twenty years ago the average hourly wage, adjusted to inflation, was $11.31. Today, the average hourly wage has gone down to $10.03. That's a double whammy! Things not only proportionately often cost more but we have less earning capacity as well!

"Because of this," observes Green, "many Americans are enduring a new kind of poverty. It's harder to take a vacation, harder to find money to go to school, harder to find the time for the kids – if it's possible to afford to have them in the first place."

This is why "Time flies ... while our wages walk!"

RECRUITING "MR. NICE GUY" AS CEO

Meet Larry Rosenberger, president and chief executive officer of Fair, Isaac and Co., in San Rafael, California.

Fair, Isaac and Co. is a rapidly growing, publicly traded, high-tech company. In a competitive industry, when first meeting Larry your question would probably be: he can't possibly be the CEO and be as nice as he seems can he?

Rosenberger lives with his wife (his high school sweetheart) in the same starter house he moved into in 1975 just before his children were born. Until recently, his office was a cluttered cubicle in a room full of cubicles, not even in the main complex where most of Fair, Isaac's employees work. Unusually, Rosenberger would rather talk about employee satisfaction and empowerment than profits, growth, and sales. Hello? Central casting? You sent the wrong guy to play the role of CEO! Or did you?

"If you look at organizations and organisms, profit-making companies need to make a profit like a mammal needs to breathe," Rosenberger says. "If we can't generate a profit, we can't breathe. If we can't breathe, we can't grow. But when people say the purpose of a company is to maximize profit, I ask: 'Is your purpose to maximize oxygen?' In my mind, the purpose of an organization isn't to breathe more oxygen. It's to deliver value."

What does Rosenberger value? The basics. The simple. The practical. An engineer by training, he drives a1986 Volkswagen van, of which a friend says "It gets him from here to there, and that's all he needs." Before a recent news photo session, he worried that he should have cut his wavy hair for the photo, but then he says, "Real people have hair that grows."

Some real people don't like neckties either. When Rosenberger became CEO, succeeding founder Bill Fair, he stayed true to his values and principles, which included a disdain for ties. "I didn't see any reason to change," he says, implying that there was no requirement that a CEO should dress a certain way. Nothing was ever said one way or the other, but the ties started disappearing in droves throughout the company after he took charge. Even as a CEO he stayed with his own lifestyle and priorities to justify his other "indulgences," such as time with his family and dedication to educational causes.

A case in point would be his ailing golden retriever. He wanted to take the family dog, Alana, to the vet. "By working sometimes long hours, and somewhat intensely, I have zero guilt (about leaving the office in mid-day)," he said in an interview, Alana at his side. "For the time taken off the last three weeks to nurse this dog, I apologize to no one."

"I wanted to see if fundamentally a nice guy could be a CEO – if, in the minimum requirements of the job, I could continue to be myself." (Fost, 1997, p. B2).

Interestingly enough, word has gotten out in the industry about Larry Rosenberger *and* Fair, Isaac as a "good place to work," a place reflecting his values: honesty, hard work, and community involvement. His enthusiasm for his company has also helped create this corporate identity. Consequently, the retention rates at Fair Isaac remain among the highest in the industry. Indeed, as the new Thoughtware says: being a good person and a good citizen, is good business!

GEN X: YOU GOTTA LOVE 'EM! ... AND YOU GOTTA KNOW 'EM!

They're more entrepreneurial than previous generations. They grew up with computers. A fax machine is a form of slow communication. They're self-reliant. They're more loyal to their work than to a firm ... and *much* more loyal to their friends than to their work! They seek balance and they "want a life." Also, according to UCLA head basketball coach Steve Lavin, himself only 33 years old, they also "don't listen very well." They are quite a package to reckon with.

In the USA, the 45 million or so people born between 1965 and 1977, were tagged several years ago with the label "Generation X" – Gen X for short. Initially, Gen Xers were described as lazy and self-centered, latch-key children of families where both parents worked. They have long since shed the "slacker" label from the early 1990s. As Bruce Tulgan, consultant and author of *Managing Generation X* (1997) describes them:

- They're flexible and adaptable.
- They're techno-literate, constantly adapting to change.
- These younger workers are more entrepreneurial.
- They aren't motivated in the same old way.
- They don't respond well to a dues-paying, ladder-climbing corporate culture.
- They are self-reliant.
- They keep their own skills sharp.

Perhaps most importantly, for those charged with managing Gen X (which I believe is a contradiction in terms), Gen Xers insist on being able to balance work with the rest of life.

Many companies aware of the new Thoughtware regarding Gen X, such as accounting firm Arthur Anderson, are changing a long-standing pay practice in order to give new hires more control over work hours.

Says Scott Wilson, partner and director of human resources in the firm's Dallas office, "Traditionally, it was base pay plus overtime for the first six years. There was a direct correlation between pay and hours worked. Now we're going to straight salary. The individual has the opportunity to do a good job or a not-so-good job of managing their own time," he said.

Department store chain Mervyn's recently revamped its manager training to be more effective for people in their twenties. One key: "more self-paced learning and practical training in stores," said spokeswoman Anne Marie Reid, herself a member of Generation X. "We like to learn at our own pace."

"Managers can win over younger-generation workers with clearly defined projects that allow them to contribute directly, and with frequent feedback," says Tulgan.

Continuous learning. Frequent feedback. Some flexibility to balance work and other life needs. "I believe this spirit is moving into the entire market for skilled workers," said Tulgan, and ... "X'ers are leading the charge." (Kunde, 1997, p.E6).

If those sound like management techniques to retain more than just Generation X workers, then you are already attuned to the new Thoughtware.

COMIC RELIEF: GEN X

The Washington Post now holds a contest in which participants are asked to tell Gen-Xers how much "harder" they had it in the good old days:

Second Runner-Up:
In my day, we couldn't afford shoes, so we went barefoot. In the winter we had to wrap our feet with barbed wire for traction.
(Bill Flavin, Alexandria, Virginia)

First Runner-Up:
In my day we didn't have MTV or in-line skates, or any of that stuff. No, it was 45s and regular old metal-wheeled roller skates, and the 45s always skipped, so to get them to play right you'd weigh the needle down with something like quarters, which we never had because our allowances were too small, so we'd use our skate keys instead and end up forgetting they were taped to the record player arm so that we couldn't adjust our skates, which didn't really matter because those crummy metal wheels would kill if

you hit a pebble anyway, and in those days roads had real pebbles on them, not like today.
(Russell Beland, Springfield, Massachusetts)

The Winner of the velour bicentennial poster:
In my day, we didn't have no rocks. We had to go down to the creek and wash our clothes by beating them with our heads.
(Barry Blyveis, Columbia)

Honorable Mentions:
In my day, we didn't have dogs or cats. All I had was Silver Beauty, my beloved paper clip.
(Jennifer Hart, Arlington)

When I was your age, we didn't have fake doggie-do. We only had real doggie-do, and no one thought it was a damn bit funny.
(Brendan Bassett, Columbia)

In my day, we didn't have fancy health-food restaurants. Every day we ate lots of easily recognizable animal parts, along with potatoes drenched in melted fat from those animals. And we're all as strong as AAGGKK-GAAK Urrgh. Thud.
(Tom Witte, Gaithersburg)

In my day, we didn't have hand-held calculators. We had to do addition on our fingers. To subtract, we had to have some fingers amputated.
(Jon Patrick Smith, Washington)

In my day, we didn't get that disembodied, slightly ticked-off voice saying "Doors closing." We got on the train, the doors closed, and if your hand was sticking out it scraped along the tunnel all the damn way to the Silver Spring station and it was a bloody stump at the end. But the base fare was only a dollar.
(Russell Beland, Springfield)

We didn't have water. We had to smash together our own hydrogen and oxygen atoms.
(Diana Hugue, Bowie)

Kids today think the world revolves around them. In my day, the sun revolved around the world, and the world was perched on the back of a giant tortoise.
(Jonathan Paul, Garrett Park)

In my day, we wore our pants up around our armpits. Monstrous wedgies, but we looked snappy.
(Bruce Evans, Washington)

Back in my day, *60 Minutes* wasn't just a bunch of gray-haired liberal 80-year-old guys. It was a bunch of gray-haired liberal 60-year-old guys.
(Russell Beland, Springfield, & Jerry Pannullo, Kensington)

In my day, we didn't have virtual reality. If a one-eyed razorback barbarian warrior was chasing you with an ax, you just had to hope you could outrun him.
(Sarah M. Wolford, Hanover)

SKILLSETS OF THE RICH, FAMOUS, AND DESIRABLE

Gen-X or not, what is the emerging skillset of the new workforce? How can you become sought after and desirable in the marketplace? Best-selling author Stephen Covey (1997, p.4) adds some new Thoughtware when he advises:

- *Behave Like An Entrepreneur.* Act as if you were in business for yourself.
- *Seek Feedback.* Get ... "a 360-degree review."
- *Move Beyond Mentors.* "Today there's so much turmoil in the workplace no one has time to be a mentor ... I call it "modeling."
- *Think Teams.* Learn to work with others, develop a range of collaborative styles.
- *Take Risks.* Don't sit back and wait, initiate. Start something.

- *Be A Problem Solver*. Anyone can describe the problem, but few can solve it. Focus on solutions.
- *Balance Your Life ...* Always being the last to leave the office does not make you an indispensable employee.

SMALLER PAYCHECKS, MORE COOKIES ... AND "CIRCLES OF COLLEAGUES"

The times they are indeed a'-changin'. So if you are a fast-rising executive and you have a picture of John Wayne on your desk, a quote from Vince Lombardi on "Winning" carefully framed on your wall, and a photo of yourself with your local politician on the golf course, you are in trouble.

If you are (or aspire to become) the CEO of a company these days, you have to think differently and look for new models of leadership and achievement. Chief executive officers today are under fire for receiving high salaries, often in the face of poor performance. We all know that. However, money is only the tip of the iceberg.

Nowadays the pressures of the marketplace are many-fold.

- Trade unions increasingly understand the value of alliances with management. The days of adversarial relationships between labor and management are outmoded at best, and diminish American competitiveness at worst.
- Customers want CEOs to do more than offer value-added products. Customers expect what I call *values*-added products and services. Little-but-important things show the customer that their business is valued, that the production process reflects environmental values, and that the company cares about the community's future.
- Employees want their bosses to listen, to recognize them when a job is well done, not to take them for granted, but to make employees part of the decision making process. I am not proposing that the new CEO be a kind of corporate "Mr. Rogers" nor that we are ushering in an age of MBAs – management by accolades. Or am I?

You see, several models are emerging that are worth tracking and, interestingly enough, they are not coming from the world of business at all!

Consider the case of the Girl Scouts of America! Did you know that Harvard Business School has been studying the revitalization process of the Girl Scouts since Francis Hesselbein took the reins of the organization? Hesselbein has infused the organization with vitality by instituting "circles of colleagues" as a way to reduce the hierarchical nature of the Girl Scouts.

By emphasizing collegiality, shared decision-making, recognition for day-to-day achievements, and the intrinsic "perk" of being involved in helping to shape the lives of youngsters, Hesselbein has created a collegial model worth watching – and emulating. All this and she sells great cookies too!

In fact, Peter Drucker, one of the foremost management thinkers of our time, recently told a reporter: "If I had to put somebody in to take over as CEO of General Motors, I would pick Francis."

THOSE WHO LAUGH ... LAST

Hidden in the myriad research snippets in a management newsletter I was reading recently was this interesting research finding.

One recent study showed that the average kindergartner laughs 400 times a day. The same study revealed than the average 40-year-old laughs 15 times a day. Pardon the pun, but that's pretty sad isn't it?

I was thinking about laughter and the relative paucity of good humor and wit. Most comic strips are not particularly funny. Most comedians aren't either. Once in a while a cartoon tickles my funny bone (like the Caldwell cartoon of a guy wearing a "Swiss Army shirt" that has twelve sleeves, something for every occasion). TV sitcoms full of racial and gender stereotypes don't make me laugh, they make me wince. It seems that most businesses and corporations are not destined to be the subject of "Ode to Joy" poems, and that's discouraging.

Then I thought of a story Paul Hawken once told. Canaries are beautiful birds and their songs bring great pleasure to all ages. Unlike any other bird, canaries also save human lives. For many centuries, miners have taken canaries into mine shafts as an early warning signal that there is danger in the air. When the canary stops singing, the miners head out of those shafts as quickly as possible.

Hawken, founder and former CEO of Smith & Hawken, then adds:

"Laughter is the canary in the mines of commerce. When the laughter dies, that company is dying too!"

The new Thoughtware knows this too. These days we have to *constantly* mix business with pleasure, because those who laugh ... last!

Chapter Ten

RETENTION

If the Gate's Open ... They'll Stay in the Yard!

"The soul spans geological time, discerning & detached in relation to the self & the other, the life & purpose of our world epoch, that the fire not go out ..."
– poet John Clarke, from the poem "The Bridge"

IF THE GATE'S OPEN ... THEY'LL STAY IN THE YARD!

I have told this story a thousand times.

When I was about to get married, I knew my wife-to-be was bright, self-confident, and had a mind of her own. That was the good news ... and the bad! One day, shortly after meeting her mother I was given the full tour of the family albums ... a sure sign of my acceptability as a future family member. I saw baby pictures, toddler pictures, junior and senior high pictures – the works!

As my mother-in-law was about to close the album, she spotted a photo of a backyard barbecue taken when my wife was about 3 or 4. I saw lawn chairs, a table, and some rather simple fencing. Pointing to the picture, she laughed and said: "One thing was always true with Catherine ... if the gate's open she'd stay in the yard!"

In beginning to organize my thoughts on the important topic of retention of top talent, I knew that my mother-in-law's advice was a good place to start. In today's marketplace, *finding* talent is only the beginning of a complex relationship. As we saw in Chapter 9, TALENT, with today's workforce, filled with bright, self-confident people, the best advice is: keep the gates open if you want retain top talent.

More and more companies are doing exactly that. The remainder of this chapter will illustrate how this is done in many industries worldwide. We'll start ... with fun!

FUN AND GAMES ... AND LOW TURNOVER

- Dave Duffield, CEO of PeopleSoft, does stand-up comedy routines at quarterly meetings, while employees are asked to join "Raving Dave's" Rock band! Says Kit Robinson from their Silicon Valley Headquarters, "We have a low turnover rate, it's a fun place to work."
- In Natick, Massachusetts, Cognex software promotes Friday afternoon mixers and free movie night. They also promote an attitude and a culture of hard work and fun times. At their holiday party this year, executive dressed in pink tutus and danced portions of *The Nutcracker*. It was not a pretty sight ... but it was fun!
- John C. Malone, president of America's largest cable TV company, TCI, works only five hours a day – and goes home for lunch too!

PROFITABLE PARTIES AND OVERHEAD BINS

Southwest Airlines CEO, Herb Kelleher believes in impromptu partying, events that "praise the goodness of the soul and bring out the goodness and altruism in people," as he puts it. "What we do (by celebrating) communicates itself to the outside world in better service and warmer hospitality." (Kelleher, 1998, p.123).

Partying is only one form of rewarding his 25,000 employees. Numerous airplanes are dedicated to his staff. When, for five consecutive years Southwest had the best on-time, baggage handling and satisfaction ratings, he put all their names on the outside of the overhead bins. Twenty-five thousand names!

At the headquarters of the $3.8 billion, Dallas-based airline, the halls are filled with more than 1500 photos of employees on the job. "Those pictures show that we're not interested in potted palms or Chinese art, but in our people." Kelleher says.

Though the airline has grown dramatically since being founded in 1971, Kelleher is determined to keep some aspects of it as personal as possible. When asked if it was true that he sends birthday cards to employees he said: "I do, and it's not just birthday cards. It's on their anniversary of employment ... it's Thanksgiving ... it's Christmas ... it's recognizing the births in families, recognizing the deaths."

Doesn't this all take a lot of time and money? Kelleher admits that the company could save money by not adding these personal touches. However, set against that is the lowest customer-complaint record in the American airline industry, and who can say how much that is worth? He adds that reducing these costs would be like "cutting out your heart!"

WORKIN' 9 TO 5: IT'S THE *POLICY*!

For many people, the 40-hour week disappeared just after the dinosaur. Not at Sterling Information Group in Austin, Texas. Co-founders Chip Wolfe and Dan Thibodeau (1998, p.97), believed that a "healthy, growing company should retain satisfied employees who have ample time for their families, hobbies, and communities. The goal was to maximize people's quality of life and at the same time create a growing business."

The commitment to a nine to five, 40-hour work week runs deep for the co-founders since starting the company in 1985, the year Thibodeau's first son was born with cerebral palsy. "Dan couldn't work very much," observed Wolfe, who himself did not want to get swallowed up by their growing company. So the policy is now firmly in place, and the bottom-line rewards from it are substantial. Says Wolfe, "It's far easier to be fair and generous to employees than to deal with 20–30% turnover ... and my employees had time for their families. The community had people with time to volunteer and give back. And the clients received excellent work. All the stakeholders in the corporation came out looking pretty good."

Many companies are similarly inclined. Daniel Maude, CEO of $10 million software services company Beacon Application Services Corp., noticed that his software consultants were working full weeks at sites a long distance away from their headquarters in Farmington, Massachusetts. Flying out on Sundays and returning late on Friday nights, "that really left them with only one day off." says Maude. (1997, p.149).

So he did what was in his power to do: he changed the policies of the company. Now, employees leave Monday morning and return Thursday nights. Fully understanding the new Thoughtware, Maude's advice is: "If you want to keep someone 5 to 10 years, you can't work them 60 hours a week."

WORK IS A RUBBER BALL

Brian Dyson, CEO of Coca-Cola Enterprises, had this to say about keeping your priorities straight and your work in perspective as he addressed a recent university graduation:

> Imagine life as a game in which you are juggling five balls in the air. You name them – work, family, health, friends and spirit – and you're keeping all of these in the air at the same time.
>
> You will soon understand that work is a *rubber* ball. If you drop it, it will bounce back. But the other four balls – family, health, friends and spirit – are made of glass. If you drop one of these, they will be irrevocably scuffed, marked, nicked, damaged or even shattered. They will never be the same. You must understand that and strive for balance in your life.

He is a wise man, and heads a company that is often listed as among the most respected in the world in the annual *Fortune* magazine polls. Finding how to juggle that rubber ball – and how to protect the glass ones – makes an employee healthy, productive, and loyal too.

LOSING SLEEP ... AND VACATION TIME?

A new study by Primark Decision Economics shows the average US worker gets 11.37 days a year in paid vacation, a steady decline from 12.17 days in 1987. Private sector employees must work 23.9 days to earn one day of paid vacation whereas they worked 22.4 days for the same benefit in 1987. (Neuborne, 1997, p.B8).

Before the invention of the electric light, Americans slept an average of 10 hours a night, according to James Maas, a Cornell University professor and authority on sleep. Today, we sleep an average of 7.1 hours a night and a third of Americans sleep six hours nightly. Yet if someone loses as little as an hour of sleep a night for a week, his productivity drops 25%. (Jackson, 1997, p.E1).

Consequently, the loss of sleep, coupled with the loss of vacation time has begun to be a factor affecting productivity. As if the sleep/vacation deprivation were not enough, when you factor in the additional workload from downsizing, and the stressful pace of the world of commerce, you have a significant problem to address.

How do you address such problems? Paul Allaire, chief executive of Xerox, says, "We found the real answer is to figure out how to restructure work, instead of helping individual employees, one at a time." For example, he says, "We restructured the work day into periods of quiet time to do individual work and other time for meetings and collaboration." Also, 320 people were allowed to arrange their own flex-time. The only caveat: the work had to get done. The result? Absenteeism dropped by 30% and creativity rose. (Allaire, 1997, p.B5).

And at The Learning Design Group in Minneapolis, Steve Cohen has "no vacation policy." Says Steve, "We allow people to take the time they need, when they need it." In seven years, no one has abused this non-policy.

AMAZING FACTS!

- IBM reports that the average cost of replacing and training a new employee is now \$125,000. At Oracle, the *direct* cost only is now \$70,000. Neither of these figures reflects the dollars lost in transition and while waiting for the new hire to attain the same level of productivity of their predecessor! (ITS, Network World)
- At MCI, they estimate that productivity in their conference call/call waiting units takes on average 15 months to bring new people up to speed on their proprietary systems. (ITS, Network World)
- The average time an employee is with a hi-tech company is now 5.2 years, down from 5.7 just a year ago. (So if it takes 1.5. years to gear up, how much productive time is left?) (ITS, Network World)

- Charles Schwab estimates that its new accounts performance support systems staff has 100% turnover every eight months! (ITS, Network World)
- In the information technology industry, one in 10 positions is open. (ITS, Network World)
- Only 22% of Fortune 500 companies worldwide have stated talent retention goals. (ITS, Network World)
- A Towers Perrin Workplace Index study (1997, p.CL41) reported that 94% of employees agreed that it was their responsibility to remain employable by continually learning new skills.
- The same study revealed that money is the *third* most important predictor of job satisfaction. The top two are: management supervisory practices and styles; and career advancement opportunities.

EMPLOYEES: THE NEW "VOLUNTEER" WORKFORCE!

Many CEOs now readily admit that the number one problem facing managers today is attracting and keeping skilled employees. This is even more of a high stakes issue in high-tech companies and their suppliers. Author Christopher Meyer (1997, p.73) summarizes a lesson of the new Thoughtware: "in knowledge work, the power often shifts from employer to employee. The focus moves from what the employee offers the company to what the company offers the employee."

If this is true, what is the attitude and the perspective needed to guide a company along the transition from an employer to an employee-based organization? Meyer quotes Ed McCracken, CEO of Silicon Graphics, a $3.5 billion workstation and supercomputer supplier, "*All* employees ought to be viewed as consultants."

Put slightly differently, the new Thoughtware teaches that if you wish to attract and retain top talent, if you want to keep them healthy, productive, and happy, you have to think of them in an entirely new way. The emerging workforce is a collection of *paid volunteers*!

Meyer understands this full well, having consulted with companies such as Intel, Quantum, Cisco Systems and Hewlett-Packard who have created systems to entice and retain their teams of virtual volunteers. Among the tools in the toolbox of these forward-thinking companies managing their volunteers are:

- Understand that these volunteers are more sensitive to the kudos of their peers than those they receive from their managers and superiors.
- At Sun Microsystems, the dress code is ... flexible. Says CEO Scott McNealy, "We do have a dress code. You must." (Marin I J, July 27, 1998, p. C3)
- Capital assets depreciate. However, *knowledge* depreciates much faster. In a rapidly changing world, good knowledge is good for business. Let your volunteers have ready access to information. Be aware that the new work force may be manic about information! Meyers refers to this behavior as "FMS ... 'fraid of missing something" syndrome.
- Feed their pride in having "made a difference" or a contribution to a body of knowledge. Meyer quotes Genentech's former CEO Kirk, who says, "money is the ultimate report card but not the incentive. What really drives highly educated knowledge workers is pride of accomplishment."
- Fuel the tools. Give the volunteers the best tools around. They are too smart – and too mobile – to settle for substandard tools while being asked to produce state-of-the-art products. At Intel, for example, knowing the value of investing in top tools, they spend about 20% of their entire R&D budget for them, and as a consequence reduce their new product development times by exponential factors.

THE NETWORKED AGE AND THE "NEW COMMODITY"

Today, in a Networked Age, people like Kelleher and Wolfe and Maude know that their employees are a different breed from those in previous eras. They know, too, that the conventional rules of hiring and retention are quickly giving way to new Thoughtware practices

B. Lynn Ware, Ph.D., is among the foremost authorities on retaining top talent. Her research, strategies and excellent training programs have helped move her company, Integral Training Systems (ITS), in Half Moon Bay, California, into the leadership role in the myriad issues affecting the retention of top employees. She is also an old friend and valued colleague, whom I often describe as a medical doctor for corporations. In fact, when asked what she does, she sometimes rightly says, "I treat corporate diseases." (1998, p.8A). Today, the epidemic disease in most companies is "unwanted attrition, which can cause a company to slowly bleed to death."

Over a long lunch, Lynn and I recently talked about the general topic of keeping top talent, a hot topic today, but until recently one which was nearly non-existent as a perceived key success factor. When I asked her "Why now ... why is the retention issue so important today?" she said, "The biggest issue is people. We are now entering fully a networked society. And this is much more complex than saying we are in the Information Age." Foreshadowing the New Thoughtware, she said, "Brains and people are the new commodity."

So people are the new asset base. "You gotta have the best people," says Lynn, "and the company *with* the best people, and who can *keep* the best people, wins."

THE "NEW COMMITMENT"

If Lynn is right, and I believe that she is, then the assumptions about the nature and substance of the search and retention game must change. Organizations now need to understand the new rules controlling this game.

- *Balancing work and "life" have become a cornerstone of an emerging belief system.* As we have seen, more and more companies are now encouraging workers to work *less* time and have more of a life; become active in charitable and community service; and to take frequent sabbaticals to up their learning curve ... and see the world. If George Lucas and Steven Spielberg can build their schedules around their children's, so can you.
- *Job descriptions are being replaced with the specification of work results that are expected.* It's not *how* work is done, but the *results* that matter most. Many companies have adopted flexible schedules and other options to enhance productivity while simultaneously giving employees greater control over their own time. At Fair-Isaac in San Rafael, California, for example, they have instituted a technological "way-station" along the main commuter routes so that during rush hour workers can drive a short distance, stop in at the "way station,"

get some work done and move on when traffic subsides. This is done in addition to their flex-time models for true telecommuters.

- *Self-employed employees are changing the labor market.* These are workers who want to be self-employed, yet also crave the stability of a regular paycheck. In effect, they become semi-permanent temporary employees. Several former temp agencies such as Fellows Placement Inc. and M2 Inc., both headquartered in San Francisco, realized this early on. In both cases they create a network of freelancers, assess and market their skills, and place them at virtually all levels in companies. Says co-founder Marion McGovern, "We're sort of a corporate 'yenta'." (*Inc.*, August 1998, p. 92.)
- *Use customer retention/service tools and strategies for keeping employees satisfied.* Most companies are quite skilled at customer relationship building and retention techniques. Yet, most of these skills are equally applicable to retaining top talent and key employees as well. At Information Access Company (IAC), a $300 million Silicon Valley software company, they understand that incentives entice customers, so they instituted cash finders-fees to any employee who is hired. In several cases, recruiting new employees became a second income stream for current employees, and created a cost-effective, win/win relationship with IAC.
- *Quickly respond to the expressed and unexpressed needs of employees.* At Prudential Insurance Company, a recent employee survey found that the lack of or slow response to questions and requests was the number one cause of dissatisfaction.
- *Measure and track the way people find employment with you and why they stay and why they leave!* At Sun Microsystems, for example, they have global divisions which are held accountable for retention goals, and bonuses and incentives are tied in part, to those goals.

THE 360 BUG

A major cornerstone in any retention perspective is the growth and development of the workforce. In recent years, the traditional performance review has fallen on hard times, and for good reason. In far too many instances, these reviews are more of an inquisition, a sophisticated form of what I call *blame-storming*. Adding insult to real injury, the focus is on:

- deficiencies not performance
- incompetence rather than competence
- weaknesses to shore up rather than strengths to enhance.

For Jack Stack, CEO of Steelcase Manufacturing, the typical annual-review process "does nothing but harm. It creates divisions. It undermines morale. It makes people angry, jealous, and cynical. It unleashes a whole lot of negative energy, and the organization gets nothing in return." (1997, p.39).

To overcome these negative outcomes, the performance review has been shifting and evolving. One such evolution is the "360 review." In this format, an employee is evaluated by a wide range of subordinates, managers, and co-workers.

More and more of the corporate world is being bitten by the 360 bug. Although only 8% of major companies now are using multi-source assessment (the fancy buzzword for 360s), 69% plan to introduce it in the next three years, according to a survey by human resources consulting firm Towers Perrin.

This new surge of interest is due in part to the increased use of teams within the business world. In a team-based environment, fellow team members often know more about each other's day-to-day performance than their boss.

The 360 review is also a backlash against earlier management trends that rewarded people strictly for meeting financial goals. Unlike those reviews, a 360 assessment focuses more on how workers do their jobs. Proponents claim it boosts productivity by giving workers a more accurate sense of their personal strengths, as well as their weaknesses.

Many employees are reluctant, however, to candidly assess a colleague if there are financial implications to their review. Consequently, many personnel experts question whether a 360 should be used as a basis for raises and promotions, or rather as a tool for employee development.

Opinions vary widely from company to company, and even within larger companies from division to division. Generally speaking, when utilized, a 360 makes the employee an integral part of structuring the review process. This is how it works:

- an employee chooses several people for her evaluation
- those people fill out anonymous questionnaires and rate the employee
- the results are tabulated by computer or neutral party
- she goes over the results with her manager, and puts together a long-term plan to enhance or improve her work.

At Intel, for example, the 360 review has been used for some time. As one employee said about the feedback she received and the picture it painted of her, "What I thought was positive, they thought was monopolizing the discussion. I got much more honest feedback than I'd ever gotten from a one-on-one review."

At Hewlett Packard, an employee acknowledged receiving the kind of "validation" review one wouldn't have received from an old-fashioned performance review. One Hewlett-Packard employee said, "The surprise came from the consistency of the feedback from totally unrelated sources, particularly on my strengths. I never felt I was being torn apart. It was very constructive coaching. It was soul-searching but not touchy-feely."

Occidental Oil and Gas Corp. found that there is always the possibility of some reluctance to evaluate or to second-guess another's work, but the temptation to engage in such thinking is far greater when companies use 360 to determine pay raises or promotions. If you just use it for development, you avoid the issue of, "I don't want to say something bad about my friend because it will jeopardize his raise."

As valuable as a 360 may be, it is a very time-consuming process. Some companies, therefore, spread the 360 process throughout the year, while others such as Intel conduct all their 360 reviews in the first three months of the year, what Illana DeBare refers to as a "once a year kind of time-sink, like tax time."(1997, p.B1).

At Steelcase Manufacturing, Jack Stack has his own version of the reviews conducted in the first quarter of every year. "I don't write anything down. I don't put any reports on file. There's no reason to. I'm not building up a record for the lawyers," he says. "I'm trying to help people take an inventory of their strengths and weaknesses." (1997, p.40).

Whether conducted at one point or throughout the year, whether done as a stand-alone or in addition to the performance review *per se*, the new Thoughtware tell us that the 360 review is an important new tool in the toolbox.

BOLOGNA AND REALITY

Every organization faces habitual moments of truth and the evaluation of employees is certainly one of them. Even in the traditional performance review, a "poor" performance by a worker is often attributable to "poor" performance by their supervisor. However, setting such subtle factors aside, at minimum the evaluation process remains one of the last great strongholds of corporate mythology. In every organization, as Harold Geneen says in *The Synergy Myth* (1997) there is the "bologna" and there is the "reality." Consider the case of ITT:

Bologna: Managers should nurture workers and strive to make the workplace a caring environment.

Reality: Managers should inspire workers and help them strive to make the company a profitable place. That way people will keep their jobs and get raises, bonuses, and other perks for working hard and showing initiative, and they'll share in the spoils. What could be more caring than that? The goal at ITT, says one executive, was always "to make the people around me successful." (ITT, 1997, p. 81).

THE "ENCRYPTION GUY"

Regardless of how good the retention plans may be, and in spite of the most advanced techniques for reviewing and nurturing employees, some key people inevitably slip through the cracks. To offer a general profile, these are quiet, diligent employees. They don't complain much, they work very hard, *and* they are generally taken for granted!

VISA recently learned a hard lesson in the retaining of such "invisible" talent when it fell prey to the myth of the organizational chart and corporate plan as being all they needed. If it was down on paper, they presumed it was real! What a fantasy!

What they discovered the hard way was that the plan had no "qualitative" side to it, no real way to assess the value of the contribution to the critical success path of a company and its products.

Enter "the encryption guy" as a case in point. When VISA was ready to launch into an emerging new market, the encryption of data for security purposes for e-commerce transactions, they made one fatal mistake. They assigned the bulk of the development work to a quiet, unassuming guy and paid little attention to him. He was invisible. Shortly before the product launch (in this case an encrypted debit card), The Encryption Guy gave two weeks notice to his boss, and left – to work for a competitor! Not only was the product launch delayed, and opportunities lost, but because they could not find a suitable replacement, they couldn't do the debit card at all for more than a year.

The unexpected departure of an unheralded – yet crucial – person is not uncommon to any large organization. Once burned is twice shy, and Lynn Ware has researched the signs of employee dissatisfaction extensively, to help colleagues and managers alike.

EARLY WARNING SIGNS – *GALORE*!

In my meetings with Lynn, she identified for me some of the early warning signs that managers and fellow-employees should be aware of, signals that are subtle but still let you know the presence or the level of dissatisfaction and disillusionment. "With unemployment and loyalty both at an all-time low," she says, "companies realize they have to be concerned about people leaving." If such concerns are real to you, here are a few of the early warning signs:

- A noticeable change in an employee's behavior patterns. (If a person who has worked on a flex schedule starts coming in at 9 a.m. and leaving promptly at 5p.m.).
- A non-complainer starts expressing personal discontent.
- The employee's productivity declines dramatically.
- The products and "culture" of other companies start to appear in an employee's conversations.
- The employee is heard repeatedly retelling an incident, need, or suggestion that was denied with "no explanation."
- The employee expresses the sudden desire to complete unfinished projects, either personal or professional.

Such signs are relatively obvious, but often only in hindsight. Less obvious though are more subtle clues such as body language (tense movements, lack of eye contact), personal appearance (major alterations in appearance from their norm), changing peer group, and increased impatience with familiar policy and processes.

RETAINING *YOUR* JOB

Best-selling author Stephen Covey adds additional new Thoughtware when he describes how to become indispensable to an employer. Even in an era of high demand for good workers, it remains true that if you have a job you love – and want to keep it – there is an emerging new skillset that you can master. Says Covey (1997, p.4):

- Behave like an entrepreneur. Act as if you were in business for yourself.
- Seek feedback. Get a 360° review.
- Move beyond mentors. "Today there's so much turmoil in the workplace no one has time to be a mentor ... I call it modeling."
- Think teams. Learn to work with others, develop a range of collaborative styles.
- Take risks. Don't sit back and wait, initiate. Start something.
- Be a problem solver. Anyone can describe the problem, but few can solve it. Focus on solutions.
- Balance your life. Always being the last to leave the office does not make you an indispensable employee.

Becoming indispensable is an attitude that is encouraged at Ritz-Carlton Hotels. The company brochure refers to "The Upside Down Pyramid." Julia Schneiderman, a director of quality at their property in Laguna Niguel in California says, "the company considers employees to be its greatest assets." Employees – referred to as "Ladies and Gentlemen" – are trained to become indispensable to the hotel management as well as to the guests (also referred to as Ladies and Gentlemen). Adding "A" plus "B," it is no wonder that the Ritz-Carlton's motto is: Ladies and Gentlemen serving Ladies and Gentlemen!

At the Ritz-Carlton, this motto is no abstraction. For example, a *waiter* who hears a complaint from a guest about a broken TV calls engineering, and then follows up to be sure the repair has been made. President Horst Schultze says, "an employee who does whatever is necessary for the guest's well-being is truly exceptional ... they will benefit."

COMIC RELIEF: DILBERT'S "LAWS OF WORK"

On one level, understanding The Rule of Three is logical and sane. The trouble is, the world of commerce these days is neither logical nor sane! Consequently, we all need additional skills and tools to play the game today. Towards this end, I offer these pearls of practical wisdom from Scott Adams: Dilbert's Laws of Work. The truth, they say, can set you free. These truths about work can also make you laugh! ... And they're easier to understand than gaining market share.

- If you can't get your work done in the first 24 hours, work nights.
- Keep your boss's boss off your boss's back.
- A pat on the back is only a few centimeters from a kick in the butt.
- Don't be irreplaceable. If you can't be replaced, you can't be promoted.
- It doesn't matter what you do. It only matters what you say you've done and what you're going to do.
- After any salary raise, you will have less money at the end of the month than you did before.
- You can go anywhere you want if you look serious and carry a clipboard.
- The more crap you put up with, the more crap you are going to get.
- When the bosses talk about improving productivity, they are never talking about themselves.
- If at first you don't succeed, try again. Then quit. No use being a damn fool about it.
- There will always be beer cans rolling on the floor of your car when the boss asks for a ride home.
- Everything can be filed under "miscellaneous."
- To err is human. To forgive is not our policy.
- Anyone can do any amount of work provided it isn't the work he/she is supposed to be doing.
- If you are good, you will be assigned all the work. If you are really good, you will get out of it.
- You are always doing something marginal when the boss drops by your desk.
- People who go to conferences are the ones who shouldn't.
- At work, the authority of a person is inversely proportional to the number of pens that person is carrying.

- When you don't know what to do, walk fast and look worried.
- Following the rules will not get the job done.
- Getting the job done is no excuse for not following the rules.
- When confronted by a difficult problem, you can solve it more easily by reducing it to the question, "How would Beavis & Butthead handle this?"
- No matter how much you do, you never do enough.
- The last person that quit or was fired will be held responsible for everything that goes wrong.

STARS AND MERE MORTALS

Every company has its stars, special people with special gifts. Some are new and fresh and on the rise, some have long track records of success. In both of these cases, they share a great deal in common, including garnering the adoration of their superiors ... and the disdain of the mere mortals who are their peers!

Stars are stars because they're in a class by themselves; they don't need to work well with others as long as they outperform your expectations by 30% or 40% or 80%. Meanwhile, the merely mortal yeoman work the mines, where performance standards keep getting higher. Author and consultant Nancy Austin (1997,p.61) writes, "We ask a lot of regular employees these days. They're expected to pack their own chutes, keep their skills sharp, and work hard because they want to. Above all, they're supposed to contribute more than they cost. No 10-year, $70 million deals for them. Journeymen's work is as plain and as filling as a ploughman's lunch: not fancy, well done and, if you ask me, deeply undervalued," she says. "We're starstruck. Not only that, we're so completely entranced by star shine that we're jeopardizing the real core of the business, the good stuff that make it green up and thrive."

Consequently, the new Thoughtware encourages us to pay attention to the best and highest role and jobs for ordinary people, just as we now do for the stars.

ODE TO JOY ... AND OY!

We began this chapter by looking at examples of fun in the workplace which contribute to profitability. As we close this chapter, I see no reason not to return to the subject once more. Perhaps you've heard that Ben & Jerry's Ice Cream Company has created a team of "Joy Ninjas" whose job it is to come up with ideas to make employees happy.

For example, they have created Elvis Presley Day, complete with artificial felt pen sideburns and oversized beltbuckles; large county fair-type picnics; and ice cream flavor naming events. The new CEO was sought via an "essay contest" on "Why I want to be the CEO of Ben & Jerry's." The founders wear T-shirts to meetings. You get the picture.

Now, for contrast, consider one of my clients, RCM Capital Management, one of the world's largest capital management companies, with managed assets of more than $30 billion. Their offices take two floors of the prestigious Embarcadero Center building in San Francisco. They are meticulously dressed, and fine art fills the hallways. Yet they have a "Joy Committee," too.

Not only have they instituted a "Joy Committee," but when people started using the Joy Committee to register complaints they decided to start an "Oy Committee" (named for the Hebrew idiom). With the two committees they were then able to foster the good news ... and respond to the bad.

In a world where change and transition are the rule not the exception, in school, in work, and at home, Joy Pays Off!

As the new Thoughtware teaches, happiness yields an excellent return on investment.

TATTOOS AND THE NEW CORPORATE CULTURE

A dozen or more times a year I am invited to come in as the catalyst for a "bunk-it junket," i.e. a corporate retreat. I have been doing this for quite a while, and just when I think I have heard every issue, or seen it all, something new happens.

Let me tell you about one recent adventure.

I was in Woodstock, Vermont, with a group of 80 top hospital executives from a major health care corporation in New England. (I will use ficti tious names because Wall Street would never understand the inherent value of what unfolded in those three days in the New England countryside.)

The Chairman of the Board, who I will call Bob Dorset, had read my articles and my last book *If it ain't broke ... BREAK IT!* and felt that many of the themes and ideas coincided with his own, so he contacted me directly. At Christmas, every senior administrator was given the book as a present in lieu, I suppose, of the annual free turkey. So Bob instructed James Thompson, President of the company, to work with me. Jim called and asked me to lead his group on a strategic planning off-site.

As is my practice, I interviewed several key participants, created a proposed agenda for the day, and worked out a contract. All the regular professional things. Or so I thought.

My first clue to what was ahead came when Jim told me that every year he and Bob organize a skit. This year they had decided to sing along to *Surfin' USA*, complete with bare chests and blonde wigs. This would kick off the morning and set a tone of "anything goes." Never one to shy away from a good laugh, I concurred.

The skit worked wonderfully and it was hilarious, complete with Jim in a bikini and a revered doctor playing air guitar on an old lacrosse racquet.

After a short break Jim turned the meeting over to me. I reiterated a piece of unconventional wisdom I made up – "Plan as we may the future has plans of its own" – and announced that I was going to begin the day by changing the agenda. Rather than five minutes as announced, we would spend the first half hour or more on introductions!

Bob and Jim looked quizzical as their New England sense of order and proper sequence took over. I had surprised them. Undaunted, and following my intuitions and experience, I pushed on.

I asked each attendee to give their name and tell one thing about themselves that no one in the room would know unless they told us. One doctor said she was runner-up to Patti Duke in an audition for the lead in the movie *The Miracle Worker*, and having lost the part, only then applied to medical school. The Chief of Psychiatry said he meditates daily and would love to try taking a one-year vow of silence. The CFO said his dad ran a tattoo parlor and mentioned in passing that he had a six inch leprechaun on his thigh! Another said he had been an All-American pitcher on the Harvard baseball team.

The half-hour stretched to an hour in no time at all. No one complained, but Bob and Jim were still somewhat puzzled and noticeably fidgety.

During the break I told them that I had noticed during breakfast that many people didn't know each other, and that in my experience it is important to invest this kind of time early on "in order to get some rubber into the walls of this corporation's culture." I apologized for the unannounced change in the "plan," but closed by saying one of a consultants favorite phrases: "Trust me!"

Well, the day moved along very, very well. We listed the company's Sacred Cows, we addressed their "core competencies," we discussed new strategic initiatives. Many new ideas and insights were generated.

Perhaps most importantly, during each break I noticed people approaching one another to share a bit about themselves. Two doctors had been pro baseball prospects and were talking about split-finger fastballs with the Harvard doc. One woman who wanted to be a ballerina was talking to the Patti Duke runner-up.

I liked what I saw, and there were innumerable compliments around the dinner table about how the day had gone.

After dinner, Bob and Jim had arranged to reserve the only bar in town, Bentley's. Already in a good mood, virtually everyone strolled the block and a half in groups of threes and fours, chattering all the way.

Bentley's is small, so 80 people filled it up quite readily. There was a karaoke machine and a left handed DJ/guitarist/comedian. It was dimly lit, and had a small dance floor. Best of all, the drinks were on the house!

Well, by 11:30 p.m. Bob had sung two or three versions of *You've Lost That Lovin' Feelin'* and a strange aberrant hybrid of the *Rocket Man* and *The Bunny Hop* had been created by a line of HealthCare professionals dancing out into Woodstock Common! Quite a scene.

Then, it happened. The Executive Director of one of the hospitals jumped onto the stage, grabbed the microphone and began to chant: DA-VID ... DA-VID ... DA-VID! Soon, the crowd raised up in one voice chanting DA-VID, DA-VID, DA-VID!

The natives were relentless. They would not stop until David Johnson came on stage and let everyone get a glimpse of the leprechaun on his thigh!

What's a CFO to do?

Yes, you guessed it. To the sounds of *The Stripper* over the PA system, David dropped his jeans, flexed his thigh, and made that little leprechaun dance! There wasn't a dry eye in Bentley's, people were laughing so hard. I hardly knew him and I had tears rolling down my cheeks!

David was a good sport, the evening wrapped up by one in the morning, and we all started to walk back to the Woodstock Inn. I caught up with Bob and said, "You were a terrific example today, Bob. I hope you understand now why I spent so much time on the introductions this morning.

"These days, a new corporate culture is not possible if you only develop a mission statement and a business plan," I said. "It is built on images of little leprechauns dancing in the hearts and minds of your people. Folks will talk about tonight for years. That's the name of the game."

"You're right on," he said. "And my challenge now is to figure out how to keep this momentum going. I think I'll start by getting a little sleep."

Wise man. Great company!
They know that "Joy Pays Off!"

Chapter Eleven

GLOBALISM

Think Globally, Act Locally ... and Vice Versa!

"... something of heaven should become part of human nature ..."
– Ogotemmeli, totemic priest of the African Dogon tribe

TAIWAN, TORONTO, AND TRINIDAD

The 1997 Annual Report from Berg Electronics in St. Louis, Missouri, a billion dollar connector supplier to the high-tech and telecommunications industry, opens with a headline proposing that Berg provides its clients with a "Global Focus and Local Solutions." Sounds like a good bumper sticker.

If bumper stickers ruled the world, certainly by now most business leaders would choose "Think Globally and Act Locally!" Makes a lot of sense, doesn't it? Sounds good on paper, right? Has a poetic ring to it, don't you think? Unfortunately, although all-of-the-above are true, this axiom only tells half the story.

Today, in a truly globalized economy, we must "Think globally, act locally ... *and vice versa*!" The new Thoughtware reminds us that in both instances, the *thinking precedes* the *action*! Furthermore, *good* thinking – global and/or local – is a rare commodity these days.

In fact, the impulsive entrepreneurial axiom of "ready, fire, aim" only complicates matters, especially when global success is the target. The grit and verve and daring of the entrepreneur, untempered by reflection and thoughtful perspectives, is a sure recipe for global – and local – frustration and failure. We live on a pluralistic planet where methodologies coexist rather than dominate, where right and wrong ways of doing things readily blur.

In such an environment: how *do* you market a product in Botswana, or Boston, or Brighton? How *do* you find good employees in Taiwan, and Toronto, and Trinidad? How *do* you provide excellent service in Sydney, or Stockholm, or Shanghai? Just how, as one unified-integrated-global company, can you achieve *all-of-the-above*? Tough questions indeed, yet there are answers being formulated, best practices to emulate, and quality Thoughtware to put to use. Although the truth is not eternal, somewhere, for some period of time, some things do in fact work! That's what is so exciting about the Network Age, "the truth is out there."

NECESSITY IS THE MOTHER OF GOOD THOUGHTWARE

We have done so much, for so long, with so little thought to it, you can only imagine the possibilities that accrue from the potent combination of attitude, perspective and keen action. Why is this so? Why must we follow the new Thoughtware in this arena as well? The answer is simple: necessity is the mother of good Thoughtware.

The "necessity" of which I speak has been driven by a combination of:

1. inadequate, antiquated business tools
2. newly emergent opportunities, and
3. viable new models of global excellence.

The remainder of this chapter examines these three elements, beginning with a brief list of inadequate business tools, including:

- *Poor business practices.* We have too often assumed that the way we do things in our own country or company is the way of the world. In global dealings, as we will see, what constitutes good business practice here may not be good elsewhere.

- *Poor information systems.* In spite of the advances in technology and data collecting, our information is often far too complex and far too plentiful to be of much practical utility in the running of a global business. The lack of systems integration on a global level is appalling.
- *Ethnocentrism.* The nature of work, the role of "jobs," and the relative importance of "careers" varies enormously from country to country, region to region, even city to city. A large, diverse metropolis may have more complexity than an entire nation. Opening a factory, in New York City, for example, can be infinitely more problematic than opening one anywhere in Denmark. Ethnocentric attitudes and biases can create barriers to productivity, profitability, and sustainable growth.
- *Volatile markets.* Products, markets, even entire industries now have a half-life no long measured by carbon dating or tree rings but in nanoseconds. Certainly this is obvious in high-tech areas, but it is also true, for example, in the retail, manufacturing, hospitality, food and beverage, and entertainment industries as well. *Every* market today is a volatile market, a moving target, a shooting star, a clay pigeon.
- *Inadequate labor supply.* The combination of an exponential increase in global business, the lack of adequate attention and funding to public education, and the rise of new attitudes towards work are but a few of the factors that have contributed to a redefinition of the very nature of work, as well as to the relative shortage of skilled labor *per se.*

FOLLOW THE "YELLOW BRICK ROAD"

"Whatever we do," the global futurists say, "will be accompanied by unplanned side effects." I'm quoting from The Annals of the America Academy of Political and Social Science, of July 1992. As the cowardly lion says in *The Wizard of Oz*, "Ain't that the truth!" This is a decidedly academic publication and the article, written by futurists Joseph Coates and Jennifer Jarratt, was entitled "Exploring the Future."

In my last book, *If it ain't broke ... BREAK IT! Unconventional Wisdom for a Changing Business World*, I made a similar point by saying: "Plan as we may, the future has plans of its own." I still believe this.

Yet, I also believe in the value of seeing far, far down the road, in exploring the possibilities of the future 10, 20, 50, 100 years from now. Fortunately for me, given this esoteric interest, I garner much of my livelihood by working with corporations and institutions that want to develop a long-range perspective. Unfortunately, such organizations are few and far between. Not many corporations, organizations, or individuals take a long enough – or zany enough – look far down the road. Let's take a journey into the global future and look at many new issues and opportunities that will shape the destiny of companies worldwide.

"ELECTRONIC IMMIGRANTS"

When thinking globally you have to understand the factors that may be less important locally but which may loom large on a planet-wide level. The demographics and data are staggering:

- According to the World Future Society (1998, p.1), publishers of *The Futurist*, a new wave of "cross-border commuters" will compete electronically against workers in more affluent countries in a wide range of jobs and industries. These "electronic immigrants" will soon become "a hot international trade issue."
- Globally the world's population will grow by nearly one hundred million people in 1999. Like compounding interest, by 2003 there'll be more than twice as many of us.
- The World Future Society forecasts that "up to 90% of the world's languages may disappear in the next century as information technology creates a global language." Though this may sound far-fetched, we have already seen the universality – and versatility – of numbers. A universal language of commerce has similar potential.
- High-tech will merge with science fiction, creating what I call "Hi-Sci-Fi," and will shape new images for our culture via new technologies that are totally unimaginable (no, make that totally non-existent) today. We can always imagine more than what exists.
- The cutting edge of the future will be conveniently located inside our DNA, minds, hearts, and souls. The breakthroughs in medicine and pharmacology alone will greatly alter the global opportunities. The so-

called "Nanotechnologies," the micromanipulation of molecular-level materials, are on the verge of releasing products that will increase life spans by a full generation, regulate moods hour to hour, grow hair, enhance memory, harden teeth, remove wrinkles, clone human organs ... the list goes on. By 2025, it is estimated that more than four thousand human genetic diseases will be controlled thanks to new diagnostic and treatment modalities. No child in the world will then have to be born with birth defects, or other congenital disorders. Pardon the pun, but Viagra raised the bar – and the awareness – of lifestyle-enhancing drugs, and it is only the beginning.

- The role and clout of the military will continue to decline as we move from a paradigm based on the preparation for, fighting of, and recovery from war to a new paradigm now being forged. E-war (my term), however, will increase, as international "attacks" on data and information systems will create information espionage of unprecedented proportions. This could range from altering satellite trajectories to jamming millions of pager links, to electronic bank robbery, to uncovering sensitive government and corporate secrets, among others.
- Women around the world will significantly, and permanently, alter the rules of the business game in the personal, social and public arena. In education, governance and policy formation, the "unplanned side-effects" of women assuming positions of power and leadership will be both substantive and far-reaching.
- New alliances between nations and global corporations will emerge, based largely upon the principles of economic partnerships now found in the private sector. These alliances will serve as the "glue" that holds the disparate parts together. The most powerful institution for planning and managing a new world order will therefore have no traditional political base. Rather it will more closely resemble the multi-national corporation.
- The longer we live, the older we get! The combination of increased longevity, and the capital assets typically held by those over 55 years of age, will alter the global economic priorities and create huge new capital-rich markets.
- Where some futurists see inter-generation conflicts on the horizon, I see the emergence of new forms of community that blend the generations in new ways. Whatever the professors, politicians, pundits and

provocateurs may say, I still believe you can't go wrong if you listen to the paraphrased wisdom of that renowned futurist, and baseball Hall of Famer, Lawrence Y. Berra, when he says: "The future of the globe just ain't what it used to be!"

CHECKING MY OLD SCORECARD

Most of us enjoy making predictions about the future. It's a civilized way of assessing where we think things are heading, even though we have little or no control over the outcome. Every once in awhile I am even *paid* to make predictions. I forecast therefore I am.

I have forecasted about new technologies, marketing campaigns, interest rates, the next vacation Mecca, trends in maternity care, and the most popular salsa ... you name it and I have probably dabbled in it. Yet after I've gazed into my crystal ball, like most trend analysts, I move on to the next forecast.

Actually, I take full responsibility for my actions and my forecasts, and I do revisit them from time to time to see where I was on target and where I was far off the mark. Recently I was cleaning out some old files and happened upon an article I had written in 1982. That's the risk of putting things in writing, the printed word has a life of its own and it can come back and visit you when you least expect it.

In the article, I was commenting upon John Naisbitt's then recently released book, *Megatrends*, saying that I found a number of his forecasts to be far afield. So, I boldly offered my own ten "megachanges" that would come to pass by the end of the millennium.

I cite these now to encourage you to do the same, to regularly play futurist and trend spotter on a global basis. Think as macro as possible, and as far forward as you wish. I'll let you be the judge of how I did.

1. From vertical organizations to horizontal organizations

Most companies are multi-layered and top down. There will be fewer layers and less top down decision-making in years to come.

2. From a youth-dominated culture to an age-irrelevant culture

The "Pepsi generation" will give way to the influence of the baby boomers, who will give way to the next generation to follow.

3. From bureaucracy to "adhocracy"

Global governmental and public institutions will increasingly be organized around specific issues and tasks, within known time limits.

4. From consumer to prosumer

Conspicuous consumption can't last forever. Impulse shopping will give way to savvy shopping. Low price will yield to high quality in making purchasing decisions.

5. From specialists to generalists

Education will shift away from the training of specialists to a curriculum more adaptable to providing a generalist education. Learning *how* to learn will supplant learning *what* to learn.

6. From goods to services

Similar to No. 4, but factors in the desire of the prosumer to have a dependable relationship with the producer of a product over time.

7. From rising expectations to sobering expectations

The wage-price spiral has gone up and up and will soon have to go down and down. We'll work more and proportionately earn less.

8. From "hard war" to software

The so-called "military-industrial complex" will be replaced to a great extent by competition on the economic battlefield, with information technology likely spearheading the changeover.

9. From belief to scrutiny

From presidents to priests, it's getting harder to find a hero anywhere and so scrutiny and skepticism will prevail unless and until new role models with decorum and vision emerge.

10. From data to intuition

Decisions, plans – even budgets – will increasingly be based upon a good hunch and a modicum of "good data."

Well, how did I do? If I was right, these changes should now be considered conventional wisdom. Do you agree with all or some of these?

So, where do *you* think we're heading? In the space provided below you may wish to make your own predictions about where we are today, and where will we be in the next ten years?

PRESENT-FUTURE

1. From to
2. From to
3. From to
4. From to
5. From to
6. From to
7. From to
8. From to
9. From to
10. From to

What do you think are the "megachanges" underway today that will affect global issues tomorrow?

CONCURRENT THINKING IN AN OXYMORONIC WORLD

In the face of the changing world marketplace, the advances in technology, and the unprecedented democratization of world political entities, there is much to be done to foster concurrent thinking – thinking globally and locally simultaneously. Several forms of Thoughtware lend themselves to facing the challenges and opportunities of globalism, many of which are contrary to conventional wisdom.

The new global Thoughtware is in fact often based on a number of oxymoronic developments that are the cornerstones to successful global business practices. All are discussed throughout this book, and all must be addressed to be globally competitive. Included in the short list are:

- encourage mass customization
- set general priorities
- understand employed volunteers
- follow local universals.

FROM PLOWSHARES TO MINDSHARE

The dramatic growth of the Internet has certainly gained significant attention, and rightly so. As a recent phenomenon, its power has scarcely been tapped. The power of true globalization has been infinitely enhanced by its presence. So, for example, if a bank in America has the best home-banking program on the World Wide Web, people in Switzerland will tap into it, and suddenly, we're using exported banking systems.

The difference though, is that on the Internet, *mind*share is at least as critical as marketshare. If you dominate a *mental* niche, (capturing the mindshare) you will certainly have the advantage when it comes to marketshare.

What about the global opportunities that are outside the realm of high-tech? What opportunities are unfolding that are a bit closer to the soiled hands of the working men and women ... in the area of the *plowshare*, not the mindshare? Where will the advantages accrue? Here too, knowledge of cultural differences, subtle knowledge at that, will make or break global enterprises. The more cultural nuances that are understood, the more likely the success. In thinking globally, the new Thoughtware advises us of a duality: to seek wisdom, more so than information, and yet to understand that even the most minute cross-cultural information may prove most crucial for global success.

TransChem Finance and Trade's executive Vice President of technology transfer Howard Kaplan understands this full well. More than seeking knowledge or reading books or researching on the Internet, Kaplan's advice (1998) is that "there is no replacement for *physically experiencing* a country," prior to a project: in Romania he ate a spit-roasted cow; rode a camel for miles in Mongolia; slept in a yurt in Turkmenistan where he sat on priceless carpets, drank vodka and ate freshly-roasted lamb! By physically visiting a country, he adds, you build understanding and relationships. "If you're going to have a comfort factor with anybody in any country in the world, you need to build up face-to-face trust."

As valuable as such trips may be, they are expensive, time consuming and exhausting. They are also impractical for most people, even if they would prefer to do so. So the next best thing is to talk to those who have recently been to a part of the globe that is crucial to your business ... but, be forewarned, you never know what you'll find out from them nor how important the smallest piece of information may prove to be.

COMIC RELIEF: GREEN IS FOR ... ADULTERY!

An article by John Flinn (1997), entitled "Don't Point: Most of the world thinks it's rude" reminded me of how some cross-cultural dos and don'ts can make or break a vacation, friendship or business deal.

- Never point the soles of your feet at anyone in Asia. Similarly, it's considered the height of rudeness in many countries to point at someone with your index finger.

- In France, it's considered rude to put your hands in your pocket while talking to someone, to cut your baguette with a knife, or to crack a joke in all but a limited number of situations.
- In the Philippines, an invitation must be repeated three times to be taken seriously. Never refer to the woman of the house as a "hostess." This term often means prostitute. Also, in the Philippines as in many other countries, laughter is often used to relieve tension or embarrassment, not as an expression of humor.
- Bad traffic in Bangkok means adding at least an hour between appointments.
- In China, never give a clock as a present, especially to an older person. The English word "clock" is a homophone for the Chinese word "funeral."
- In Indonesia, standing with your hand on your hips or your arms crossed is a sign of defiance or arrogance and is considered insulting.
- The symbolism of color varies enormously. Whereas in the United States, green is associated with money and success, it may mean something very different elsewhere. For example, a US exchange student in China who, with the best of intentions, presented his host father with a green and gold Oakland A's baseball cap. What he didn't know was that green signifies that someone in the family is committing adultery.
- You'd think that the simple act of giving flowers couldn't get you into trouble, but you'd be wrong. In Europe red roses denote a serious romantic interest; and in Russia a bouquet containing an even number of flowers would only be appropriate for funerals .
- In Bangkok, the Year 2000 deadline (software not programmed past 1999), some bankers will tell you, does not apply. In the Thai calendar Y2K happened over five centuries ago.
- Don't expect to eat dinner before 9 p.m. in Latin America, and don't expect to get quickly down to business over the meal either. Your potential business partners need to get to know you before they will consider doing business with you.
- Remember too that the working week in Muslim countries is Sunday through Wednesday, and there is no alcohol consumption.
- In Hong Kong, never stick your chopsticks straight up in your bowl of rice. This is how rice is offered to deceased ancestors by Buddhists. Doing this casually "is like desecrating the cross."
- In much of Asia, a clean plate or an empty glass is a clear signal you desire more. Unless you leave a little unfinished, your host will keep

bringing more food and drink until you burst. However, global-travel expert Ruth Stanat (1998) says that in Thailand, "it is an honor to take the last bite of food during a meal ...(yet in China) you are supposed to leave food ... You don't want to ruin a business deal in China because you've cleaned your plate."

TEST YOUR GLOBAL IQ

So, now that you are in the mood for cross-cultural trivial pursuit, let's test your global IQ. Answer the following questions, and then score at the end.

1. "You're never fully dressed without a smile." is a familiar phrase in the United States. True or false: A smile is a universal expression of genuine pleasure.
2. Japan is a "high-context" culture, where small gestures convey great meaning. Which is an appropriate behavior in Japan?
   A. covering your mouth when you laugh
   B. winking to convey agreement
   C. speaking in a loud, forceful voice.
3. True or false: never keep your left hand in your pocket while shaking hands with your right in Germany.
4. Spitting is grotesque in many places, but is actually against the law in which country?
   A. St. Thomas
   B. St. Martin
   C. Singapore.
5. You are the sole passenger on a bus in Bahrain. A man enters, and chooses the seat next to you. True or false: he intends to start a conversation with you.
6. You are greeting a new associate in France. As you firmly grasp his hand, heartily pumping it up and down, he looks a bit bemused. The reason?
   A. he's relieved you didn't kiss him
   B. the French handshake is more of a handclasp, with no pumping action
   C. he wishes you had kissed him.

7. In the United States, men sometimes slap each other on the back, backside, arms, or shoulders. True or false: This is totally acceptable in the Netherlands.
8. True or false: Before female executives travel to Brazil, they should be certain their nails are well-manicured.
9. You feel good after your big sales call in Stockholm, Sweden. It's a surprise to you, then, when they don't accept the deal. This could be because during the meeting, you:
   A. leaned backward in your chair and crossed your arms
   B. rested your ankle on your knee the whole time
   C. laughed loudly
   D. all of the above.
10. True or false: Snapping your hand downward is used to emphasize a point in Spain.

Answers to your cultural IQ

1. False. In much of Asia, a smile can be used to cover up embarrassment, shock, or fury.
2. A. You are not supposed to display the inside of your mouth in Japan.
3. True. Don't even talk to someone with your hands in your pocket in Germany.
4. C. Singapore also prohibits chewing gun, jaywalking and smoking in public places.
5. False. Solitude feels unnatural in many parts of the Middle East. Complete strangers often sit close to each other.
6. B. The French don't strongly grip each other's hands, nor do they "shake" them up and down so much.
7. False. Dutch men are formal, and usually don't demonstrate their feelings with exuberant slapping gestures.
8. True. Manicured fingernails are an integral part of a woman's professional image in Brazil.
9. D. Informal body language and raucous laughter don't impress the Swedes.
10. True. Snapping the hand downward is also a very common gesture in much of Latin America.

(Adapted from Morrison and Conaway, 1997, pp.165,196)

A BONUS QUESTION: WHAT IS "THE RULE OF THREE?"

Jagdish Sheth and Rojenda Sisodia wrote an interesting article in the *Manager's Journal* entitled: "Only the Big Three Will Thrive."

The stunning announcement precipitating the article was that Daimler-Benz and Chrysler were to merge to form the world's fifth-largest automobile maker, and that this merger is a harbinger of things to come – not only in automobile manufacturing but also in numerous other globalizing industries. "Industry after industry," they say, "is being reorganized according to the Rule of Three: In competitive, mature markets, there is room for only three major players along with several (in some markets, many) niche players."

Together, according to their research, three "inner circle" competitors control approximately 70% of the market. The top three are "volume-driven generalists" who compete across a wide range of products and services, while the smaller companies are "margin-driven" and thrive as specialists in a small number of markets or products. Having an excessive number of "majors" in an industry tends to lead to rivalry, over-capacity, and low levels of profitability. With only three majors, competitive intensity is strong but not excessive, market structure thus provides a good balance between efficiency and high levels of competitive rivalry. "Duopolies" (twosomes, as opposed to monopolies or threesomes), by contrast, tend to engage in collusive behavior.

Their Rule of Three can be observed in numerous industries, including beer, rental cars, cereals, tires, insurance, aluminum, oil companies, chemicals, airlines, pizza chains, soft drinks and athletic shoes. Current merger activity in banking, pharmaceuticals, telecommunications, and airlines is leading inexorably in the same direction. To be viable as volume-driven players, companies must have a critical-mass market share of at least 10%.

At market shares of less than 5%, financial performance turns out to be "inversely correlated with market share: The smaller the market share, the higher the return on assets." In between these two percentiles lies a "Bermuda triangle" of doomed strategies and failed ambitions. Hence, companies that fall below the 10% level must make the transition to specialist status in order to survive, or merge with another company to regain a market share above 10%. Market share is, therefore, a complex matter.

For example, trailing badly behind Boeing and Airbus in the global commercial aviation market, McDonnell Douglas had four options: to try to gain viability via a strong Asian partner (an option ruled out by the US government); become a specialist producer of short-haul jets; exit the commercial aviation market; or merge with one of the big two competitors. McDonnell Douglas chose the last option, merging with Boeing.

In a market with slow or negative growth, the fight for market share between No. 1 and No. 2 often sends No. 3 company into a tailspin. In soft drinks RC Cola wound up losing, and in beer Schlitz lost out. Nevertheless, a *new* No. 3 full-line player usually emerges, especially if the market becomes globalized. In soft drinks, the combination of Cadbury-Schweppes, Dr. Pepper and 7-Up has resulted in the creation of a viable new No. 3 player, with approximately 17% market share.

THE AUTOMOTIVE TAILSPIN

These lessons apply to the auto industry. In its late nineteenth-century infancy, more than 200 manufacturers were building cars in the US alone, none on a national scale. It took the Model T and Henry Ford's innovations in mass production to trigger the process of industry consolidation. Almost immediately, the number of manufacturers dwindled to 70 or 80. Within a few years, the market had consolidated further into three full-line players – General Motors, Ford and Chrysler – and several smaller players such as American Motors (which failed in its attempts at becoming a generalist and was acquired by Renault and then by Chrysler), Checker and Studebaker. Eventually, the Rule of Three prevailed, with GM, Ford, and Chrysler dominating the US market. Chrysler's crash in the 1970s had little to do with Japanese competition and everything to do with the fight between GM and Ford. It went into the ditch, and then re-emerged as a marginal full-line player in the Lee Iacocca era following its government bailout, thanks to an emphasis on minivans and jeeps.

Chrysler could have remained in the ditch, giving Honda or Toyota an opportunity to become the No. 3 player in the US market. However, Chrysler pulled ahead through its acquisition of AMC, while Honda failed to rapidly expand its product line to include minivans and sports utility vehicles.

"When a market globalizes," say Sheth and Sisodia, "many full-line generalists that were previously viable as such in their secure home markets are unable to repeat that success in a world-wide markets context. When this happens, there are typically three global survivors – one from the US, one from Europe and one from East Asia." To survive as a *global* full-line generalist, "a company has to be strong in at least two of the three legs of this triad."

The automobile market is currently being globalized. The big, broadly defined players are Toyota, Nissan and Honda from East Asia; General Motors, Ford and Chrysler from the US; and Daimler-Benz, Volkswagen, Renault, Peugeot and Fiat from Europe. The strongest contender for one of the top three global spots is Toyota, followed closely by Ford. None of the European companies have shown so far that they can become a major presence in the US market (at one point, VW's US market share slipped to just 4%), so they're unlikely to become global full-line players unless they ally with other firms.

Consider General Motors. It's numerically the world's largest automaker, but it has thin margins. The broader problem for GM, say Sheth and Sisodia, is that it is "poorly integrated in terms of both operations and market identity." Globally, relatively few know the GM brand *per se*. Rather, they know the company only through its divisions, such as Chevrolet, Opel, Cadillac, and Vauxhall. GM essentially operates as eight more-or-less independent car companies, none of which can rival the efficiencies of scale of Toyota's globally integrated production and marketing system. (The same Toyota assembly line can produce Tercels, Camrys, and Lexus LS400s.) GM's current lead is based on profitless market share, which means that its lead is ultimately not sustainable.

A "FULL-LINE" ... OF TWO: A CASE STUDY

Full-line generalists, another oxymoron, really need only two major brands: an upscale brand and a broad-based brand that is typically the corporate name. Thus, we have Toyota and Lexus, Ford and Jaguar – and now Chrysler and Mercedes. "Facing the challenge of keeping up with the big boys," say Sheth and Sisodia, "Chrysler had three options:

(1) It could remain a market specialist providing a full range of products to the North American market, with minimal ambitions overseas. (2) It could become a global product specialist, leveraging its relatively secure niches in sport utility vehicles and minivans. (3) It could try to enter the inner circle on a global scale by merging with complementary companies. Daimler-Benz, for its part, could have remained a luxury-car specialist. By merging, Daimler and Chrysler are trying to become one of the top three global, full-line companies."

At the time of the merger, as evidenced by the strong positive reaction from the stock market, presents some strong synergies. Chrysler's strengths in supplier partnering, low-cost production and product design mesh well with Daimler's global presence and emphasis on quality, both of which were weaknesses for Chrysler. Of course, the challenge comes in blending the two different cultures.

As the auto industry evolves and foreshadows truly global competition, the Rule of Three would predict that DaimlerChrysler must find an Asian partner, such as Mitsubishi or Honda, while Toyota needs a strong European partner. Ford is well positioned, given its stake in Mazda and its strong European presence; it is also well on its way toward integrating its operations globally.

The auto industry is a high-stakes instance of an emerging phenomenon: a truly global marketplace wherein three top companies will likely emerge. By looking at it closely, you can learn many lessons for other industries facing similar immanent changes. In commerce, unlike love, three seems to be a charm ... at least until Africa opens, then we may see the Rule of Four!

ON BEING A PROPHET, AND MAKING A PROFIT

As tough as the emerging global marketplace is, and as common as the Rule of Three is operative, it never ceases to amaze me that in the search for *profit*, nations and corporations still seek out *prophets*. One of my earliest memories of Sunday School was a lesson that it's tough to be a prophet in your own land. Somehow, I always remembered this and so I take my own prognosticating, theories, and forecasts for other nations with considerable preparation, and a large grain of salt. That's why I was both cautious (for I was going to another "land") and flattered when I was invited to be the keynote speaker at the annual meeting of the Canadian Hospital Association held in Halifax, Nova Scotia.

My host was asking me "informally" to identify trends in American HealthCare that would hold for Canada too. Specifically, they were seeking the essential factors in any new managed-care health delivery system that the US had experienced that could be a model for Canada. They wanted me to be a prophet in *their* land.

It was a challenging assignment – and one I thought about at length, since Canadian health care is often a model. I accepted their kind invitation and presented to their members several key factors endemic to HealthCare delivery. The speech, entitled "Seven Ps in the HealthCare Pod," by way of summary, offered this:

1. *Protocol-based* delivery systems free physicians up to handle more complicated cases and are more cost-effective.
2. *Partnerships* and team-delivered care touching all levels of the HealthCare system – administrators, nurses, paraprofessionals, physicians, vendors, suppliers, insurers, educator, etc. – are imperative for efficiencies of both scale and cost.
3. *Property* must be de-emphasized so that the "hospital-as-hub" and "edifice complex" of many models (which is very costly to maintain and fully utilize) can be kept under control.
4. *Primacy* of mission must be the driving force, and the basis of rewards and incentives. The mission serves as a reminder of *why* the system exists, *who* it is serving, and *what* it must do to meet the needs of the patient population.
5. *Patient outcome data* becomes the measure by which we know if the mission has been achieved. Outcomes, related to the mission, are revised and upgraded regularly and enable patient and provider alike to better answer the question: "How did we do?"
6. *Patient-focused care* (not physician, insurer, or employer-focused care) shifts the attention to the "end user," to the customer. To mix metaphors, in many managed care models the patient is still pretty low on the totem pole while the doctors are treated as royalty.
7. *Principle-based* care assures that ethical and prudent decisions are made that emphasize and reward a team approach to the total wellness

> of every patient. Such a model is more holistic, educational and service oriented. It strives to change *behavior* as well as treat symptoms, and it puts "hospitality" into the "hospital."

That evening there was a reception line where I shook nearly a thousand hands. Broad smiles, meaningful eye contact, and brief allusions to their favorite part of my speech were common. I was pleased.

Then, ten days later I got the evaluation! The ratings were quite good, but slightly lower than I had thought. So I called my host to ask for more specifics and more feedback. She told me they "liked your manner and style and liked you as a person," but they thought that it was not "formal" enough. Remembering it was she who suggested an informal tone, I remarked "But everyone I met was so enthusiastic and complimentary. You were in the line next to me. Was I imagining this?" She laughed: "O, they were just being very Canadian! We're very polite you know."

After I hung up, I knew two things: it is really hard to be a prophet in your own … or another land … and my Sunday School teacher was right!

ASK NOT, SUCCEED NOT: SEVEN QUESTIONS BUSINESS LEADERS SHOULD ASK

In hindsight, one of the reasons for my having missed the Canadian mark was that I had failed to get a wide range of perspectives from prospective attendees – a practice I normally follow – and had not asked nearly enough tough questions. *Inc.* magazine writer Tom Richmond reminds us that thinking globally, like all other varieties of Thoughtware, often begins with good questions. When he reads books, for example, one of his criteria for good writing is does the author have a "powerful inclination to ask questions." (Richmond, 1998, p.112).

In asking questions from a business perspective, he reads to find books that explore "why to" questions rather than "how to," because few of us "give enough thought to the why before plunging right in." Then he adds, "to ask *how* is to get someone else's answer; to ask *why* or *what if* … is to seek your own."

In my 20 years of consulting, I have worked and traveled in more than 80 countries. I have found that some questions hold up well and when asked at the right time make all the difference between success and mediocrity! Here I recap some of the questions raised in Chapter 2, THE FUTURE, and add some more:

1. What business are you in?

Many companies are in more than one business (Disney, Sony) and/or offer a variety of products and/or services without knowing it (see the example of the law firms cited below). Others have a single focus (Coca Cola) or a few well-conceived products or services. It is important to understand the business you are in, and the most innovative practices in your industry.

2. What other business are you in?

Many companies do not see their business through a wide enough lens. They fail to capitalize on other business opportunities that can accrue from little more than a change in thinking, not knowing that you can tilt the field ... by tilting your head.

As long ago as 1960, Harvard Business School professor Ted Levitt argued that businesses often succumb to tunnel vision, failing to see the big picture because they are myopically looking at the details. For example, certain railroads did not understand they were in the *transportation* business, they thought they were in the railroading business. In the 1950s and 1960s, some motion picture companies thought all they did was make movies, and thus they didn't notice they were in the *entertainment* business. Pardon the pun, but you get the picture don't you?

At Ford Motor Company, they discovered that 89% of their operating profits came from Ford Financing, raising the intriguing further question, "Has the production of the Ford motor car become the loss leader for the more profitable *financing* of the motor car?"

Hospitals, too, are often really in the business of family counseling and patient services, yet they frequently focus more time and energy upon physicians, and insurance company needs.

School teachers are in the business of educating, but frequently have to spend most of their time on parenting, policing and disciplining children.

3. What are your core competencies?

Knowing what M.K. Prahalad and Gary Hamel (1990) described as the taproot or core competence of your company will give you an incredible advantage.

What are your strengths, things you can do or provide that separates you from others? At a fast growing start-up, for example, a major competence might be the nimble ability to relocate. At Berg Electronics, a billion dollar company, much of their skyrocketing growth came via an unnoticed core competence: the ability to acquire companies and customers.

Your core competence is not a "product" or a widget; it is a unique resource, knowledge, or technique that gives you an advantage. It is part of your intellectual capital and knowledge resource base that propels a company to excel.

4. What are your core values?

Isolating and identifying core values is crucial. If your core value is short-term profitability, you need to organize your company accordingly. If you value long-term relationships with customers, this will require a different strategy, compensation program, and organizational chart, especially when allowing for cross-cultural differences.

5. Which competitor will be your next partner?

Necessity is the mother of odd couplings. It may be to your advantage to form a strategic partnership on a specific product or R&D with a competitor in order to remain a player in your field. The world has changed, and a past competitor can be a future ally.

6. Are your short-term goals and long-term strategies aligned?

Public companies tend to think quarter to quarter in order to please financial analysts and shareholders. The pressures of the next quarter too often conflict with the opportunities of the next few years. Companies need to learn how to align both short-term results with long-term profitability, short-term profits with long-term customer satisfaction.

7. Do your answers to questions 1–6 complement (or negate) one another?

Too often a company will provide a viable answer to one or two of these questions. The real advantage, however, will go to the company that continuously examines itself in the context of all six areas. In other words, are core competencies, goals and values working together to meet both long and short-term goals?

These are not easy questions, nor are their answers cast in stone. I advise managers to ask these questions – all of them – at least twice a year. Even if the answers have not changed significantly, at minimum you will be thinking on the right level with some regularity. Then, once you have the perspective this combination of answers will offer you, you are ready to act and make hard decisions because you will know *why* you are doing what you are doing.

BUSINESS BEYOND THE OBVIOUS: WHEN A LAW FIRM IS NOT A LAW FIRM

Let's examine a case in point and see how the answers to the first two questions above further your likelihood of success. Moving beyond the obvious to the less obvious business you are in can be the key to profitability and success in these hectic and tumultuous days. Ted Levitt's timeless description of "marketing myopia" has more relevance to other industries and businesses, large and small, than you may think.

In my experience, every business is actually engaged in multiple businesses concurrently, often without consciously realizing it, or worse still, without capitalizing on it.

As an example: most global law firms do much more than legal work. Let's look at the following three "other" businesses that nearly every global law firm is in today:

1. Hospitality

The San Francisco offices of Pillsbury Madison & Sutro (as mentioned earlier) realized that they were not only lawyers, they were in the hospitality business as well. On a given day the firm arranges more meetings, caters more lunches, and responds to more interpersonal needs of staff and clients than a mid-sized hotel. So they hired a local concierge to help them offer better customer service. With the concierge's help, they reinvented their receptionists as "client service assistants," set up new databases to track information and resources, and in so doing altered their perception of themselves in the process. In short, they played Robin Hood, taking what they needed from the rich (the hotel industry) and giving it to the "poor."

They also discovered that it isn't just the job of the Customer Service Assistants to be in the hospitality business. Every young attorney and senior partner is in the hospitality business too. Retaining clients and obtaining new ones frequently is correlated with how the client feels they were treated by the firm, from first phone greeting to final legal outcome. A little hospitality goes a long way.

2. Publishing

The sheer volume of printed matter coming out of a law firm is staggering. The gifted, prolific novelist would love to be as productive as the average, bright lawyer in terms of the amount of writing accomplished daily. If novelist Michael Crichton spent an afternoon at Townsend & Townsend, an intellectual property firm headquartered in San Francisco, I would imagine that she would be quite envious.

Yet most firms do very little to upgrade, enhance and otherwise continuously improve the writing skills and research methodologies of their staff. In fact, quite the contrary is true. They take writing ability for granted.

A savvy firm, on the other hand, would do well to "benchmark" the management and training practices of a mid-sized, local publishing house for clues on how to qualitatively and quantitatively improve their writing, editing and publishing capacity. Unfortunately, in this arena, most firms are clueless, "clue impaired."

3. Counseling

If a senior partner at a law firm asked a seasoned general contractor or an astute architect "What other business are you in?" they might answer "psychotherapy, just like you!" Few things are more stress-inducing on individuals, families, or companies than the building or remodeling of a home or office; the only exceptions are major illness … and preparation for a court appearance.

If you want to see the human personality at its worst or best, few occasions offer more insight than the days leading up to a major trial. When the going gets tough, the tough can get *very* weird. Stress stalks us all. As my attorney, Bill Ibershof, of Ibershof & Dole, says "there is more stress associated with litigation than with any other legal activity. Clients worry about possible outcomes and expenses that they seem unable to control."

This gives the attorney what Ibershof refers to as "a natural opportunity to help them work through this period. Interacting with clients under stress can bring out the best in a lawyer who is also a skilled counselor."

Hospitality, publishing, and counseling are but a few of the possibilities for a law firm. Give some thought to how you would answer the question "What other business(es) are you in?" in your field. Then, having answered that question, spend some time assessing what you have to do to repackage your organization (and/or yourself) to take advantage of this. You'll find that it is time well-spent.

HOW CHINA'S SUPREME COURT JUSTICES CAME TO AMERICA

Bob Roos is a caricature of a Renaissance man. He holds both a doctorate in social work and a doctorate in law. In other words, he is a lawyer with a heart, and some would say that is a rarity indeed! He has his own non-profit foundation, The Delta Institute, and has served for several years on the California State Parole Board. As part of this job he has literally looked mass murderer Charles Manson in the eye and said, "You ain't goin' nowhere." One Christmas I got a card from him that included a form letter encouraging me to enter into a network marketing program a friend of his was organizing!

You're beginning to get the picture? He is not your run-of-the-mill attorney. This guy is up for anything. That's his greatest strength ... and a minor weakness. From law to the parole board to foundations to network marketing, there is never a dull moment around Bob Roos.

I met Bob early in 1987 when he asked me to consult with him on several fund development projects for The Delta Institute. During this period of time he co-chaired the Bar Association of San Francisco's China Law Committee and had just returned from Shanghai as a delegate to its sister city exchange program with San Francisco. Bob had been to China before, but this time upon his return he told me of the incredible reforms going on in their judicial system. China, he said, was totally engaged in the process of shifting its entire legal system to one that more closely resembled that of the United States and England. These changes, he said, were going all the way up through the Chinese Court. "Well," I asked, "have the Shanghai judges been to the USA for first-hand observation?" He said that they had, but wondered aloud if the Supreme Court Justices had been on American soil recently. "I'll find out," he said. He asked around and no one could recall such a visit. As it turned out, no member of the Supreme Court had ever been to the United States! Bob and I discussed this and the next day sent off a short telex of inquiry to the Offices of the Supreme Court that read:

TO: Mr. Ren Jianxin, Vice President, The Supreme People's Court of the PRC, Beijing, China.

GREETINGS: Proposed: Visits to the United States by representatives of the Supreme People's Court.

August 2–16, 1987, 2 of your highest judges, one interpreter and one assistant (to speak English if possible).

Nine days later Roos got an answer:

ATTENTION: DR. ROBERT ROOS, DELTA INSTITUTE.

THANK YOU FOR YOUR TELEX. WE ACCEPTED YOUR INVITATION WITH GREAT PLEASURE AND DECIDED TO SEND A FOUR-MEMBER DELEGATION LED BY THE MEMBERS OF THE TRIAL COMMITTEE OF THE SUPREME PEOPLE'S COURT ... WE'D LIKE TO EXPRESS OUR SATISFACTIONS (sic) AND THANKS ... ON THE ITINERARY OF VISITING AMERICA.

The rest, as they say, is legal history. Roos had proceeded exactly backwards from J.R. Kinsella's maxim "If you build it, [they] will come." They *were* coming and nothing yet had been built except a tower of chutzpah!

In the days and weeks that followed, there was a flurry of letters, dozens of phone calls, and attendance at innumerable meetings to arrange the proper protocol, obtain necessary security, set the diplomatic groundwork in place, and rally the necessary financial resources.

As each day unfolded, we received more and more support and commitment. Law firms in Los Angeles and Washington, D.C., agreed to underwrite portions of the visit. A luncheon here, a dinner there. Air transportation was then set, as was a series of high level meetings with legal and political dignitaries. By the time of their arrival, we *had* built it and here they were!

In August of 1987, Chief Justice Wang Qi and Senior Justice Shan Chang-Zong and two associates came to San Francisco as honored guests of the American Bar Association convention, then continuing on to Sacramento, Reno and Los Angeles. As their visit played out, they met with two US Justices and attended special seminars at the National Judicial College in Reno. They then circled back through Sacramento for meetings, before finally heading on to Washington, D.C. for the last leg of their visit before returning to the People's Republic.

As a special treat we also arranged for them to spend half a day in a rural coastal area of Marin County, California, walking amongst the redwood trees and along the beaches, where they also visited a residential treatment center for adolescent boys called Full Circle Programs. At Full Circle we were led around the property by San Francisco attorney, Judd Iverson, then president of the Full Circle Board of Directors. The Justices met the counselors, staff and children at the ranch, and later told us that their time in Northern California was the highlight of their visit.

Several years have now passed but I think about those early sessions with Bob Roos and the musings about the remote chance of bringing the Justices here. Though I rarely am in contact with him, I marvel at how quickly it all happened and how everything fell into place. I remember well the conversations about the minutia and logistics, the diplomatic maneuverings and protocol. Of course there were the seemingly interminable long waiting periods for final decisions to come through from prospective hosts and sponsors.

We couldn't wait by the phone for a response, we had to move on and move forward, always trusting that the "work to be done," the seeds we were casting, were going to bear fruit. I'll tell you this, Norman Vincent Peale – bless his soul – would have been very proud of us. We took the power of positive thinking to new heights!

Only recently did I realize the lessons I learned from that experience that I use almost daily in running my company. Only now, many years later, can I articulate them in a succinct way. It's just "common sense," but worth stating nonetheless. They work for me, and I think they are solid Thoughtware:

1. it never hurts to *ask*!
2. always assume the answer will be "yes," and
3. if they're coming, build it right!

THINK, THINK, THINK

Stan Davis wrote a now-classic book, *Future Perfect*, which has a far-reaching premise for global strategy that resonates well with the new Thoughtware: From the future-perfect perspective, the present is already the past. Those who are present-oriented, therefore, are always in a reactive mode, playing an endless game of "catch up." If you think only in the present, he proposes, time is a constraint.

If you think in the present you think in increments, in steps, in sequences, in logical progressions. Unfortunately, the world today doesn't work that way! What the new Thoughtware teaches is that if you think incrementally you will get only incremental results, and that will not give you a global advantage. For those who think from the perspective of the future, time is a resource, and hence, future-perfect thinking is now a "given" in a global economy.

What global competitors ought to think about, says Tom Richman, (1998, p.114) "is not, say, reducing the time from order to delivery but eliminating it; not the miniaturization of mass but its elimination; not many-place delivery but any-place delivery."

Jerry Kaplan, in his delightful book *Startup: A Silicon Valley Adventure* (1994) adds an entrepreneurial spin to this when he points to a clock on the wall and says "If you're the first one there you will get to say what it is that others will see."

Stan Davis calls such thoughts "transformative" thinking, and my term for it is "Break-It! Thinking™." Call it what you wish, the common denominator which makes it suited to a global economy is *that it imposes no limits on its own results*. For this reason the new Thoughtware says: Think globally *and* think locally ... but whatever you do ... Think. Think. Think!

Chapter Twelve

!EADERSHIP

To Lead, You Must *Lean* Into Life!

"You cannot blow an uncertain trumpet!"
– Rev. Theodore Hesburgh

THE PARABLE OF THE DIVER

Greg Louganis approached the platform for his final Olympic dive with more than a modicum of pressure and emotion.

A three-time gold medallist, Louganis was trying for an unprecedented fourth medal, breaking the previous record held by his own coach, Sammy Lee. His chief competitor, an unknown 14-year-old from China, was slightly ahead in points … and half Louganis's age.

Adding to the high drama of the day was Louganis's announcement before the Games began that he was retiring from competition. Imagine what must have been going through his mind, as he was about to attempt the final dive of a long career.

There was more to this moment. It was happening in public – not an office or boardroom behind closed doors – but rather, before the eyes of the world, with an estimated two *billion* people watching him, live. More eyes were on him than there had been on Abraham Lincoln at Gettysburg, Queen Elizabeth at her coronation, and Babe Ruth when he hit his sixtieth home run – combined!

There was yet one more factor. As he walked along the pool's edge the crowd could see several stitches in Louganis' partially shaved scalp from where he had hit his head on the same platform the day before!

How will he deal with the pressure? Is he in pain? How will he keep his focus? What will his strategy be? Can he overcome the trauma of the whack on the back of his head?

Four billion eyes and ears asked these questions collectively as he approached the diving platform for his final dive. It was high drama.

In Olympic diving competition, "playing it safe" is, literally, a *calculated* risk. Because competitors can multiply their score by the "degree of difficulty" of the particular dive they attempt, the riskier the dive, the higher the possible points.

In this sense, diving is an interesting metaphor for life these days, and competitive diving gives us all an insight into challenge, fear, defeat, and victory.

What viewers did not know was that Louganis made two apocryphal decisions prior to climbing that platform in Korea. The previous evening, after the stitches were put in, when his friends and coaches had offered to show him the videotape of the frightening meeting of head and platform, Louganis politely refused. Instead, he asked that they bring him some footage of a tough dive that he had "nailed" in the preliminaries. That was the dive he wanted to watch over and over again. That was his first decision.

His second decision was an equally graceful and gutsy one. Approaching the judges, he notified them that he would be attempting a very difficult dive which, if executed flawlessly, would assure his final gold medal before retiring from competition.

Any number of easier dives would have been a safer bet and guaranteed him a bronze or silver medal. After all *conventional* wisdom says: a silver bird in the hand is worth two gold ones in the bush, and a bronze medal is better than no medal at all. However, during his long career Greg Louganis had never shied away from adversity or the challenges of performing under pressure and he surely was not going to change for his last competitive dive.

He knew himself too well. He knew what it takes to win. He understood that *playing it safe is dangerous!*

He calmly and confidently approached the platform, climbed the nine stairs to the top, walked to the edge, turned, and set his back to the water. The full weight of his muscular body was supported by the last three inches of his feet.

He took one deep, confident breath, and pushed off into the steamy air of Seoul's Olympic pool. In a split second he curved and twisted in mid-air until he cut through the water's surface like a fine crystal knife.

As his stitched head came out of the still water the spellbound crowd knew they had witnessed one of the most dramatic moments in Olympic history. Greg Louganis was the greatest diver in the history of this highly competitive sport.

LEADERSHIP AS AN ART

Four times a year, the officers of furniture manufacturer Herman Miller Inc. meet to reflect on results and set a course for the next quarter. As one such meeting was about to begin, Max De Pree, CEO and son of the founder, received a thank-you note from the mother of a handicapped employee. Touched by it, De Pree thought he should read it aloud at the meeting. In his book *Leadership Is an Art*, De Pree describes what happened:

"I almost got through this letter but could not finish. There I stood in front of this group of people – some of them pretty hard-driving – tongue-tied and embarrassed, unable to continue. At that point, one of our senior vice presidents, Joe Schwartz – urbane, elegant, mature – strode up the center aisle, put his arm around my shoulder, kissed me on the cheek, and adjourned the meeting." De Pree then asks: can you imagine having a company where, under similar circumstances, a Joe Schwartz would kiss you? He answers his own question, stating that every company needs a Joe Schwartz, and offers a sound piece of new Thoughtware. "The signs of outstanding leadership appear primarily among the followers."

Peter Drucker, one of the foremost thinkers on the subject of leadership was impressed enough by De Pree's book to write a cover endorsement, saying that the book "says more about leadership in clearer, more elegant, and more convincing language than many of the much longer books ... on the subject." High praise coming from a true pioneer in the field.

Drucker, of course, is long-remembered for his classic book, *The Practice of Management*, published in 1954. His insights into the nature and substance of management at many points dovetail with my term, *!eaders*. By using an exclamation point (!) I hope to draw attention to the new forms of leadership now emerging.

Etymologically, the word "manage" is rooted in the Latin word for "hands," and was associated with using the hands to rein in a horse. Unfortunately, far too many people still assume that that is the principle role of management and leadership ... to command and control, to tightly grip the reins. Quite the contrary, today, using a horse-racing analogy, the new *!eaders* know that you have to "give your horse his head," loosen the grip, and let him run!

A half century ago, Drucker understood this, and his words still ring true. When he speaks of "manager" it is also true of !eaders.

> The final function of managers is to manage workers and work ... This implies organization of the work so as to make it most suitable for human beings, and organization of people so as to make them work most productively and effectively. It implies consideration of the human being as a resource – that is, as something having peculiar psychological properties, abilities, and limitations that require the same amount of engineering attention as the properties of any other resource, e.g. copper. It implies also consideration of the human resource as human beings having, unlike any other resource, personality, citizenship, control over whether they work, how much and how well, and thus requiring motivation, participation, satisfaction, incentives and rewards, leadership, status and function. And it is management, and management alone, that can satisfy these requirements."

CEOS LEAD ... AND LEAVE!

Not everyone is as astute as Peter Drucker, nor as savvy and inspiring as Max De Pree. Quite the contrary. Many CEOs, for example, have no *!eadership* abilities whatsoever. All they know how to do is pull in the reins, cut-cut-cut, or bring on various forms of organizational triage. I used to think I was dealing with a skewed sampling of senior managers, but in reading a *Harvard Business Review* study of "The Way Chief Executive Officers Lead," by Charles Farkas and Suzy Wetlaufer (1996, pp.110–122), I saw that mine was not an isolated sample.

"There is no school for CEOs," say C. Farkas and F. Wetlaufer, "except the school of experience. Chief executives must learn on the job how to lead a company, and they must learn while every stakeholder is watching." Sad, but true.

Given the on-the-job, idiosyncratic nature of the position, one might think there are an infinite array of leadership styles. Not so, say the researchers. In fact, after interviewing 160 CEOs from around the world, they have identified the five most common forms of leadership:

1. *The Strategy Approach*: These CEOs (such as former leader of Coca Cola Roberto Goizueta, and Dell's Michael Dell) believe their job is to "create, test, and design the implementation of long-range strategy ... (devoting) approximately 80% of their time to matters external to the organization."
2. *The Human-Assets Approach*: These CEOs (such as Pepsi-Co.'s Roger Enrico, Gillette's Al Zeien, and Herb Kelleher of Southwest Airlines) see their primary job as the imparting "to their organizations certain values, behaviors, and attitudes by closely managing the growth and development of individuals." In addition, "their goal is to create a universe of satellite CEOs."
3. *The Expertise Approach*: These executives (such as Ogilvey & Mather's Charlotte Beers) focus chiefly on "selecting and disseminating within the corporation an area of expertise that will be a source of competitive advantage ... (and) "they hire people who are trained in the expertise ... possess flexible minds, lack biases, and demonstrate a willingness to be immersed – *indoctrinated* is not too strong a word – in the expertise."
4. *The Box Approach*: CEOs in this category (such as Fortis's Maurice Lippens, HSBC/Hong Kong Shanghai Banking Company's John Bond, and French-based international insurance company AXA Claude Bebear) believe they add value by "creating, communicating, and monitoring an explicit set of controls – financial, cultural, or both – that ensure uniform, predictable behaviors and experiences for customers and employees." Most of their time, therefore, is spent tracking and correcting "exceptions" to their organizational controls via detailed and prescriptive policies and procedures.
5. *The Change Approach*: This style of CEO leadership (such as Tenneco's Dana Mead, and former W.R. Grace's J.P. Bolduc) believes in creating "an environment of continual reinvention ... (by focusing) not on a specific point of arrival (in contrast with the Strategy Approach) for

> their organizations but on the process of getting there." Consequently, they spend the majority of their time "using speeches, meetings, and other forms of communication to motivate members of their organization to embrace the gestalt of change."

The research also makes a clear distinction between the "personality" of the CEO and the "approach" they use. If he or she senses the need for a "dominant approach" that differs from their personality, they will use it as a "compass and rudder," and the "dominant approach" therefore "can and should change over the course of his or her tenure."

As one of their interviewees, Edzard Reuter, CEO of Daimler-Benz, told them: "A business is a living organism. There will always be a point where the environment changes, the competition changes, something critical changes, and you must realize this and take the leading role in meeting change."

Intel's Chairman Andy Grove (1993, p.59) echoes this, saying "A corporation is a living organism, and it has to continue to shed its skin. Methods have to change. Focus has to change. Values have to change. The sum total of these changes is transformation," he says. "One of the biggest lessons I have learned is that it is always easier to put strategic changes into action than to declare them as a policy."

Fortunately or unfortunately – and as often as not – these days it is the arrival and/or departure of CEOs that is the major catalyst for change! "Between 35–50% of all CEOs are replaced within five years," say Farkas and Wetlaufer. In today's volatile world of commerce, says the new Thoughtware, the motto of CEOs seems to be: "Lead 'em ... and Leave 'em!"

YOGI BERRA, CEO

For decades Yogi Berra has been the object of considerable attention for both his performance on the baseball field and his malapropisms off it. You could write a book – and he has – that chronicles his wit and wisdom.

At an airport book store I bought his autobiography called *The Yogi*

Book. It's the best $3.95 I've spent in a long time because the crazy wisdom is hilarious and because the charm and warmth of the man come through loudly and clearly. That alone would be enough.

As I read on I realized how applicable Yogi's insights are to the wacky world of business today. Taken together they form the nucleus of a very sound strategic perspective on a global economy that changes faster than a Roger Clemens curve ball. Here are several of my favorite Yogi-isms that helped influence my sense of !eadership today.

1. "It ain't over 'til it's over."
2. "The future just ain't what it used to be!"
3. "It's *deja vu* all over again."
4. "A nickel isn't worth a dime anymore."
5. "If the world was perfect, it wouldn't be!"
6. "You can observe a lot just by watching."
7. "If you come to a fork in the road, take it!"

So, when you see Yogi doing Pepsi and Pringles commercials, think twice about what he says. The media has cast him as the innocent fool, but I believe he could make a great CEO, ... if (as Yogi once observed while looking at a Steve McQueen movie) he's offered the job before he dies.

INVISIBLE !EADERSHIP

Tell me your admired leaders, and you have bared your soul.
– George Will

From Harvard researchers to Yogi, regardless of the style or approach, the good news is that it is increasingly true that most of the directionality and success of a company today comes from the "many" not from the "few," from the "invisible" leaders rather than the "visible" ones.

When most people think of "visible leaders" they conjure up images of FDR, Churchill, JFK, or Gen. Colin Powell – all men, all in positions of authority, all projected as larger than-life-figures who tower over those around them. They are charismatic, dramatic, and even dogmatic. That, in part, is what leadership has traditionally meant.

The irony today is that as nations dial up for more traditional leaders, there's no one home to answer. In fact, there is a global void in traditional leadership: In countries as diverse as Britain, Russia, Japan, Germany, Mexico, Italy, Brazil, Israel, and France the enthusiasm for elected leaders has met with only sporadic support. What does this tell us? Perhaps, as we near the end of the twentieth century, the traditional model has outlived its usefulness.

I believe there is new Thoughtware that is emerging, and a new understanding of (and criteria for) alternative forms of leadership as well. It is a quiet, nearly invisible, yet escalating call that is now going out.

Why is traditional leadership diminishing and the call for !eadership increasing? Why now? The possible answers are unlimited. Some have proposed the relative lack of a common enemy that accompanies the end of the so-called Cold War. Others say media scrutiny has proven too intense for anyone to reach heroic proportions. Still others suggest it is the global digital village, the Internet, the direct access to people and information – on line and on command – that has eliminated an intermediary level of power and authority. Whatever the reasons, leadership, like the future, just ain't what it used to be.

So the question becomes, if it ain't what it used to be, what is it now? What is the new, invisible !eadership model that is emerging?

I see at least three characteristics rising to the surface: a strong preference for, and trust in, mutual aid and human cooperation; the ability to harness what I call "pent-up rapport"; and the readiness to engage in small, leaderly acts – being, as my friend, poet Duncan McNaughton says "on duty" – day in and day out. In combination, these three factors define small "*l*" leaders. To differentiate the traditional from the small-"l" leaders, for the remainder of this chapter I will use the new spelling – !eadership.

MUTUAL AID

On a flight from Washington, D.C., I came across an article in *Scientific American* entitled "The Arithmetic of Mutual Help" (Nowak, May and

Sigmund, 1995) which documented a series of computer experiments that show how cooperation rather than exploitation can "dominate the Darwinian struggle for survival." However, it was not the article that lingered with me, it was the wonderful lead photo that I cannot get out of my mind.

Amidst the open rafters of a roof-raising in Lancaster, Pennsylvania, I counted no less than 33 Amish carpenters, nearly one per beam, voluntarily building part of a collective dream, their black clothes silhouetted against the light pine and oak wood like so many crows on aspen trees. As I squinted at the picture of these sure-footed, focused, and busy men doing hard, physical work, it occurred to me that the page resembled a symphony score, with 33 black notes per measure.

I wanted to throw on a tool belt and climb those rafters, for that was where the real action was. Charles Darwin would have been pleased, for he wrote in *The Descent of Man* that "the small strength and speed of man, his want of natural weapons, are more than counterbalanced by his ... social qualities, which lead him to give and receive aid from his fellow-men."

!eaders today thrive in opportunities to foster and contribute to mutual aid. Such altruistic leadership is not driven by ideology, or the desire for personal recognition, but rather by the desire, as poet Charles Olson put it, to be "of use." Today's invisible !eaders, like the 33 Amish carpenters, would very much rather be "of use."

PENT-UP RAPPORT

In his book *No Easy Victories*, John W. Gardner looks at the role of the leader in society. Gardner says leaders are symbols of "moral unity" ... and "can express the values that hold the society together." He adds, "Most important, they can conceive and articulate goals that lift people out of their petty preoccupations, carry them above the conflicts that tear a society apart, and unite them in pursuit of objectives worthy of their best efforts."

While people and organizations love to complain, the new *!eader*, while motivated by the internal desire to be "of use," recognizes that just beyond the horizon of the whining is a vast heartland of rapport.

I am continually overwhelmed by the raw energy of "pent-up rapport." People want to help, people want to get along with each other. People want to make a contribution, even make a difference. They want their actions to *count*! Every day, random acts of "rapport" are perpetrated upon someone else.

In my neighborhood, in just the last month I saw it happen several times:

- A British tourist helped my wife crack the code on our van's tire jack to replace a flat tire.
- A teen gang at the county fair was challenged by a dad for cutting into line in front of him and his son. This lead everyone in the front and back of the line to heckle the gang members until the teens rolled their eyes and headed off to another line.
- Three dinners were left anonymously at the front door of a family whose 10-year-old boy was diagnosed with a rare form of cancer.

That's pent-up rapport! It doesn't make headlines, but it does make a difference.

LEARN TO LEAN INTO LIFE

In *On Becoming a Leader*, Warren Bennis notes that "The ingredients of leadership cannot be taught. They must be learned." Therein lies the paradox of leadership: that which can't be taught must be learned. How? ... by living a life, by "using yourself completely" says Bennis," – all your skills, gifts and energies."

TV innovator Norman Lear once said he admired his father because he had learned to "lean into life." Juxtaposing Bennis and Lear into new Thoughtware, *you learn to lead by leaning*. Though this kind of *!eadership* cannot be taught it is pent-up inside all of us. That's why Bennis prods us to "strike hard, try everything, do everything, render everything" Today's !eaders are able to harness the inherent good in people – their pent-up rapport – and draw it out of them by their actions. As my mother used to say "When there's nothing else to do there's always work to be done."

ON DUTY

The third (and related) element of *!eadership* is that *!eaders* are always "on duty." To get at what it means to be "on duty" I'll let Duncan McNaughton do the talking. In a recent conversation he told me that in his experience of !eadership "there are always a certain number of invisible 'poles' that the human and other universes depend on moment to moment, and those individuals don't know who they are and so the poles shift moment to moment ... so therefore everybody's obliged to be on duty – because for the next 15 minutes – *it may be you*, it may be your turn."

So today might be *your* day, your lucky day, the day you've prepared for by leaning into life. You stay ready, are responsible for seizing the opportunity to lead, and from time to time you become an invisible pole around which the world, from moment to moment, revolves. That's pretty abstract, so I offer a more direct metaphor: *!eaders* are like magnets in the sand: one at a time, while shining in the sun, they attract parts of the world to them.

THE "DEMOCRATIZATION" OF LEADERSHIP

Most of us grew up with relatively narrow and certainly very pedestalized notions of what constituted *real* leadership. With the decline of the larger-than-life, heroic politician, military icon or business tycoon, the void has been filled by the average citizen, and leadership is now in the able hands of the many rather than the few. In short, what we have been witnessing is the slow and steady *democratization of leadership*. As the new Thoughtware teaches, never before have so many owed so much ... to so many!

So there is emerging a profile of the new *!eaders*, including:

- *Possessing an aesthetic that is "hands on."* To paraphrase Forrest Gump, they believe that beauty is as beauty does. They don't keep score, and they derive *intrinsic* rewards from the activity itself. *Doing* is rewarding.

- *Driven by values not pedagogy; vision, not political ideology.* The painter Braque was right in saying that "the only thing that matters in art cannot be explained." *!eadership*, like electricity, is easier to measure than define. You know it when you see it, but you can't readily explain it or define it. Knowing what you value helps you know what to do.
- *Acting locally, but in universally recognizable ways.* Tolstoy once observed that "All happy families resemble one another." The same is true of the new *!eaders*.
- *Being active is not an act.* Leaders are always a reflection of ourselves and of our values. Seventeenth century philosopher Thomas Hobbes described human existence as "solitary, poor, nasty, brutish, and short." The new *!eaders* work on a different premise and on a different scale. What they do when they are "on duty" incorporates active listening, active vision and an active imagination – rather than the nasty, brutishness of a bygone era.

The new *!eaders* make change their ally, they unleash their best and the best in others, and they stand ready to do so again and again. Somewhere, right now, someone needs a roof raised. Today, *!eadership* rests more in the heart and hands than in the authority of the position or the power of the gavel. And so, the democratization of !eadership spreads.

TOM BROWN'S E-BOOK: VIRTUAL *!EADERSHIP* ON-LINE

The press release tells you the basics:

NEW BOOK CHALLENGES OLD LEADERSHIP: First Book Of Its Kind Written Totally On-line

QUICK SUMMARY:

- [WHO?] Tom Brown, veteran author and website editor
- [WHAT?] ... just completed a year-long pioneer experiment writing an e-book about leadership "live" on The Web, with readers reacting to regularly-posted chaplets.
- [WHEN?] ... THE ANATOMY OF FIRE began February, 1997; it was completed May, 1998.

- [WHERE?] ... the entire book, including color graphics and audio files, is copyrighted but can be accessed without any charge by the website on which it appears: http://www.mgeneral.com ...
- [WHY?] ... the author – disillusioned with current trends in leadership and, despite a boom economy, saddened by the dispirited, angry mood of today's workplace – concludes that too many "leaders" today are really placeholders and that the next century demands a new model of leadership. He defines the future of leadership in the book, using free-and-open twenty-first century technology to broadcast his findings.

That's the basics, but as usual, the basics tell only part of the story.

Tom Brown took some quiet and bold steps in order to elevate the level – and the accessibility – to dialogue on the topic of leadership.

"Today's leaders need more 'fire' to take society into the next century," he says. In his wonderful electronic book, composed in "virtual time" on-line, he spurns today's "leaders" as "placeholders" and demands fresh thinking about the fundamental question: "What *is* a leader?"

After studying the idealized forms of leadership developed over hundreds of years, Brown concludes, "Leadership is not about creating and extracting wealth for the benefit of the few. Nor is it about the raw exercise of power. It's about the discovery of new and better ideas for improving life for all. Generating widespread enthusiasm for better ways, finding the resources to turn them into reality, and being resilient in the face of setbacks are the qualities of tomorrow's leaders." Most importantly, he says, "making a contribution to society – improving the human condition – will be what separates leaders from mere placeholders in the future."

Jim Collins, who co-authored the best-selling book *Built to Last: Successful Habits of Visionary Companies* (1994) writes in the Foreword to Tom's book that Brown's definition of leadership is distinct.

"Tom argues that true leaders in any discipline choose exploration over exploitation, rallying over ruling, imagination over inventory, achievement over compliance, and giving over taking."

In this pioneering e-book process, Tom used new technology to transmit his thoughts about new leadership via short "chaplets" to which readers responded, thereby helping to shape a final, virtual, and interactive manuscript! It represents therefore, an entirely new way of democratizing knowledge.

At heart a humanist, Tom believes deeply in the power of people, individually and collectively, to make our world better. He believes, says Collins, "that all of us have creative capabilities – usually squashed by the institutions we work in – and that anyone can grow into leadership roles."

"The e-book concept," says Brown, "is potent. For readers, it provides access to fresh writing on a just-in-time basis; for authors, it provides feedback about content and style when it can be most helpful; for publishers, it's a unique way to test the market for new books before deciding how many to print.

"The greatest lesson, however, may be that an e-book creates a new way for people to communicate with one another," Brown notes. (Please send e-mails to mail@mgeneral.com) "The potential for reading text while viewing colorful, even animated, graphics, while hearing simultaneous audio, and (soon) while glimpsing video clips, means that the message of a book can combine with the electronic power of the on-line medium to create whole new vistas for readers."

Bernie Nagle, for example, gave Brown periodic appraisals of his thinking and writing as the e-book progressed. At one point, Nagle responded:

"It's been a long time since I tingled so, at the reading of a passage. I can only sit here in awe and pray that the complacent, the powerful, the condescending, the self-absorbed, the detached, the insulated, the ruthless, the greedy, the compassion-impaired, and the doers of churn – by some holy intervention – become consumed by 'the fire.' "

THE HARD WORK OF SOFT MANAGEMENT

I know of few people who have given more of their professional and personal lives to leadership development than my good friend, Bernie Nagle. In Bernie's book on leadership, *Leveraging People and Profit*, co-authored with Perry Pascarella, there is a telling subtitle that is both insightful and instructive: Leadership today is *The Hard Work of Soft Management*. In the Foreword to the book, the inimitable Warren Bennis remarks that "Interest in leadership has never been higher than it is today.

Yet the public image of leadership has seldom, if ever, been lower. What has gone wrong?"

Bernie and Perry believe we are on the "front edge of a wave" which has been building for more than two decades. During this time, *!eaders* have been emerging and are recognized via the following traits:

- "altrupreneurial": A conspicuous – and high – regard for the welfare of others
- participative management style
- collaborative
- strong spiritual roots.

These traits are well-aligned with the sense of leadership espoused by Herb Kelleher, CEO of Southwest Airlines, who is quoted in the book. "The servant leader is exactly what's needed in any business. Whatever you do," he says, "you do it to satisfy an inner desire for excellence and fulfillment. In a way, I am talking about a religion. If you're in the service business, you're looking for altruism, too."

TRAINED CHANGE AGENTS

There is no escaping the reality that in the past, present and foreseeable future, leaders will have to foster change. "While I was at Ameritech," says Bob Knowling (1997, p.66), who ran the Ameritech Institute that trained change agents, "Our CEO made it clear that this wasn't change for the sake of change. We had to make the business perform. He took that stock from 36 to 92; it split, and when I walked out the door to join US West, it was back up to 63. That's because the CEO embraced and led change."

The profile of the change agent, says Charles Fishman (1997, p.72) can thus become another element in the emerging picture of the new *!eaders*. They:

- Create an environment where people gravitate in the direction you want them to go.
- Model the change you espouse in others.

For example, as Bob Knowling found at Ameritech, once he embraced his role as change agent, the CEO not only came to rely on him more, but also to demand more from him, both were traits he valued.

- *Even if the company doesn't change, you will.* Most change efforts fail because companies know intuitively that one of the scarcest resources they have is the person who can help them through a period of turbulent, fast-paced change.

Bob Knowling even went so far as to draft a *Change Manual* (Tichy 1997, p.78). In it, he offers his advice: "First, you never announce that you're launching a change agenda ... I immersed myself in the organization: I touched people ... Second, asking for permission is asking to be told 'no.' Don't ask permission. Third, the system is stacked against you. Never underestimate that. Pick your battles. Fourth, have a model of change. Fifth, deal with the political issues of change. That means they have to understand that being an effective change agent is not about being a kamikaze pilot. A change agent who's looking over the edge at the next opportunity isn't going to succeed. Sixth, it's about talking about the issues that we don't want to talk about, the ones that drive the business. It's about moving people out of their comfort zones. Seventh, a change agent has got to walk the talk."

THIS CEO EARNS A DOLLAR A YEAR!

Walking the talk is crucial to the new *!eaders'* style. Netscape Communications' chief executive Jim Barksdale did just that when he said he would accept only $1 in salary one year, counting instead on the company's stock to increase his personal fortune.

In a document filed with the Securities and Exchange Commission, Netscape said that Barksdale will forgo his salary and bonus because he "believes that his compensation should be linked to the long-term interests of the company's stockholders." (Einstein, 1997, p.D1).

In so doing, Barksdale is not only modeling the commitment and confidence he has in his own leadership abilities, he is also sending a clear message that he believes in his company as well. As the "David" in a

"Goliath" battle with Microsoft, every little bit of extra motivational leverage helps.

JOIE DE VIVRE ... HOTELS

In addition to occasional motivating acts, the new *!eaders* are frequently contrarians. "Three-and-a-half to four years ago, people wouldn't have thought of investing in hotels," said Stephen "Chip" Conley, founder and CEO of Joie de Vivre hotels (see also p. 18). "Everything for us has to work in a circle," he explained. "You have to take into account three major parts of the circle: the employees, the guests and the investors. If you don't get all those things in sync ... it doesn't make any sense." (Tanaka, 1997, p.B1).

It's difficult to find a building in San Francisco, the home base for his company, which hasn't already been worked over. Yet Chip's found a lot of them. Like other new *!eaders,* Chip generated the support and investors he needed, and created a market niche. Much the same way the Kimpton Hotels took run-down properties, remodeled them, and put a five star restaurant on each of the premises, Chip has created a series of "theme" or "boutique" hotels, each with special target markets (such as rock musicians or woman business travelers). Though there is no ready formula for "how" Chip does what he does, he leads by demonstrating a certain ... Joie de Vivre! Like most !eaders, Chip is a bit ephemeral. As Warren Bennis, professor at the University of Southern California, would say: "The reason is that leadership is squishy, hard to get your conceptual arms around." (Finegan, 1997, p.46).

READY, AIM, FOCUS: THE RODEL WAY

As "squishy" as Chip's leadership is, there are lessons to be learned, and many other examples that shed light on the new *!eaders* . For example, Lloyd Pickett of Rodel Inc., has cited the core values he calls the "Rodel Way." More than a mission statement, the Rodel Way is the articulation of a set of principles that have guided Rodel's transformation. The Rodel Way describes behavioral norms that apply to everyone in the company.

"The fulfillment of our vision requires this out-of-the-ordinary, collaborative way of working together," (Pickett,1997, p.53). These five commitments constitute the heart of the Rodel way:

1. "*Listening generously*: Learning to listen for the contribution in each other's speaking versus listening from our own assessments, opinions and judgments."
2. "*Speaking straight*: To speak honestly in a way that forwards what we are up to. Making clear and direct requests. Being willing to surface ideas or take positions that may result in conflict when it is necessary to step toward reaching our objectives."
3. "*Being for each other*: Supporting each other's success. Operating from a point of view that we are all in this together and that any one of us cannot win at the expense of someone else or the enterprise."
4. "*Honoring commitments*: Making commitments that forward what we are up to. Being responsible for our commitments, holding others accountable for theirs, and supporting them in fulfilling their commitments."
5. "*Acknowledgment/appreciation*: Each member commits to be a source of acknowledgment and appreciation for the team; this includes giving, receiving, and requesting."

The Rodel Way, a testimony to the adage that "less is more," fills one sheet of paper. It articulates a goal to which everyone in the company can aspire: "Personally and collectively owning Rodel's objectives ... (in order to) obtain the extraordinary results we need will come when we are all heading in the same direction, playing the same game, fulfilling the vision."

The Rodel Way is more than a simplistic version of "team building" or quality circles. When people say *synergy*, says Harold Geneen, they usually mean productive use of assets or efficient allocation of manpower and resources, and that requires sitting down and studying the situation – looking at all the steps in a process and improving them, eliminating them, or combining them. That, of course, requires hard work, determination, and strategic thinking – in short, strong management. (For more on synergy, see *The Synergy Myth and Other Ailments of Business Today,* by Harold Geneen with Brent Bowers.)

TED TURNER: THE TENDER-HEARTED TYCOON

Strong management frequently comes with strong convictions, values, and actions, and can arise from any one at any point in time. Says Ted Turner, "I was never No. 1 in my class. I tried, but I never got straight 'A's. I was a middle-of-the-road student ... When I was a kid, people wanted to be president of the United States. Or be a college president. Or be a millionaire. Be a big executive. Or be a movie star. Or be the best in sports. You know, you want to win the Heisman Trophy if you're a football player. You want to win the Stanley cup if you're on a hockey team."

After making a fortune in a well-documented career of innovations, in recent years Turner has developed a philanthropic side. "Scrooge was very rich and he was much happier when he started giving money away." Like a redeemed Scrooge on a proselytizing mission, Turner has begun challenging his peers to ante-up.

He is not alone. Viacom owner, Sumner Redstone is a multi-billionaire who lives in the same house he lived in more than 40 years ago. He hasn't changed his lifestyle at all. "You can't spend billions of dollars. So you can invest billions. You can only drive one Rolls-Royce at a time. That's $200,000. I drive a Ford. I deliberately keep my life simple. Why? Because I enjoy that. I never really liked ostentatious wealth." (Stossel, 1997, p.4).

Says Turner, "basically, the very, very rich usually weren't good athletes, weren't particularly handsome. Basically, they were like I was: looking for something that they could do well, that they could excel at. They were deprived of success. Then, when they got into making money, they found something they could do."

AFTERWORD: IT'S NOT HOW MUCH YOU KNOW ...

As mentioned earlier in this chapter, Warren Bennis has long been articulating the distinct attributes of leaders and how they differ from managers. His generous and wise perspective has for decades been at the front edge of our understanding of leadership. I recommend his Foreword to Nagle's *Leveraging People and Profits* for a skillful overview of the traditions and lineage of the constantly evolving relationship between a leader and a period in history. He describes some of the qualities of the emerging new small "l" leaders. The new Thoughtware teaches that capital "L" Leadership – the "command and control," top-down, testosterone-driven variety – is but a remnant of an archaic and outdated way of working with people.

In contrast, the new *!eaders* are neither macho ... nor myopic ... nor motivated solely by personal gain. They do what they do not at the *expense* of others but rather with conspicuous – and high – *regard* for others. It is these *!eaders* who are at the vanguard of a major, quiet revolution. It is they who build relationships for the long haul, who know how hard it is to be soft sometimes, who prefer asking the right questions to having all the right answers. These are the invisible leaders who, like fine strands of gold filigree, hold our schools and neighborhoods and companies together. It is they who we must now acknowledge, cultivate, emulate, and reward. They are today's real heroes.

Guess what? These "servant leaders," as Bennis calls them, these softies, they have found a way to make a profit while making a difference. They touch people's lives daily in a thousand small and unobtrusive ways, because they have the right attitude, a clear perspective, and tremendous peripheral vision and common sense which enables them to take things from idea to fruition. They understand, for example, the ripple effect of the loss of a single key employee or client, the incredible cost of replacing either, and the tremendous leverage that accrues from long-term (yes, even spiritual) commitments within an organization as well as between human beings. It is they who dare to dream while others stare ... and scream.

Having spent most of my life in California, I have developed a fairly sophisticated "touchy-feely detector." I live amidst a veritable breeding ground for the fad-of-the-day and the buzzword-of-the-month, a region where countless academicians and theoreticians vie with one another to make their mark.

So is it refreshing to be graced with the opportunity to write a book about real people, in real situations, making real things happen. These are the new heroes, the new *!eaders*. These are the men and women who have a little dirt under their fingernails. These are your friends and neighbors who, like a jackdaw, have the special ability to look for shining objects with which to build a nest for others. These are the solid citizens who know from experience and wisdom that it is, indeed, much more important to be useful than correct. They know what's right and they do what's right. They are !eaders by their attitude and perspectve.

Their work every day encourages us to keep up the good work too, to join with them in small, decisive acts. It is they who dare us to be bold and public and exemplary in holding others in "conspicuous and high regard." The cast of hundreds in this book is, I am delighted to say, only a very small dot in a very large picture. These !eaders have demonstrated that the human spirit is alive and well, even in the sometimes dark, dank corridors of commerce. It is they who live out daily that which basketball legend John Wooden once taught me, "No one cares how much you know ... until they know how much you care." And to show how much they care the new !eaders don't compete ... they tilt the field!

Appendix A

THE NEW TILTSET

1. THE 2 × 4 (TO, BY, FOR)

One of the most common issues facing today's !eaders is how to make decisions quickly and/or solve problems. The new Thoughtware has taught me that sometimes the best place to begin to solve a problem isn't with the solution! When I was first starting out a client, a woman in her sixties, told me that she was a "master of getting people's attention" and that was the crucial first step in the decision-making process.

"What I do," she said with a straight face, "is take them into my office one at a time and hit them over the head with a 2 × 4! *That* gets their attention every time and gets decisions made really fast!"

Years later the 2 × 4 metaphor surfaced again for me. I was collaborating with Terry Pettengill, (now President of Oculus Consulting in Mill Valley, California) on helping a client develop a mission statement for their strategic plan. Reaching an impasse with the senior executive team, Terry stepped up to the flip chart at the front of the room and said "Ladies and gentlemen, I need your attention, and I happen to have a 2 × 4 here to get it!" All eyes focused on him, as he proceeded to write and then circle three words on the flip chart:

TO, BY, FOR

Hence, the birth of the TO, BY, FOR exercise. Step one is answering "To ... DO what?" Step two is describing "BY what means?" Step three – the most important and most often omitted step – explaining "FOR what purpose?"

In other words, it is not enough to state "what" (step one) you want to do, nor to say "how" (step two) you will do it. The anchoring concept is to know "why" (step three) you are doing what you are doing in the manner in which you are doing it.

There is one further step I will offer. If you really want to make all of this To, By, For "real"... add a final step four: come back to the "BY" page and add: By WHOM? and By WHEN? Suddenly, when someone becomes accountable and responsible for the implementation, things start to happen!

So effective is this simple organizing tool, that I will employ it in describing the tools in the TILTset which follow.

2. PAPER AIRPLANES

TO: To encourage team building and problem solving amongst two or more groups of people. Also has elements of creativity to it.

BY: Using blank sheets of paper of any size, the groups are asked to work as quickly as possible to design and build and decorate a paper airplane. The challenge is to make a plane that can travel at least 15 feet. Two masking taped lines are therefore made on the floor 15 feet apart. One group completed the challenge in less than 10 seconds! One person said, "Scribble on the paper!" Another said, "Yeah, then give it to me." He *crumpled* the paper in a ball ... and *threw* it the 15 feet!

FOR: The value is to think quickly and decisively, to work together, *not* to worry about what the other group (the competition) is doing.

3. THE FISHBOWL

TO: To keep meetings moving, to open up new lines of discussionwhen there are lulls.

BY: Ask participants to write out their biggest concern, the largest barrier faced, and/or the toughest question/topic they want addressed. All are written on small pieces of paper and dropped in a fishbowl. At random times or as needed ... someone reaches in and, *bingo*, a new topic emerges.

FOR: The purpose is to keep invoking new and important issues, to encourage discussion and communication.

4. BRANDSTORMING

TO: To encourage participants to look at brands within and outside the industry.

BY: Ask each person to tell which brands are synonymous with quality, or profitability, or innovation (or a similar relevant topic). Then ask each to use one or two words to describe the key attributes of this product (such as consistent quality, low cost, durability, and so on). Then, look at your own products or brands and compare their attributes to the best brands.

FOR: The value is to encourage a comparative perspective on your own products or services by looking outside your company for "best practices."

5. THE ABUSEMENT PARK

TO: To encourage the creation of new products/ideas.

BY: Make a list of products or brands that participants know were created for one purpose but are used in other ways. For example, *Avon skin-so-soft* is widely used as a mosquito repellent, and Coca-Cola can be used to remove minor forms of rust. Then, list a variety of random products and ask them to invent another use for them (for example: a floppy disc makes a pretty good Frisbee). Finally, take your own company's products or services and repeat steps one and two.

FOR: The purpose here is to allow for lateral thinking, to move out of the confines of logical or linear concept formation.

6. THE SNOWFLAKE EXERCISE

TO: To help people understand the complexities of communication, and the role of good listening and good explanations in accomplishing a goal.

BY: Each person is given a standard piece of blank typing paper. The !eader then asks them to follow his instruction, but with their eyes *closed*! The !eader says: "Now, with your eyes shut, take the paper in your hands and fold it in half. Now fold it again in half. Now fold it a third time in half. Now, tear off the top left corner and the middle of the bottom too. Now open your eyes, unfold your page, and hold it above your head for all to see."

Since everyone received the same simple instructions, all the pages ought to be identical, right? W*rong*! As you look around the room you see every page is as different and unique as a snowflake, some dramatically so! It makes for a good discussion of differences and similarities amongst individuals, the nature of communicating expectations and outcomes, and the ability of the group to listen selectively. Just imagine what can happen with a complex, corporate problem!

FOR: This exercise quickly and memorably demonstrates the value of good communication and listening skills. It also shows the tremendous diversity in a room, the uniqueness of all, and the vast potential for new solutions to old problems.

7. ANAGRAM IT!

TO: To enable people and/or groups to provide answers to difficult questions by giving them a mechanism to break the ice ... or the impasse of too much familiarity with the topic.

BY: Select a topic, for example, new kinds of compensation packages. Ask for one example of the topic, in this case let's say the example is a "bonus." Then, write the letters "B ... O ... N ... U ... S" on a large sheet or white board. Then ask each person to list some form of compensation that you have ... or could have ... that begins with each of those letters For example, B might elicit perks such as "banking privileges," "birthday's off," and so on. When you are done, you have five ideas from every participant.

FOR: The purpose of this exercise is to get people to work within a random, imposed structure (the five letters in "bonus") to force them to look anew and/or to reframe an old problem.

8. BLUE, RED, GREEN

TO: To anticipate and minimize potential barriers.

BY: You can look at any given action plan, agenda, or strategy – by colors. The *blue* view spells out the vision, the goal, the planned direction, or outcome sought. The *red* view looks at the *blue* and asks: "What can stop this, what are the roadblocks, where are the barriers, how many sacred cows are there?" The *green* view looks at the *red* and spells out what needs to be done to remove the barrier.

FOR: The value of this is to identify quickly some obvious obstacles to the results that are desired. Usually, as you explore the *red* and *green* views, the discussion will open up substantive areas previously not seen.

9. BACKCASTING

TO: To develop a plan or direction for future action.

BY: First, use the typical techniques of forecasting: Take a look at recent historical performance or revenue or other factor. Then examine current levels. Then project current levels into an agreed upon future time frame, such as three years ahead. That is *fore*casting. Then, repeat this in inverse order: Start with a year or quarter, such as three years ahead. Then, *assume* the desired result has happened. Then *back*cast from that future date, identifying benchposts and key actions taken that enabled the outcome or goal to be reached. Finally, align the two processes, forecasting and backcasting.

FOR: The benefit of backcasting is that it is not limited by past performance in determining future steps. It is not a projection of the past into the future, but rather is an instance of *inventing* a future, then figuring out how to make it happen. Combining the best of forecasting (data, projections, logic, and so forth) with backcasting (vision, innovation, and flexibility) makes a more viable planning tool.

10. EXTREME VOLLEYBALL!

TO: To encourage people quickly to work co-operatively rather than competitively.

BY: Begin by having the group divide in half and play a typical game of volleyball ... complete with "spikes," "kills," and "digs." Then announce that we are about to play "eXtreme Volleyball" and that there have been a few rule changes. First, divide the players into two groups by any method you wish (alphabet, number off "1" and "2," by height, etc.). Second, ask any player to pick a number between 15 and 21, then tell them that that selected number (for example, 19), when reached, constitutes a "win." Third, tell them that the game begins with a serve ... and that a point is scored every time the ball goes over the net! Both teams should yell out the score each time the ball passes the net, i.e. "1,2,3, ... 19!" If the ball hits the ground, you start over ... until you hit it 19 consecutive times over the net. When the initial goal is reached ... raise it! Pick a score between 21 and 100. Lastly, when you are done "playing" the game, gather everyone and ask them what they have learned from the experience, about business, competition, etc.

FOR: eXtreme Volleyball encourages a group to play by new rules, develop a new strategy of co-operation, and to see the familiar game of volleyball with new eyes. To "win," both teams must work together. It is also an exciting way to get some exercise and blood circulating.

11. ELINA'S SOLUTION

TO: To enable people to see there are many ways to approach and/or solve a problem.

BY: Draw the figure below on a flip chart or slide.

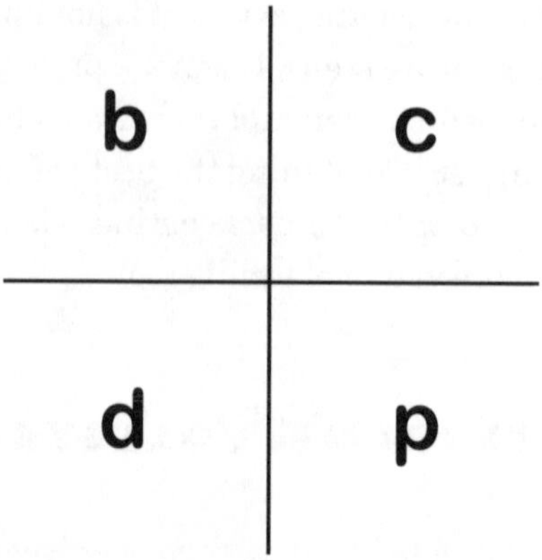

Then say to the group "When Louis Patler's daughter Elina was in Kindergarten and learning to read, her teacher asked the class to answer the following question: Which of these letters (in the drawing) is the most out of place?" Take a moment and study the choices and 1) select one letter, 2) be prepared to say why you chose that letter, and 3) keep your answer in the privacy of your own mind...do not call out your answer."

Give people about 15 seconds then ask for a show of hands. "How many of you say the letter that is most out of place is the 'b'?" Why? (Select one or two to volunteer why. If no one chooses the "b," move on). Repeat the process for the "c," "d," and "p," in each case asking "why" they selected a given letter. The "c" and the "p" usually are selected. Then talk to the group about how a variety of solutions are often possible when faced with a problem – even when you are learning to read and write.

Then say to the group: "I suppose someone would like to know what the teacher felt was the right answer. Well, the teacher felt it should be the "p," and on Elina's paper the had crossed out Elina's answer, written in the letter "e," and drawn a 'frowning face'. (Pause for a few seconds, then say) "Oh, incidentally, Elina felt that the letter that was the most out of place was [pause] the ... 't'!"

Now discuss with the group how the "simple and the most obvious" solutions are often the most difficult to see. Other topics and "lessons" will arise during this discussion.

FOR: This exercise is wonderful for discussing problem-solving, communication, diversity, flexibility and leadership styles in a humorous but poignant manner.

Appendix B

THE NEW THOUGHTWARE

An Irreverent Compilation

Preface: Be Somebody

1. If you really want to "be somebody" ... you have to be more specific. (p. xi)
2. New times call for new thinking. (p. xi)
3. The wild, roller coaster world of business today is in a state of perpetual flux. (p. xii)
4. Technological advances have altered the nature and substance of commerce forever. (p. xii)
5. Globalization of the market, once only a dim light on the horizon, now fully brightens the night sky. (p. xii)
6. Given today's business environment, there is no such thing as a level playing field. (p. xii)
7. If you want to "tilt the field" ... simply tilt your head! (p. xii)

Prolog: Horse Sense

8. If your horse dies, dismount! (p. xiii)

9. If you are too focused on the saddle or the jockey or the competing horse, too often you forget about your own horse's health, the changing conditions of the track, and what it will really take to win the race. (p. xiv)

PART ONE: ATTITUDE!

Chapter 1: ATTITUDE!

10. Learn to place lightbulbs in the snow. (p. 3)
11. Paradigms shift! (p. 4)
12. 90% of business is half mental. (p. 5)
13. Find the wrong direction in order to be on the right track. (p. 8)
14. Turn important things upside down and proceed counter-intuitively. (p. 9)
15. Management is the last stronghold of amateurism. (p. 8)
16. If it ain't broke ... BREAK IT! (p. 10)
17. Today, "business as usual" means "business as unusual." (p. 10)
18. Most problems can't be solved by using the same kind of thinking that created the problem. (p. 11)
19. Experience can often be the best – and the worst – teacher. (p. 10)

Chapter 2: THE FUTURE

20. There are no prizes for predicting rain. (p. 13)
21. Plan as we may, the future has plans of its own. (p. 14)
22. Invent – rather than fear – the future. (p. 15)
23. Learn to think like a child. (p. 16)
24. Look for the SECOND, "best" solution. (p. 17)
25. Break old habits, break new ground, then break the mold! (p. 18)
26. Ask the tough OBVIOUS questions. (p. 18)
27. Learn from the carpenters: Measure twice, cut once. (p. 20)
28. Ask the right questions ... at the right time. (p. 21)
29. A principle of good communication: say *exactly* what you mean. (p. 24)
30. Neither whining nor workaholism are sustainable business strategies. (p. 25)

31. Utilize "novice consultants" with "fresh eyes." (p. 25)
32. There is nothing sacred about sacred cows. (p. 27)
33. Develop double standards – for the best, and for the rest. (p.28)
34. Be practical, spread your wings. (p. 29)
35. Dropping the ball is not the enemy. Fear of dropping is. (p. 29)

Chapter 3: SERVICE

36. Service is as service does. (p. 31)
37. To be competitive today is more complex, and more simple, than ever before. (p. 31)
38. Service is a "Golden Rule" profession: Do to others what you want them to do to you. (p. 33)
39. One size fits ... one! (p. 33)
40. The customer may be right, even when they are wrong. (p. 33)
41. Service never sleeps. (p. 33)
42. Give the customer more than "the Works." (p. 35)
43. Attend to the details, they all have meaning. (p. 35)
44. The crisis in the poem is everywhere in the poem. (p. 35)
45. Good service requires a thick skin and a warm heart. (p. 35)
46. The best deserve the best. (p. 36)
47. A little comic relief when you least expect it never hurts. (p. 41)
48. Watch consumers in their "natural habitat." (p. 41)
49. Reward service that is Above and Beyond the Call of Duty (ABCD). (p. 42)
50. The customer is the boss, and "fires" us simply by taking their business elsewhere. (p. 43)

Chapter 4: "GOOD LUCKY"

51. When the going gets tough, the tough get ... lucky! (p. 51)
52. Go after good luck, don't wait for it to find you. (p. 52)
53. Lure luck out of hiding. (p. 53)
54. Information is like money: you don't reap its benefits until it is put to good use. (p. 53)
55. Mistakes are a good investment. (p. 53)
56. Failure is success in the making. (p. 53)
57. If you want to succeed, double the rate of failure. (p. 53)

58. Good things come to those not set in their ways. (p. 53)
59. Get into the habit of breaking your habits. (p. 54)
60. Anything worth doing is worth overdoing: Learn from your excesses. (p. 54)
61. Do something backwards every day. (p. 54)
62. Learn to leverage your luck. (p. 54)
63. Most good ideas arise from the passionate pursuit of irreverent intuitions. (p. 55)
64. Spoon-feed your hunches. (p. 55)
65. Chaos is order in the making. (p. 56)
66. Pay attention. Then pay attention to what you pay attention to. (p. 56)
67. Take the time to notice what you notice. (p. 56)
68. You can observe a lot just by watching. (p. 56)
69. Children ... and good business people ... always ask "why?" (p. 57)
70. Being lucky is rarely a matter of luck. (p.58)

PART TWO: PERSPECTIVE

Chapter 5: IDEAS

71. Let the clouds touch the bottom line. (p. 63)
72. Telling someone to be more innovative is akin to telling them to be wealthier: The goal is admirable, but the pathway lacks specificity. (p.63)
73. Don't ignore the little guys. (p. 64)
74. The seeds of innovation are often in a single idea, from a simple source, at unexpected times. (p. 64)
75. Innovate ... or die! (p. 64)
76. The gateway to success depends on chronic innovation and implementable ideas. (p. 65)
77. Focus on creating a chronically innovation-conducive environment, not on creating "results." (p. 65)
78. Ideas are usually rooted in experience, laced with flexibility, and seasoned with large quantities of chutzpah. (p. 65)
79. To catch up you need to ask the right questions. (p. 69)

80. To get ahead, find the right answers to the right questions. (p. 69)
81. To stay ahead, find the right answers at the right time. (p. 69)
82. The more unsettling the questions ... the better. (p. 69)
83. Incessant idea-generation is crucial in today's global marketplace. (p. 71)
84. In a fast changing market, at any moment you have to give up what you "are" for what you could be. (p. 71)
85. What you "could be" in the future is often limited by what you "are" today. (p. 71)
86. Ideas, like a good garden, require watering, good soil preparation, the right climate ... and a half-way decent gardener. (p. 71)
87. There IS such a thing as a bad idea ... which has given rise to many a good one. (p. 72)
88. Ideas are the raw material for a solution, they are not the solution. (p. 72)
89. Sometimes, the customer is rarely right. (p. 74)
90. Any idea worth keeping is worth keeping track of. (p. 74)
91. If ideas are a dime a dozen, it may take a fist full of dimes to find the right one. (p. 78)
92. Ideas are not just for the chosen few, ideas are everybody's business. (p. 76)
93. Creativity "yanks convention inside out." (p. 77)
94. Repeatable success is the by-product of an innovative organization where ideas and implementation meet. (p. 77)

Chapter 6: INNOVATION

95. Learn how to back into a clearing. (p. 79)
96. Innovation, like "electricity" or "intelligence", is easier to measure than define. (p. 79)
97. Success often breeds complacency ... rather than further success. (p. 79)
98. The innovation process is part perspiration, part exasperation and part motivation. (p. 80)
99. "Creativity" and "innovation" are *not* the same. (p. 82)
100. An innovation is an idea brought to fruition that tilts the field. (p. 83)

101. Most companies are much better at "blaming" than they are at encouraging employees. (p. 83)
102. The tool doesn't matter, so long as the job gets done. (p. 84)
103. De-pedestalize innovation. (p. 85)
104. In business, notice especially that which runs contrary to conventional wisdom. (p. 85)
105. It is a common trap to believe that creativity is the delegated pursuit of novelty. (p. 85)
106. Imitation can expedite creativity. (p. 86)
107. Doggedly pursue innovations without attaching emotional baggage to what fails – *or* to what succeeds. (p. 86)
108. Creativity is a springboard ... not a podium. (p. 86)
109. What's private is public, and in public is where you behave. (p. 87)
110. Look for the "strange attractors" amidst today's chaotic times. (p. 88)
111. An idea left unimplemented has never yielded an innovation. (p. 88)
112. Low organizational-esteem is no different than low self-esteem. (p. 89)
113. Innovation can be taught, encouraged and rewarded. (p. 90)
114. Ideas regarding the technological future come when they're completely impractical. (p.91)
115. One formula for success today is: innovation and steady management. (p. 91)
116. Contrariness pays off. (p. 93)
117. The best way for a company to stay healthy is to stop getting sick. (p. 93)

Chapter 7: STRATEGY

118. It's better to be useful than correct. (p. 95)
119. Good strategy is like good philanthropy, it becomes "good" only when freely given. (p. 95)
120. Strategy is a dynamic process, more than just a plan, and greater than the sum of its parts. (p. 96)
121. Effective strategy is a "win-win" strategy. (p. 97)

122. The best time to partner with change is when you are riding high. (p. 98)
123. As the *position* of "manager" is downsized, the *skills* of good management are in even more demand. (p. 99)
124. Management skills can be taught, but enthusiasm to use those skills is "caught". (p. 99)
125. Every new challenge is a new opportunity ... to think. (p. 100)
126. Metaphors are strategy's ally. (p. 102)
127. Learn from analogies, such as basketball: see the whole court; move without the ball; use the backboard; make your free throws; know thy teammates. (p. 104)
128. These days, as in skeet shooting, we have to shoot *ahead* of the target in order to hit it. (p. 105)
129. Most strategy benefits from input from a "diagonal slice" of an organization. (p. 106)
130. The best strategy is to plan on changing your plans. (p. 107)
131. Strategy progresses when perceived by "other than ordinary sight." (p. 109)
132. Don't wait on success ... go ahead without it! (p.111)
133. In pure strategy, the collective whole is much greater than the sum of the individual parts. (p. 111)
134. Knowledge accumulates *within* organizations, but *between* individuals. (p. 111)
135. Today, the rate of change is exponential, not incremental. (p. 112)
136. Things will never get "back to normal". *This* is normal. (p. 112)
137. Plan as we may, the future has plans of its own. (p. 112)
138. Organizations that "learn how to learn", ask the right questions at the right time, and find out how to find the answers will thrive in a global economy. (p. 113)
139. Strategically productive organizations value flexibility, diversity, integrity, cooperation, and innovation. (p. 113)

Chapter 8: PERSPECTIVE

140. Don't compete ... tilt the field! (p. 115)
141. Wisdom doesn't always come with age, sometimes age shows up all by itself. (p. 115)
142. Reflection and perspective are separate and not equal. (p. 116)

143. The power of reflection is revealed through a perspective that is wise enough to be made real. (p. 116)
144. Perspective is like a jackdaw: it helps you to gather up that which sparkles and use it to feather your nest. (p. 116)
145. A winning perspective is one wherein as you run down the corridors you see the doors first and know which of them to enter. (p. 117)
146. With perspective comes a greater sense of sequence, and with the right sequence there comes greater likelihood of success. (p. 118)
147. Perspective thrives on continuous learning and insatiable curiosity. (p. 118)
148. Under the malaise of massive amounts of information, simplicity succeeds. (p. 120)
149. The word "criticism", in Chinese, means "medicine for the ears." (p. 122)
150. To gain perspective, treat a metaphor as a fact, and facts as metaphors. (p.123)
151. When you run into a brick wall, find the first loose brick. (p. 123)
152. "No profit grows where there is no pleasure taken." (p. 127)
153. Perspective, like experience, is a wonderful thing. It enables you to recognize a mistake when you make it again. (p. 127)
154. Humor and serendipity are perspective's good friends. (p. 127)
155. Perspective allows us to make a "To Do" list ... as well as a "Don't Do!" list. (p. 130)
156. Stand back far enough, long enough, and often enough. (p. 131)

PART THREE: !EADERSHIP

Chapter 9: TALENT

157. The waves are in the water. (p. 135)
158. Finding and keeping top talent is the name of the game today. (p. 135)
159. Fun pays off. (p. 136)
160. The reserve labor reserve is dropping. (p.137)
161. People make a business run, it does not run all by itself, nor by systems and software. (p. 138)

162. Today, "the long haul" has a horizon line of three to five years. (p. 138)
163. Today's labor force has few loyalties, and even fewer regrets. (p. 139)
164. Retaining top talent is a goal that applies in a "boom" or a "bust" economic cycle. (p. 139)
165. Hiring smart, and hiring smart people, may be the smartest thing you'll ever do. (p. 139)
166. The new skillset requires attitude, perspective, tenacity and humor. (p. 140)
167. The search for top talent – much like raising good children – is incessant. (p. 142)
168. Finding talent is everybody's job. (p. 142)
169. The workforce has become a "free agent", everyone for themselves. (p. 142)
170. You can change you life in an afternoon. (p. 143)
171. Don't forget the "rest" who may not be the "brightest" as you focus on the "Best and the brightest." (p. 143)
172. Chutzpah attracts talent. (p. 144)
173. Pay attention to the fringe benefits ... and the "fringe *deficits*" of a job. (p. 144)
174. "Meaningful" work heightens a sense of loyalty. (p. 145)
175. When recruiting, maximize lifestyle-relevant choices. (p.145)
176. Treat your company's "culture" as if it were a "brand." (p.145)
177. "Mass customize" your benefit plans ... and the challenges of a project. (p. 146)
178. When making an employment decision, trust your first impression ... and your "gut" reaction. (p. 146)
179. Time "flies" ... but, comparatively speaking, wages "walk." (p. 148)
180. Organizations are like organisms, so generating a profit is how they "breathe." (p. 149)
181. The purpose of an organization is to deliver value to customers, employees, and the community. (p. 149)
182. Being a good person and a good corporate citizen is good business. (p. 149)
183. Gen-X employees will choose "lifestyle balance" over "bucks." (p. 150)

184. Better managers can manage Gen-Xers ... and by managing Gen-Xers they become better managers. (p. 151)
185. Act as if you are in business for yourself and your title is CEO of your domain. (p. 153)
186. Take a 360 degree look at yourself regularly. (p. 153)
187. Think "team", think "collaboration." (p. 153)
188. Take risks. Don't wait. Start something. (p. 153)
189. Anyone can describe a problem, far fewer can solve it. (p. 154)
190. Laughter matters: It is the "canary" in the mines of commerce. (p. 156)
191. Constantly mix business and pleasure. (p. 156)
192. Those who laugh ... .last! (p. 156)

Chapter Ten: RETENTION

193. If the gate's open ... they'll stay in the yard! (p. 157)
194. Praising the goodness of the soul is also good for the bottom line. (p. 158)
195. Long hours and little rest will burn out even the best. (p. 160)
196. Remember that "work" – unlike family, health, friendships and spirit – is a rubber ball: drop it and it'll bounce back. (p. 160)
197. Restructuring the nature of "work" is more crucial than restructuring an individual job. (p. 161)
198. Loyalty – like career development – now resides with the individual rather than the organization. (p. 162)
199. The emerging workforce is an oxymoronic and eclectic collection of "paid volunteers." (p. 162)
200. Capital assets depreciate. Intellectual capital depreciates even faster. (p. 163)
201. Higher pay is but the "report card", pride of accomplishment is the real incentive. (p. 163)
202. In a Network Age, brains, intelligence and quick access to the right information are a much in demand commodity. (p. 164)
203. The companies that have ... and can keep ... the best people, win. (p. 164)
204. Job descriptions matter, but completed work matters even more. (p. 164)

205. Customer retention and service tools and strategies also work for keeping employees satisfied. (p. 165)
206. The slower the response to an employee's problem, the faster they may exit. (p. 165)
207. Measure, track and reward retention goals when met. (p. 165)
208. The typical performance review is better understood as "blame-storming." (p. 165)
209. Encourage and reward competence, not incompetence. (p. 166)
210. Celebrate, model and learn from high performers. (p. 166)
211. Spend more time building on strengths rather than on shoring up weaknesses. (p. 166)
212. More often than not, a "poor" performance by a worker is attributable to an equally "poor" performance by their supervisor. (p. 168)
213. In every organization it is useful to know the difference between what's bologna ... and what's real. (p. 168)
214. Putting things down on paper does not make them real ... only good implementation can do that. (p. 168)
215. Not so coincidentally, unemployment and employee loyalty, are both at an all-time low. (p. 169)
216. Learn from medicine: there are early warning signs of employee dissatisfaction. (p. 169)
217. The world of commerce today is neither safe, nor sane ... so keeping your tongue-in-cheek is a practical tool. (p. 171)
218. If you are looking only at your "star" performers, you may well trample all the others. (p. 172)
219. Find the best and highest roles and jobs for your ordinary people. (p. 172)
220. A corporate culture can be built by a single leprechaun dancing in the hearts and minds of its people. (p. 175)
221. Happiness yields an excellent return on investment. (p. 176)

Chapter Eleven: GLOBALISM

222. Think globally, act locally ... and vice versa! (p. 177)
223. Adopt a global focus with local solutions. (p. 177)
224. Thinking precedes action, and good thinking – local or global – is rare. (p.177)

225. We live on a pluralistic planet, where methods coexist rather than dominate, where "right" and "wrong" ways of doing things readily blur. (p. 178)
226. Although the truth is not eternal, somewhere, for some period of time, some things do in fact work. (p. 178)
227. Necessity is the mother of invention ... and good Thoughtware. (p. 178)
228. Every market today is a volatile market, a moving target, a shooting star. (p. 179)
229. Whatever we do will be accompanied by unplanned side effects. (p. 179)
230. Few organizations or individuals take a long enough – or zany enough – look far enough down the road. (p. 180)
231. There is emerging an international language of commerce. (p. 180)
232. We can always imagine more than what exists. (p. 180)
233. The cutting edge of the future is conveniently located inside our DNA, minds, hearts and souls. (p. 180)
234. The multinational corporation may become the basis of a new world order and have no traditional political base. (p. 181)
235. The longer we live, the older we are ... and a multigenerational future lies ahead for all of us. (p. 182)

We continue to move:

- 236. from vertical to horizontal organizations (p. 183)
- 237. from bureaucracy to ad hocracy (p. 183)
- 238. from specialist to generalist (p. 183
- 239. from consumer to "prosumer" (p. 183)
- 240. from "hard war" to software (p. 184)
- 241. from belief to scrutiny (p. 183)
- 242. from data to intuition. (p. 184)

243. Think globally and locally concurrently. (p. 185)
244. Encourage mass customization. (p. 185)
245. Set general priorities. (p. 185)
246. Understand paid volunteers. (p. 185)
247. Follow local universals. (p. 185)
248. Today, with the growth of the Internet, mindshare is at least as critical as market share. (p. 185)
249. Seeking wisdom will prevail over seeking information. (p. 186)

250. In mature, established markets there appears to be a "Rule of Three" – the top three will dominate. (p. 190)
251. Today, a generalist's full line of products often consists of but TWO. (p. 193)
252. A mission statement serves as a reminder of "why" the system exists, "who" it is serving, and "what" it must do to meet the demands of its customers. (p. 194)
253. Good thinking begins with good questions, and asking "why to" is to seek your own answers, while asking "how to" merely provides you with someone else's answers. (p. 195)
254. When it comes to understanding "what business you are in?", most companies are "clue-impaired." (p. 199)
255. It never hurts to ask. (p. 203)
256. Assume the answer will be "yes." (p. 203)
257. If they're coming, build it right! (p. 203)
258. From a future-perfect perspective, the present is already the past. (p. 203)
259. "Incremental" thinking gives incremental results, which is not very useful in a world of exponential change. (p. 203)
260. "Break-It!" Thinking™ imposes no limits on its own results. (p. 204)

Chapter Twelve: !EADERSHIP

261. Learn to "lean" into life! (p. 205)
262. You cannot blow an uncertain trumpet. (p. 205)
263. Playing it safe ... is dangerous. (p. 206)
264. The signs of good leadership appear primarily among the followers. (p. 207)
265. A business is a living organism. (p. 210)
266. It's easier to put strategic changes into action than it is to declare them as policy. (p.210)
267. The success of many companies is more attributable to the "many" than the "few," to the "invisible' more than the visible and charismatic. (p. 211)

Today's new !eaders share:

268. a strong preference for, and trust in, mutual aid and cooperation (p.212)

269. the ability to mobilize "pent-up" rapport (p. 212)
270. the constant readiness to be "on duty", to engage in small "leaderly" acts. (p. 212)

271. !eaders know that you don't need to make headlines in order to make a difference. (p. 214)
272. The elements of leadership cannot be taught, they must be learned. (p. 214)
273. When there's nothing else to do, there's always work to be done. (p. 214)
274. What we are witnessing is the slow and steady democratization of leadership. (p. 215)
275. For !eaders, "doing" is intrinsically rewarding. (p. 215)
276. Today's new !eaders are driven by values not pedagogy, vision not ideology. (p. 216)
277. Like happy families, all !eaders resemble one another. (p. 216)
278. Being "active" is not an act. (p. 216)
279. The desire to make a contribution – a difference – separates !eaders from "mere placeholders." (p. 217)

True !eaders choose:

280. exploration over exploitation (p. 217)
281. rallying over ruling (p. 217)
282. imagination over inventory (p. 217)
283. achievement over compliance (p. 217)
284. giving over taking (p. 217)
285. changing over the status quo (p. 220)
286. the "walk" over the "talk." (p. 220)

287. !eadership is the hard work of soft management. (p. 218)
288. Leadership today is "squishy" ... hard to get your hands around. (p. 221)
289. !eaders hold others in conspicuous ... and high ... regard. (p. 224)
290. Today's real leader's know – and do – what's right. (p. 225)
291. No one cares how much you know until they know how much you care. (p.225)

The New Tiltset

292. Sometimes the best place to start to solve a problem isn't with the solution. (p. 227)

293. Take a "2 by 4" (To, By, For) to most problems in order to know "what", "how", and most importantly "why". (p. 228)
294. Many "best practices" are found outside you own company. (p. 229)
295. With ideas: abuse 'em, or lose 'em. (p. 229)
296. A random, imposed structure can yield focused and free-wheeling ideas. (p. 230)
297. One benefit of "backcasting" is that past performance needn't limit future steps. (p. 231)
298. Combine forecasting (data, projections, historical performance) with backcasting (vision, innovation, flexibility, confidence). (p. 231)
299. See the familiar with new, unfamiliar eyes. (p. 232)
300. The most useful solutions are often hardest to find because they are too clear and too obvious. (p.234)

Epilog

301. Poet Robert Duncan ("The Opening of the Field", p. 79, *New Directions*, 1973) gets the last word:

"Go write yourself a book and put
therein first things that might define a world."

REFERENCES

Chapter 1

Kriegel, R. and Patler, L. (1992). *If It Ain't Broke ... BREAK IT!* New York: Warner.

Kuhn, T.S. (1962). *The Structure of Scientific Revolution.* University of Chicago Press.

Meadows, D.H. (1997). *Whole Earth Review*, Winter, pp. 78–84.

Chapter 2

National Association of Suggestion Systems (1992). *Executive Edge*, August, p. 7.

Prahalad, C.K. and Hamel, G. (1990). The core competence of the corporation. *Harvard Business Review*, May–June, pp. 80–91.

Schnieter, F. (1992). *Getting Along With the Chinese for Fun and Profit.* Hong Kong: Asia 2000 Ltd.

Chapter 3

Deming, W.E. (1982). *Out of the Crisis.* Cambridge, Massachusetts: MIT Press.

Gorman, L. (1998). *8th Annual Customer Service Conference Brochure*, January, p. 15.

Griffin, J. (1998). *Customer Loyalty: How to Earn It, How to Keep It.* quoted in *8th Customer Service Conference Brochure*, January, p. 18.

Heil, G. (1996). *One Size Fits One: Building Relationships One Customer at a Time*. New York: John Wiley & Sons.

Kasten, T. (1997). *Fortune*, November 24, p. 294.

Spurrior, J. (1998). *8th Annual Customer Service Conference Brochure*, January, p. 11

Chapter 4

Beattle, A. (1989). *Picturing Will*. New York: Random House.

Useem, J. (1997). Help wanted: smart CEOs, no ideas necessary. *Inc.*, March, p. 29.

Chapter 5

Diller, B. (1998). *Independent Journal*, Jan 26, p. C-1.

Gates, W. (1998). *Independent Journal*, Feb. 2, p. C-1.

Greco, S. (1998). Where great ideas comes from. *Inc.*, April, pp. 76–90

Hirsch, Y. (1994). *Stock Traders Almanac*. Old Tappan, New Jersey: Six Deer Trail.

Lebovit, M. (1994). *Volume Reversal Survey*. Arizona: Sedona.

Spitzer, T. Quinn (1997). quoted in *San Francisco Chronicle*, June 22, p. CL23

Weil, E. (1994). The future is younger than you think. *Fast Company*, April/May, p. 104

Chapter 6

Mall, E. (1997). Talkin' about the webolution. *Your Company*, April/May, p. 23

Covey, S. (1989). *The Seven Habits of Highly Effective People*. New York: Simon & Schuster.

Gates, W. (1997). *Independent Journal*, September 29, p. D1

Schnaars, S.P. (1994). *Managing Imitation Strategies: How Later Entrants Seize Markets from Pioneers*. Glencoe: The Free Press.

Hamel, G. and Prahalad, C.K. (1994). *Competing for the Future*. Cambridge, Massachusettes: Harvard Business School Press.

Chapter 7

Clifford, D. Jr. and Cavanaugh, R. (1991). *The Winning Performance: How America's High-Growth Midsize Companies Succeed.*

Commission on Industrial Productivity, *Endicott Report* (1989). Massachusetts Institute of Technology, as reported in *Fortune*, May 22, pp. 92–97.

Olson, C. (1978). *The Journal of the Charles Olson Archives*, Number 10, Fall, University of Connecticut Library, p. 24.

Chapter 8

Austin, N.K. (1997). What balance? *Inc.*, April, p. 38.

Collins, J. (1997). Pulling the plug. *Inc.*, March, pp. 76–77.

Hammer, M. (1997). The power of reflection *Fortune*, November 24, p. 291

Rubin, H. (1998). Peter's principles. *Inc.*, March, pp. 62–68.

Schnieter, F. (1992). *Getting Along with the Chinese for Fun and Profit.* Hong Kong: Asia 2000 Ltd.

Weil, E. (1994). The future is younger than you think. *Fast Company,* April/May, p. 104.

Zaslow, J. (1998). Straight talk. *USA Weekend,* November 28–30, p. 22.

Chapter 9

Bailey, G., Interim Services, Tippen, M., Tressa, S., and Weinstein M. (1998). Quoted in *Independent Journal*, Jan 15, p. B8.

Covey, S. (1997). How to succeed in today's workplace. *USA Weekend*, August 29–31, p. 4.

Fost, D. (1997). A nice guy can finish first. *Independent Journal,* May 26, p. B2

Gates, W., Allchin, J. and Ballmer, S.A. (1992). Quoted in *Business Week,* February, p. 24.

George S. May International Co. (1997). The challenge of recruiting. *Inc.*, March, p. 102.

Kunde, D. (1997). Meeting generation X halfway. *Dallas Morning News*, reprinted in *Independent Journal*, August 24, p. E6.

New York City Department of Consumer Affairs, Mark Green.
Ottenweller, M., Swonk, D., Guthrie, T., and Glandon, P.J. (1998). quoted in *Wall Street Journal*, April 22.
Tulgan, B. (1997). *Managing Generation X.* Oxford: Capstone.
Ware, L. (1998). *Half Moon Bay Times*, Feb 2, p. 8A.

Chapter 10

Allaire, P. (1997). Concern for employees reaps higher productivity. *Independent Journal,* Feb. 26, p. B5.
Austin, N.K. (1997). Starstruck. *Inc.*, September, p. 61.
Clarke, J. (1987). The Bridge. *From Feathers to Iron.* Tombouctou/Convivio, p. 86.
Covey, S. (1997). How to Succeed in Today's Workplace. *USA Weekend*, August 29–31, p. 4.
DeBare, I. (1997). 360° of evaluation. *San Francisco Examiner*, May 5, p. B1.
Geneen, H. and Bowers, B. (1997). *The Synergy Myth and Other Ailments of Business Today.* St. Martin's Press.
ITS Network World.
ITT, (1997). *Inc.*, March, p. 81.
Jackson, M. (1997). Sleeping on the job? (AP), *Independent Journal,* May 18, p. E1.
Kelleher, H. (1998). *Inc.*, May, p. 123.
Maude, D. (1997). *Inc.*, December, p. 149.
Meyer, C. (1997). *Relentless Growth: How Silicon Valley Innovation Strategies Can Work in Your Business.* Free Press/Simon & Schuster Inc.
Neuborne, E. (1997). Worker vacation time shrinking. *Independent Journal,* March 12, p. B8.
Stack, J. (1997). The curse of the annual performance review. *Inc.*, March, pp. 39–40.
Towers Perrin Workplace Index Study, (1997). *SF Chronicle*, Dec. 7, p. CL41.
Ware, L. (1998). *Half Moon Bay Times*, Feb 2, p. 8A.
Wolfe, C. and Thibodeau, D. *Inc.*, April, p. 97.

Chapter 11

Anonymous author (1998). Social and technological forecasts for the next 25 years. *World Future Society Newsletter*, May, p. 1.

Coates, J. and Jarratt, J. (1992). Exploring the future. *The Annals of the America Academy of Political and Social Science*, July.

Davis, S. (1997). *Future Perfect.* Perseus Press.

Flinn, J. (1997). Don't Point: Most of the world thinks it's rude. *San Francisco Examiner,* May 18, p. T-16.

Griaule, M. (1965) *Conversations with Ogotemmeli.* Oxford: Oxford University Press, p. 58.

Kaplan, H. (1998). *Time*, May 25, p. 56.

Kaplan, J. (1994). *Startup: A Silicon Valley Adventure.* Houghton Mifflin Co.

Levitt, T. (1960). Marketing myopia. *Harvard Business Review*, HBR Classic reprint edition.

Morrison, T. and Conaway, W.A. (1997). Your cultural IQ. *American Way,* June 1, pp. 165, 196.

Prahalad, C.K. and Hamel, G. The core competence of the corporation. *Harvard Business Review*, May-June, pp. 80–91.

Richman, T. (1998). *Inc.*, May, p. 114.

Sheth, J. and Sisodia, R. (1998). Only the big three will thrive. *Manager's Journal*, May.

Stanat, R. (1998). *Time*, May 25, p. 63.

Chapter 12

Bennis, W. (1994). *On Becoming a Leader.* Perseus Press.

Berra, L. (1998). *The Yogi Book: "I Really Didn't Say Everything I Said."* Workman Publishing Company.

Collins, J. (1994). *Built to Last: Successful Habits of Visionary Companies.* HarperBusiness.

Darwin, C. (1852). *The Descent of Man.*

De Pree, Max (1990). *Leadership is an Art.* DTP.

Drucker, P. (1954). *The Practice of Management.*

Einstein, D. (1997). Netscape CEO skips pay and bonus. *San Francisco Chronicle*, May 1, p. D1.

Farkas, C. and Wetlaufer, S. (1996). The way chief executive officers lead. *Harvard Business Review*, May/June, pp. 110–122.

Finegan, J. (1997). Ready, aim, focus. *Inc.*, March, p. 46.

Fishman, C. (1997). *Fast Company*, April/May, p. 72.

Gardner, J.W. (1982). *No Easy Victories*. Stanford.

Geneen, H. and Bowers, B. (1997). *The Synergy Myth and Other Ailments of Business Today*. St. Martin's Press.

Grove, A. (1993). *Fortune*, February, p. 59.

Knowling, B. (1997). *Fast Company*, April/May, p. 66.

Nagle, B. and Pascarella, P. (1998). *Leveraging People and Profit: The Hard Work of Soft Management*. Boston: Butterworth-Heinemann.

Nowak, M. and May, R. and Sigmund, K. (1995). The arithmetic of mutual help. *Scientific American,* June.

Pickett, L. (1997). *Inc.*, March, p. 53.

Stossel, J. (1997). *USA Weekend*, November 28–30, p. 4.

Tanaka, W. (1997). It's the inn thing. *San Francisco Examiner*, April 13, p. B1.

Tichy, N. (1997). *Fast Company*, April/May, p. 78.

ABOUT THE AUTHOR

Award-winning author, speaker and consultant, Louis Patler, Ph.D. is president of The B.I.T. Group, an international consulting, strategic research, trend analysis and corporate training company. Through his work with clients, his keynote speeches, and writing, Louis brings pioneering technologies for !eadership development, strategy formation, practical problem solving, and quality service initiatives to Fortune 500 companies, multinational corporations, and foreign governments. He writes frequently for newspapers, magazines, and management newsletters in the USA and abroad on the most innovative individuals and companies. England's BBC-TV and Canada's CBC-Radio praised him as one of America's new breed of business mentors. Recently, J. Walter Thompson Agency named him one of "The 20 Most Creative Minds in America."

He is also co-author of the *New York Times* best seller, *If it ain't broke ... BREAK IT! Unconventional Wisdom for a Changing Business World* (Warner Books, 1992) which has been widely acclaimed by reviewers such as Tom Peters, Steven Covey, and Paul Hawken, professional coaches Pat Riley and Tony La Russa, and CEOs of Fortune 500 companies such as Hewlett-Packard and Coca Cola. It was the second best-selling business book of 1992, with a Spanish and Chinese edition published in 1994. Excerpts from the book have been translated into 17 languages and 28 million copies. His exciting training program, 'Break-It!' Thinking™, reveals the new mindset, skillset and toolset needed for today's fast-changing world.

Louis is listed in several national and international *Who's Who* editions, has twice received awards from the National Endowment for the Arts for his writing, and was the editor of a prestigious American trend report.

A former professional baseball prospect, and member of several Community Boards, he lives with his wife and five children in Mill Valley, California.

ABOUT THE BIT GROUP

The B.I.T. Group
219 E. Blithedale Avenue, Suite Four
Mill Valley, CA 94941 USA
Tel: 415/388–3282
Fax: 415/388 4342
e-mail: bit@nbn.com
www.theBITgroup.com

In a global economy that changes constantly, our mission is to enable you to use your resources to generate and implement new ideas, products and strategies, solve problems in effective ways, and maximize your human and organizational productivity. The B.I.T. Group was founded to provide innovative and timely solutions that offers clients a solid return on their investment.

Our work in organizational innovation, strategic planning, and leadership development has been widely acclaimed. Our products and services reflect and embody the skills, beliefs and values so vital in today's world: innovation, flexibility, vision, integrity, enthusiasm, and cooperation. We offer clients the most current business knowledge gleaned from over 20 years experience; original research on market trends, thriving companies and highly productive people; and an extensive team of highly skilled associates and colleagues.

B.I.T. Learning Technologies

- "Break-It!" Thinking
- Training in "Leadership Perspectives"©
- "New Dimensions in Service"©
- Customized Corporate Training

B.I.T. Learning Technologies provides corporate and public education and training through customized or proprietary ('Break-It!' Thinking™, Healthcare Management Strategies©, and 'Ultimate Service'© and '!eadership Perspectives'©) programs, seminars and workshops throughout the world. For information, please contact our principle training colleagues:

Worldwide
The Learning Design Group
A Division of Dove Associates
600 S. Highway 169
Suite 1630
Minneapolis, MN 55426
612-595-8689
612-595-8550 (fax)
e-mail: scohen@tldg.com
www.tldg.com

UK and Europe
People Skills International
Longdene House
Haslemere
Surrey GU27 2PH
United Kingdom
(+44) 01428-651165
(+44) 01428-651150 (fax)
email:psi@peopleskills.co.uk
www.peopleskills.co.uk

B.I.T. Management Consulting

- Strategic Processes
- Core Competency Assessment
- Business Transformations
- Creative Product Development

B.I.T. Management Consulting offers research and consulting services in: strategic planning; leadership development; management processes; innovation skills and innovation assessment; organizational productivity; and initiating and implementing structural change – on premise, at retreat sites and at conferences throughout the world.

B.I.T. !eadership Resources

- Research and Publications
- Audio and Video Materials
- Speakers and Seminars
- Executive Leadership Retreats

B.I.T. !eadership Resources provides speakers, audio and video presentations, and special project/new product development to diverse businesses, associations, foundations and organizations, as well as working with athletes, and educational institutions. For information re speaking appearances by Dr Patler contact The B.I.T. Group or in the UK/Europe, contact People Skills International at the above location.

B.I.T. Unlimited

- Trend analysis
- Market making
- New theoretical models
- Innovative problem solving
- Start-ups

B.I.T. Unlimited, our research and development group, continually seeks to discover ... or invent ... the most current and creative strategies, materials and products in order to meet the special needs of our clients and friends, in the belief that innovation and steady management are the cornerstones of leadership. Our research findings and trend forecasts are widely respected and we regularly take on special projects and assist start-up companies.

- Unconventional Wisdom for Tomorrow's Business Leaders!

Selected international client list

AdvantageHEALTH Corporation
American Compensation Association
American Express/TRS, IDS, IISG
Bank of America
Bank Marketing Association
British Airways
California Medical Association
California Department of Food and Agriculture
Canadian Hospital Association
Dell Computers
Deloitte & Touche Inc.

Diriventas, Colombia, South America
Edmonton, Alberta, Public Schools
Electronic Arts
Emery Worldwide
CareMark Inc.
The GAP
The Golden State Warriors/NBA Basketball
Hughes Aircraft Federal Credit Union
Hewlett-Packard
Information Access Company
International Council of Shopping Centers
International Facilities Management Association (IFMA)
International Festivals Association
The Kimpton Group, Hotels Division
Lam Research
Les Clefs d'Or, Paris
McLaren School of Business, University of San Francisco
Minister of Labour, Alberta, Canada
National Restaurant Association: Marketing Executives Group
Pacific Bell/Pacific Telesis/Pacific Bell Information Services
Puma Sporting Goods, S.A.
RCM Capital Management
Sybase
Sun Microsystems
Supreme Court, People's Republic of China
University of California, School of Medicine
Williams-Sonoma, Inc.

INDEX